Cautious Rebel

Susan Clay Sawitzky, 1932

Cautious Rebel

A Biography of
Susan Clay Sawitzky

ᴡ

Lindsey Apple

THE KENT STATE UNIVERSITY PRESS
Kent, Ohio, and London, England

Library of Congress Catalog Card Number 97-3112
ISBN 0-87338-579-9
Manufactured in the United States of America

"Mariner" by Susan Clay Sawitzky first appeared in POETRY © 1941 by The Modern
Poetry Association, and is reprinted by permission of the editor of POETRY.

Poems from "The Circling Thread" are reprinted courtesy of the Kentucky Poetry
Review.

Photographs are courtesy of Elizabeth Clay Blanford.

LIBRARY OF CONGRESS CATALOGING-IN-PUBLICATION DATA

Apple, Lindsey.
    Cautious rebel : a biography of Susan Clay Sawitzky / Lindsey Apple.
        p. cm.
    Includes bibliographical references (p.) and index.
    ISBN 0-87338-579-9 (cloth : alk paper) ∞
    1. Sawitzky, Susan Clay, 1897–1981. 2. Women—Kentucky—Lexington—Biography.
3. Lexington (Ky.)—Biography. I. Title.
F459.L6A66 1997
976.9'47043'092—dc 21   97-3112
[B]   CIP

British Library Cataloging-in-Publication data are available.

Gift

Must the bleached ankles of rushes
Or the span of a lily stem
Measure my shallowness,
When the sky itself comes into me
and hollows me out of its own immensity?

I feel the clutch of roots
In dull grey mist of mud,
But miles within me
Lies the ooze of cloud,
And in the night the sharp-edged, time crushed stars
Sink to their height in me,
Settling like sand across a floorless deep.

Contents

Acknowledgments

〜

In 1984, Professor and Mrs. Woodridge Spears introduced me to Elizabeth Clay Blanford, who wanted a historian to look at some papers found at the time of her sister's death. I learned that Mrs. Blanford was the great-granddaughter of the Great Compromiser of antebellum days, Henry Clay. Any materials related to that family would interest historians. Those three individuals, who were responsible for the origins of this book, continued to offer their expertise and their moral support throughout its preparation. Professor Spears lived to read a first draft of the manuscript. A poet himself, he appreciated Susan Sawitzky's work and some of the problems she faced as a poet. He also understood the effort involved for me in teaching twelve hours and preparing a manuscript simultaneously. His suggestions, encouragement, mentoring, and friendship are treasured gifts of the development of this book. Eve Spears continued the encouragement begun with her husband. She, too, writes poetry. From the eastern Kentucky mountains, she also recognized the importance of family and place in one's upbringing, particularly that of a woman.

Elizabeth Clay Blanford shared so much of herself and her knowledge of the Clay family that she must be considered a major source for the preparation of this book. In phone conversations and interviews she provided an oral record of her family's history and, since she shared many of the events, Susan Sawitzky's upbringing. She loves her family dearly and tells their stories in a favorable light. Such material must be used carefully, but even the great pride she exhibits is important to the study. The factual details have been verified by other sources. Quick to caution when unsure of a date or a name, Mrs. Blanford's accuracy enhances her credibility. If there is a fault, it is in leaving out information that might cast someone, family members or otherwise, in a bad light or create a negative impression. That is a part of the gentility she and her sister learned as children. That approach also indicates how lessons were taught and learned in the Clay homes.

I offer my deepest appreciation to the Spearses and Mrs. Blanford. Without their help this book may never have been written, and thus I dedicate it in their honor.

Others have also been very gracious in offering their time, expertise, and encouragement. William Blanford has shared his knowledge of the family, even at time's tempering the nostalgia of his wife. Bettie Kerr, a director of the Henry Clay Home, worked with me in preparing a series of oral history interviews with Mrs. Blanford and introduced me to other members of the Clay families in Lexington. William Marshall and Terry Birdwhistell, Margaret I. King Library, University of Kentucky, helped me receive a grant from the Kentucky Oral History Commission and offered invaluable advice about the manuscript collections available at the University of Kentucky. Similarly, the staffs at the University of Louisville, the Filson Club, and the Kentucky Historical Society have been most generous with their collections and their expertise. The library staff at Georgetown College has embraced my research as if it were their own. Terry Martin, the late Darlene Cummins, and Richard Burtt were most generous and patient. To Mary Margaret Lowe, I owe special thanks. Always cheerful and eager to help, she has been at times more research assistant than librarian.

Attempting to complete research and write while teaching at a small liberal arts college requires major support. I have had the good fortune to have wonderful teaching colleagues. Fred Hood, Melissa McEuen, Stephen Leist, and Craig Thompson Friend of the History Department and Todd Coke and Michael Campbell of the English Department read portions of the manuscript at various stages. Gwen Curry, English Department, shared with me a grant from the Kentucky Humanities Council to conduct a series of programs on Sawitzky's poetry, and she offered valuable interpretive advice relative to the poems and bibliographical advice in the areas of women's poetry and women's studies. I appreciate as well the advice and encouragement of Steven May of the English Department, who read sections of the manuscript in the later stages of development but also knew enough from his own experiences to share his time and enthusiasm for scholarship. Other colleagues offered their moral support. If a heavy teaching load, advising, and committee work are the lot of a faculty member at a small college, the support of faculty from areas as diverse as music, chemistry, and physical education is the reward.

Special appreciation must also be extended to colleagues in the profession. Margaret Cowling, who loves the grand stories of history, particularly those of the Bluegrass region, read the manuscript in its earliest stages. William Ellis and John Kleber offered criticism, encouragement, and advice. Melba Porter Hay and Robert Seager shared the vast knowledge of the family they acquired while editing the Henry Clay papers. Carol Crowe-Carraco and Wade Hall read the manuscript in its entirety. Professor Crowe-Carraco, a historian of southern origins, offered personal testimony that made me realize I had significant things to say in this book. James C. Klotter, Director of the Kentucky Historical Society and State Historian, helped shape the manuscript through careful reading and insightful comments. Despite many responsibilities of his own, he always has time to give to others in the field. Equally important, he seems intuitively to know when a phone call or a word of support is most needed. Larry Prather shared his photography expertise.

Mary Buchanan, Vicki Cooper, Leila Dailey, Cynthia Bell, Jennifer Walker Brater, Jennifer Folden, and Sarah Hardin spent many hours preparing the manuscript. Cynthia Bell began as a student typist but became, after finishing her graduate education, an insightful reader.

I would also like to thank the staff of The Kent State University Press. John T. Hubbell, the director, will never know how important his kind words were in the early stages of the publication process. Linda Cuckovich guided the manuscript and me with clear, efficient, and sensitive direction. I wish also to thank Trudie Calvert, whose editorial skills have been invaluable in addition to saving me from some glaring mistakes. Authors often note how aggravating the publication process can be. My experience, thanks to the people at The Kent State University Press, has been a most pleasant one.

All authors profit from the support of their families. To my wife, who knows what it is to grow up southern, I offer my thanks for her patience but mostly for her advice and her willingness to discuss Susan Sawitzky and southern women. I have learned much from her. My children have literally grown to maturity with this project. Dinner conversation has often been about some aspect of the Clay family, and summer vacations were frequently spent at research sites. They too are an important part of the project. In fact, my daughter Lisa, a promising young artist herself, may have gained more from the education of her father than anyone.

I remain, of course, responsible for errors of fact. The interpretations are mine and until convinced otherwise I am comfortable with them.

Genealogy

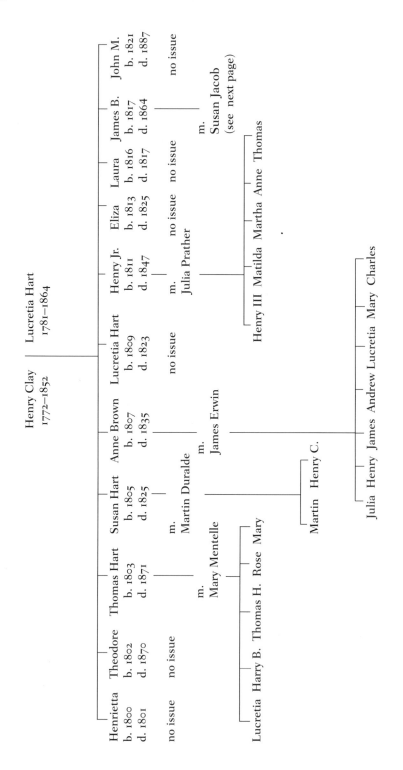

James B. Clay
1817–1864

Susan M. Jacob Clay
1823–1905

Lucy	James B.	John	Henry	Lucretia	Thomas J.	Susan	Charles D.	George H.	Nathaniel
b. 1844	b. 1846	b. 1847	b. 1849	b. 1851	b. 1853	b. 1855	b. 1857	b. 1858	b. 1862
d. 1863	d. 1906	d. 1872	d. 1884	d. 1924	d. 1939	d. 1863	d. 1935	d. 1934	d. 1863
	married						married		
no issue	no issue	no issue	no issue	no issue	no issue	no issue		no issue	no issue

Mariah Pepper

Susan	Charles Jr.	Robert P.	Elizabeth
(Mrs. William Sawitzky)	1899–1922	(Mary Martindale)	(Mrs. William Blanford)
1897–1981		1903–77	1904–

Robert P. Jr.   Lucy   Susan
b. 1941
d. 1973

Introduction

❧

IN THE FEBRUARY 1941 issue of *Poetry: A Magazine of Verse,* Charles Dillon included a poem by an unknown poet, Susan Clay Sawitzky. That issue contained works by Robert Penn Warren, Theodore Roethke, and others with established reputations or who were in the process of gaining for themselves some recognition in the world of poetry. Sawitzky's poem, "Mariner," begins with a descriptive account of retired sailors sitting at the dock dreaming of the times they went to sea. The poem creates images and captures the nostalgia of those who have visited New England fishing ports. It is not until the fourth stanza that she introduces the real theme of her poem. Her disarming descriptions mask a struggle within her mariners, a struggle, it seems, that much of humanity experiences.

> By still harbor water
> Where boats and their down-turned images
> Lie like open shell valves
> Joined at the water's surface,
> And sails hang shriveled
> Like old hides flayed off the wind,
> With all their creases brittle
> As dry leaves,—
> And chains stuck link to link in rust
> Dream of old plunging in the sea:
>
> You wait, O voyagers returned,
> Sitting on sea driven poles

At the wharf's edge
Like gulls
Unable to go inland;
Your thoughts still whirling about masts
And going out to meet each fishing boat
Heavy beneath its silver,
As though a leak had let
The leaping ripples of the sea
Across its floor.

The confident grip of earth set feet
Is not for you,
You who can never lose
The reeling sense of vast velocity;
Who know a step unmeasured
By a larger
Is land men's bondage.
For under you
A huge and certain stride
Throbbing in darkness
Through a boarded hull,
With rhythm
That made your small, contrary step
Falter and lurch against it,
Has loosed the feeling of finality
From man's aggressive tread:
And sometimes, vision of a crouching ocean
Swept round the sun
Is yours
In the watches of the night.

Only one who has felt the flood of infinite wonder
Against the tick of reason in a skull
Can know your loneness,—
Wanderers of ocean over narrow boards,
Withheld from freedom and beholding it.[1]

Sawitzky wrote the poem after visiting the fishing port at Gloucester, Massachusetts, then labored over it for several years, as was her custom, altering phrases, exchanging words, seeking more descriptive or more beautiful language with which to tell a somber truth. Her mariners, too old to go to sea, wait at the dock. They do not see the beauty the poet sees. They long for the open sea but are bound to the docks by physical limitations. Phrases such as "gulls / Unable to go inland," "earth set feet" and "land men's bondage" create a sense of confinement. Suddenly, she frees her sailors through the power of the mind which carries them to sea. Her sailors' thoughts whirl about the ships' masts. Mental images of bountiful silvery harvests and rippling seas transport them beyond their physical limitations.

There is nothing somber about the poem to this point, but she is not finished. The sailors are confronted with new realities. They tread the decks feeling the power of the sea as the vessel rises with each swell. Reality confronts the sailor with his own weakness in comparison to the power of the ocean beneath him. Moreover, the decks confine; they create a prison. Every glance confronts the mariners with the vastness of ocean, yet their movement is limited to the narrow boards of the deck. The author then expands the scope of her theme. Humanity beholds freedom, defines it, dreams of it, yet never accomplishes it. Humans are, like mariners, "Wanderers of ocean over narrow boards, / Withheld from freedom and beholding it."

The poem is, however, more than a pretty expression of a human dilemma. It is a metaphor of the life and work of the author. "Mariner" was Sawitzky's last published poem. She had written for thirty years before its publication and would write and edit poetry for another thirty years. "Mariner" reflects the style and the theme of her collected work. Romantic description masks an ongoing struggle between a sense of confinement by forces outside oneself and a longing for freedom.

Like the poem itself, her life had a surface romanticism to it. The great-granddaughter of the antebellum statesman Henry Clay, she grew to maturity on thoroughbred horse farms in the Bluegrass region of Kentucky. In the first decades of the twentieth century, Lexington, Kentucky, still sought to practice the social style of the southern planter class. Susan learned the romantic antebellum myths from her Grandmother Clay and her Aunt Teetee, who longed for the grandeur of that earlier time, and from the very ladylike, unmarried women who taught her formally. Talented, beautiful, and confident, she played the belle almost to perfection. She learned to view the world in which she was to live as beautiful and orderly. Family and community protected her from the ugly or what they considered unseemly.

Though her world was "filled with King Arthur and rainbows,"[2] it had, as in her poem, a somber side. Susan Clay Sawitzky's life paralleled that of the fictional character Sinclair Lewis created in Carol Midland Kennicott of *Main Street.* Born in 1897, Susan reached maturity at the height of the first women's movement and lived more than a decade into the second effort to achieve equality for women. A voracious reader, she consumed magazines and books that told her of the new opportunities for women and the women who pursued them. Like Carol Kennicott, she dreamed of accomplishing great things. She, too, dabbled at philosophy, wrote poetry, and painted. She experienced the criticism of her peers and the rebuke of parents and teachers when her creativity carried her beyond the role a young woman was supposed to play. As a sixteen-year-old, in her first published piece, she wrote, "No one seems to realize that beneath our little blue calico outsides, we all have individual souls."[3]

Again like Kennicott, she fled to Washington, D.C., to become a professional woman. She married an older man, at least partially to escape what one of Lewis's characters called "the village virus," a malady that suffocated bright people, whether in Kennicott's Gopher Prairie, Minnesota, or Susan Clay's Lexington, Kentucky. She would later find the same malady in New York and New England. She wanted to break free, to share her abilities, to control her own destiny, but because of upbringing, personality, duty to family, caution, isolation, fear, or a hundred other complicated reasons, she, like Carol Kennicott, found it expedient to compromise, most of the time.

Sinclair Lewis related the plight of the young twentieth-century woman in small-town middle America more accurately perhaps than the historians of his era or since. His fictional account captures the complex interweaving of factors that made it so difficult for women to break from traditional values and institutions even when they exhibited a strong desire to do so. Carol Midland Kennicott, however, is a fictional character; Susan Clay Sawitzky was a real woman. For over fifty years, roughly from the first to the second women's movement, she struggled with the external forces that limited self-expression, and she fought a battle within herself—a war between her traditional views and values and a desire to enjoy the opportunities promised modern woman. For nearly fifty years there were two Susan Clay Sawitzkys; each checked the happiness and intellectual fulfillment of the other.

Traditionally, women's historians have not been very interested in women like Carol Kennicott or Susan Clay Sawitzky. In a relatively new discipline, historians have preferred to chronicle the opportunities for women, emphasizing progress, particularly when created by women themselves. Biographers have chosen strong, successful women. Recent scholarship has identified specific issues or groups, and a new interest in political issues has developed, but the emphasis of women's studies has been on making visible the strong role women have played.[4]

The vast majority of women, however, were not activists. Consequently, they have received little scholarly attention. Some historians place them with that group of women who opposed change. Others merely acknowledge their existence. Nancy A. Hewitt and Suzanne Lebsock in *Visible Women: New Essays on American Activism* state: "We cannot say why some women were able to see while others were not, but we can offer instructive examples of women with exceptional vision." Similarly, in an excellent new history of southern women, *Daughters of Canaan*, Margaret Ripley Wolfe frequently notes the existence of women "haunted by the specter of 'the southern lady,'" but she enthusiastically pursues the southern activist woman. In an earlier article published in the *Register of the Kentucky Historical Society*, Wolfe wrote, "For every woman in Kentucky, the South, or America who has actively challenged the status quo there are thousands who have supported it, and passively opposed change; still others, *whatever the reason*, have been too helpless to be involved."[5]

Historians, then, have been slow to study what Sinclair Lewis noted over a half-century ago: tradition and modernity, continuity and change can and do exist simultaneously. Moreover, that coexistence creates tremendous complexity in the lives of individuals.[6] The life story of Susan Clay Sawitzky is an instructive example of those who, at least by current definitions, did not see, and it gives insight into the reasons

why many women were "too helpless to be involved." In fact, it suggests the existence of a group of women who may have realized more
about their circumstances than they have been credited for as well as
the existence of a pool of discontent the women's movement failed to
use to advantage. Susan Clay Sawitzky is no model—no Charlotte Perkins
Gilman, Margaret Sanger, or Elizabeth Cady Stanton. She did not equal
her "cousins"—Laura Clay and Madeline McDowell Breckinridge—or
fellow Kentucky writer Elizabeth Madox Roberts, who had fewer advantages and more success. She is instead a case study in how heritage, family, region, self, and many less significant forces can combine
to restrict the talent of a human being. Surely, such a life can also be
instructive.

This book is possible because a detailed record of her life remains.
Historically, more than any other group, women have failed to see the
value of their records.[7] In 1984, Elizabeth Clay Blanford gave me ac-
cess to Susan Sawitzky's papers and to family records still in her possession. No historian had used those papers. The family had also placed
a large collection of materials in the care of the Library of Congress.
This family correspondence presents a solid picture of three generations of the Clay family, their values, personal relationships, and, most
important, the folklore that becomes a part of each new generation's
understanding of the past. One of the reasons they saved the records
so faithfully was a belief that some member of the family would restore the prominence Henry Clay had known. Susan learned that lesson as clearly as her brothers. She preserved much of her correspondence, journals, notebooks, newspaper clippings, drawings, and
numerous edited versions of her poetry.

The poetry is particularly important and in fact opens each chapter.
The interest it generated, particularly that in the highly respected *Poetry: A Magazine of Verse*, indicates that she had ability even if few of
her poems were published. A second purpose of this biography is to
present her poetry so it can be evaluated by literary critics. I must note
that the poetry is used primarily for its historical rather than its literary
value. Generally the last versions of a poem are used, but when an
earlier version reflects the development of her thought or a particular
reaction to events in her life I have made an exception.

The poetry speaks to women's issues, and it is clearly autobiographical. Her early poetry helped define a growing rebellion against that "perfect" world presented by family and community. Like the nineteenth-century women poets studied by Sandra Gilbert and Susan Gubar in *Madwoman in the Attic,* Susan used spatial imagery to define a vague sense of confinement and a desire to understand and experience freedom.[8] The reader senses the direction of her thought before she knew it herself. Eventually, she attacked more openly the traditional institutions—family, community, religion, and the myth of the southern lady. By the time "Mariner" was published, she was exploring the restrictiveness of time, space, God, natural law, and other forces not on women alone but on humanity, regardless of gender. Moreover, her poetry seems to imply the irony of creating artificial barriers against women when all humanity shares so many limitations.

From these sources, the events of Susan Sawitzky's life can be chronicled, her mind explored, her struggle explained. The difficulties she experienced are astonishing. She faced not one obstacle but a series of barriers that arose unpredictably, acted on her subtly, or fell easily only to rise again. Traditional values that she rejected intellectually often returned to affect decisions at the height of crisis. Her life suggests that the tendency to compromise may not have been owing to lack of desire but to bewilderment, guilt, fatigue, and the very complexity of the issues.

Susan Clay Sawitzky's life spans so much of the twentieth century that she speaks to many of the major issues women of her generation faced. Educated primarily in the period before World War I, she assimilated values better suited to the nineteenth than the twentieth century. Women's studies scholarship has developed so rapidly, its results compiled so quickly, that some gaps develop from the very lack of time to consider ideas completely. Older interpretations are rejected, often with great alacrity, as new ones appear. Some need to be reconsidered. Some aspects of Barbara Welter's "cult of true womanhood" were very much alive in the homes and schools where Susan learned her values. Once instilled, the duties of "piety, purity, submissiveness and domesticity" were not easily discarded. Similarly, no one would have more quickly noted the impossibility of living completely the image, or images, of the southern lady than Susan's grandmothers, aunts, or mother. Yet the "myth" remained their model of behavior and an essential element of Susan's education. As Linda Kerber has argued, the old order continued to be "patched up" and "reconstructed."[9]

It is easy to dismiss such "myths" from the objective position afforded by hindsight, but Americans, and particularly southern Americans, have turned myth into "their" history.[10] The degree to which Susan Clay absorbed such lessons is apparent in the poems and short stories she wrote as a child. In epic dramas worthy of Arthur and Guinevere, or antebellum heroes and heroines, right triumphed over evil, nobility over baseness, and beauty over the commonplace. The seductiveness of the myths is apparent in the carefully orchestrated social life created for the gentry youth of central Kentucky. That idyllic worldview, and the desire to recapture it, affected Susan Sawitzky's actions and her writing throughout her life. In her poetry, for example, she wanted to write about issues important to women—the physical act of love, pregnancy, miscarriage, death, God, freedom—thirty years before Anne Sexton and Sylvia Plath broke the barrier erected by the men who defined "women's poetry," yet that same poetry contained the beautiful wording and imagery characteristic of an earlier time. She rebelled against family and shocked Bluegrass society by eloping with William Sawitzky, a divorced émigré Russian seventeen years older than she. He was her means of escape from the suffocation of small-town Lexington and her father's home. Yet she carried with her a traditional view of marriage and her role in it. Instead of pursuing her own dreams of success, she would lay her poetry aside to help Sawitzky establish his significant reputation in the field of art history. In fact, she published more in his field than in her own.

Susan Clay Sawitzky's life illustrates the tenacity of southern values even as far north as Kentucky. The glories of the "lost cause" were strong in her youth. Progressivism might bring some change even to middle America, but its impact was selective. Kentucky women participated in the woman's suffrage movement on a national level. Education and health reform also gained widespread support. But the same women who argued for the vote maintained much of the value structure of southern life.[11] The new film industry and literature also romanticized the South and its ways not only in the southern region but for the nation as a whole. Those ways were deeply entrenched. Anne Firor Scott, an eminent historian of southern origins, stated in an essay that her own southern "conditioning" led to a thirty-year effort "to come to terms with a historical reality that is very different from what I grew up believing."[12] She spoke of history, but in the South history and values were inseparable, and Susan Clay Sawitzky did not have the advantage of Scott's graduate education. Susan Clay Sawitzky left Kentucky to live for over fifty years in New York and New England, but the South never left her.[13]

The role of the family is also revealed in informative ways. Its impact on the assimilation of values has already been noted. Loyalty to family in its various forms may have been the major deterrent to Susan Clay Sawitzky's achieving success. The Clays bore the legacy of Henry Clay like an albatross about their necks. More than one descendant of a famous man has lived with the burden, but women were not immune to such demands. Her immediate family demanded adherence to modes of behavior vastly outdated as the 1920s approached. Susan rebelled in adolescence, but a family rupture is more easily anticipated than accomplished. Nearly thirty years old, she risked such a rupture to marry William Sawitzky. The rupture did not happen, nor did she escape the protectiveness of the male head of the house. Sawitzky, though more subtle, was equally protective; he was also the principal decision maker.

Protectiveness begets the need for protection regardless of gender, and Susan experienced a lifetime of it. Other factors also limited her effort to achieve freedom. Her writing became a pastime while she helped her husband establish his career. She suffered a miscarriage that enhanced a sense of self-doubt and guilt even as she cried out that she had done nothing to cause the loss of her child. She also experienced the grinding poverty and accompanying anxiety of the Depression years. Through most of the 1930s the central issue was survival, not freedom, and that was true of many human beings, regardless of gender.

Susan Clay Sawitzky would spend the last thirty-four years of her life as a widow. Sawitzky died from emphysema in 1947. At age fifty, Susan had no economic support and few skills to provide an income. The record reveals her efforts to function independently. Those efforts do not always provoke admiration. She relied heavily on the goodwill and sensitivity of others, sought relief in alcohol, and acted so irrationally at times that her sanity can be questioned. She did, however, cope with difficult issues—grief, a sense of personal inadequacy, financial need, loneliness—and she survived.

Several notes of caution must be raised. The definition of the word *success* can vary greatly. It is used here much the way Carolyn G. Heilbrun used it in *Writing a Woman's Life*.[14] Susan Sawitzky perhaps cannot be considered an "exceptional" woman as Heilbrun uses the term, but she was more successful than many women. She published poetry in several prestigious journals; her poetry caught the attention of several significant editors and poets. She helped with the research that earned her husband great respect in his field, and she published journal articles based on that research. She also had a successful marriage. At the end of her life, however, she lamented her lack of success. The discontent and uncertainty that characterized her poetry and her correspondence indicate that she did not think she had achieved her goals. A corollary to this note of caution involves the definitions of strength and timidity. Strength should never be equated with success or timidity with failure. Personality and the difficulty of obstacles must be considered.

A second note of caution involves interpretation. One of the complexities of her life, perhaps of the study of women or any minority, is that one interpretation invites a contrary response as criticism. As a young woman Susan Clay could easily have made a "good" marriage— she turned down several proposals—and made the transition from society belle to society matron. Many of her peers did that, even those whose parents were modern enough to let them leave Lexington to attend college. Had she really wanted a career, she could have chosen it over marriage. Marriage and career have long been "at odds."[15] She did not choose the option. Furthermore, as Heilbrun notes, the very success of some women is often used against others. The argument goes that since some women have been successful, the opportunity is there for any woman of talent, energy, and ambition. Failure must be, therefore, the fault of the individual. Ironically, that constitutes another justification for this biography. By emphasizing exceptional women, women's studies risks giving oblique credence to that argument.

To study the limitations to success, conversely, risks the possibility of portraying women as victims, which, understandably, the women's movement and women's historians have been reluctant to do. The paradox of individual responsibility versus environmental deprivation has been the classic "catch-22" for minorities seeking equal opportunity. All human beings are products of their past to some degree yet are responsible for personal success or failure to another. The issue establishes a false test, which in the process denies the complexity of women's struggle and robs women's history of its richness and vitality. As Sheila Wolfe has said of Emily Dickinson, Susan Clay Sawitzky could have done more to alleviate her discontent; under more equitable circumstances she would have been required to do less.

A third caution involves the tendency of women's studies to separate women into categories. Some will argue that Susan Clay Sawitzky cannot epitomize the majority of women of her age because she was southern, or aristocratic, or a poet. Catherine Clinton, however, in *The Plantation Mistress,* warned against the regionalization of women's studies.[16] Antebellum values blended easily into Victorian values, which were shared by the middle and upper classes largely without respect to region. Protective fathers, miscarriage, and the death of a spouse seem hardly less catastrophic by region or class. Women, regardless of class, were encouraged to limit their ambition and accept traditional roles. Betty Friedan wrote about the concerns of college women in the 1950s, but Susan Clay knew "the problem that has no name" in 1914. It had little to do with class but concerned restricted opportunities for women. Susan Clay was a poet, but the primary difference between her and most other women was that she could write in clear and moving terms what she felt as a woman. Few women who have experienced a miscarriage will fail to appreciate her poems on the subject. Few who have lost a beloved spouse will fail to understand her haunting interpretation: Inadmissible vacuum—Lesion in breast of God.[17] Susan Clay Sawitzky's experiences suggest that while the pattern of discrimination and women's reactions to it may vary by class, region, or intellectual inclination, the fabric is much the same.

A final caution or perhaps a request is directed to my colleagues in the profession. Susan Clay Sawitzky's life can speak to many women and perhaps to men who have observed sisters and daughters growing up in traditional family settings. Such people, I think, want to read the story. To avoid obstructing that story, references to secondary studies have been relegated for the most part to the notes. Susan Clay Sawitzky's life can be seen in the context of that literature, but I hope colleagues will use their own knowledge to draw the comparisons.

Biographers too often start with accomplishments and find their causes. Few lives are so focused. Few issues are so simple. This study begins at the beginning and traces a winding path with false starts and blind trails because it took years and a special style to instill traditional values to such levels. Achieving modernity with the millstone of tradition weighing upon one's shoulders was a task only a few accomplished. The life of Susan Clay Sawitzky in its unfolding speaks to the complexity of the issue.

CHAPTER ONE

✴

The Setting

IN THE SUMMER OF 1897, Elizabeth Pepper closed her twenty-two-room home in the historic district of Frankfort, Kentucky, and moved her six daughters, servants, and assorted visiting aunts and cousins to their country place, the Cliffs. The rustic, sprawling summer house occupied high ground near the settlement of Thorn Hill just outside Frankfort. It was quiet and peaceful there. Summer breezes cooled the house, and aged oak and elm trees provided shaded areas about the large lawn. Flower gardens, tended by a longtime servant, seemed to bloom continually from spring through late fall. Eleven servants assured the beauty of house and gardens as well as the leisurely pace for the pleasure of residents and guests. Those elderly aunts and cousins visited for a month or more at a time and local people always seemed present. In the afternoons, the ladies who resided on the square, a part of Frankfort which dated to frontier times, generally came together in a carriage to chat away a lazy summer day.

While the elderly women occupied themselves with casual conversation, a younger set gathered on the porch or lawn in groups of two or more. Elizabeth Pepper's beautiful and popular daughters as well as her own open, engaging manner assured a steady flow of young men and women. Many of Frankfort's young gentlemen had pursued a prospective bride walking the lawns or seated on the wicker chairs and settees scattered about it. Aristocratic and Victorian values blended in the most pleasant sense at the Cliffs. Life moved smoothly, genteelly, far removed from the hustle and bustle of a rapidly industrializing America. At the Cliffs, the clocks were set by guessing the approximate time of the day.[1]

The Peppers' Frankfort home contained twenty-two rooms and provided a gathering place for both the young and the old among Frankfort's gentry. The dwelling was razed some years ago.

Susan Jacob Clay was born into this setting on July 21, 1897. She was the daughter of Charles and Mariah Pepper Clay. They, too, had courted at the Cliffs in the summer of 1895 and married at the Pepper Frankfort home in September 1896. Charles Clay was a professional soldier, but this child was too important to be born in an army camp, so Ria,[2] as family and friends called her, came home that summer to the comfort of family, servants, and the physician she had known all her life.

The Peppers and the Clays were members of the gentry class of the Kentucky Bluegrass region. The people of the region and the class thought of themselves as southerners and embraced a style generally associated with antebellum days. If possible, the area and its gentry were more devoted to a rigid interpretation of that body of social norms and forms than antebellum southerners had been.[3]

Kentuckians were not always so southern, or perhaps it would be more accurate to say that Kentuckians were selectively southern. It was truly a border state influenced by characteristics of both regions.

The gentry, though it attempted to live in the style of the southern planter elite, was much more flexible in practice. It consistently assimilated new money made in business, commerce, and industry. Susan's great-grandfather Henry Clay epitomized the attitudes of his region. The owner of a large plantation worked by slaves, he dabbled in business interests and encouraged the adoption of the American System to encourage commercial and industrial development in the western states.

The border mentality became even clearer when the Civil War began. Kentuckians proclaimed their neutrality, a policy doomed from the beginning though it certainly expressed sentiment in the state. Best estimates suggest that approximately ninety thousand Kentuckians fought for the Union and another forty thousand joined Confederate forces. Nevertheless, both North and South questioned the loyalties of the state and occasionally the courage of its citizens. The example of the Clay family may best describe the situation in the state. Of Henry Clay's sons, James B. Clay supported the Confederacy, Thomas Hart Clay served Abraham Lincoln as a diplomat to Central America, and John Morrison Clay stayed home, pouring invective on both sides. According to the family, he complained, "The Rebels steal my horses, the Yankees steal my slaves and I don't give a damn for either side."[4] It truly was a brothers' war for Kentuckians. Crittendens, Clays, and a host of "lesser" folk sent fathers, husbands, and sons to fight on opposing sides. Kentuckian met Kentuckian across battle lines at Shiloh, Chickamauga, and hundreds of skirmishes in between. Bad feelings, such as those that became the basis of Annie Fellows Johnston's Little Colonel books, separated Kentuckians for years.[5]

After the war pro-Union sympathies waned. Though Kentucky had not seceded, many of its citizens resented the freeing of the slaves. Union governor James F. Robinson harshly criticized the Emancipation Proclamation and later, as a member of the Kentucky legislature, advised the state to reject the Thirteenth Amendment. Kentuckians also resented the harsh military occupation led by Kentucky-born Union commanders Stephen G. Burbridge and John M. Palmer. They threatened secession when the government imposed Reconstruction policies after the war and turned the state over to its own Bourbon regime, the Kentucky colonels.

Kentuckians were not alone, however, in redefining attitudes. The myth of the lost cause developed rapidly in the South to rationalize both the causes of the war and the defeat at the hands of the Union. By the turn of the century some of that rationalization influenced northern thought as well. In 1877 the nation tired of Reconstruction and nationwide prejudices reappeared. The Supreme Court altered the definition of the Fourteenth Amendment, and by 1896 Jim Crow and separate but equal had received a national blessing. Accompanying the legal erosion was a softening of social attitudes. The myths of southern ladies and gentlemen, benevolent masters, and genteel living gained national acceptance. Kentuckians played no small part in the creation of the myths. Annie Fellows Johnston published *The Little Colonel* in 1895, the first of thirty-eight novels glorifying the South and southern values, particularly those relating to the role of women.[6] In 1915 David Wark Griffith produced *The Birth of a Nation,* a film that portrayed the Ku Klux Klan as heroic and enshrined nineteenth-century stereotypes. By the time of Susan's birth, popular culture made southern values and attitudes quite acceptable.[7]

Kentuckians had long advocated southern social values. From frontier times the Bluegrass gentry had sought to make itself and Lexington, the hub of the region, distinctive. Most proclaimed kinship with Virginia's tidewater aristocracy so they easily adopted the planters' social values as a means of setting themselves above a more common crowd. The early settlers built a respected university, established a public library, created literary, musical, and horticultural societies, and built fine homes and estates for themselves.[8] The contradiction between democratic rhetoric and aristocratic pretension seemed lost on Kentuckians though it was noted by some visitors and newcomers. Madame Charlotte Mentelle, for example, welcomed by the gentry because she was a refined and cultured Frenchwoman, described them as hypocritical in a letter to relatives in France.[9] The contradiction remained one the Bluegrass gentry did not care to explore.[10]

The social system that characterized the antebellum South was not destroyed by the Civil War. Indeed, in Lexington the maintenance of the civility called for by the code justified the belief that southern life was superior to that of the industrial North and that the South should not have lost the war. An air of defensiveness, then, made any violation of the code virtually as serious in 1897 as in 1847.[11]

In the Bluegrass world at the time of Susan's birth, society continued to revolve around the grand homes of the region.[12] Faithful black servants had replaced faithful black slaves, but little else had changed. These servants performed the labor that allowed the gentry to live in relative leisure. The male was the head of the household, provider, protector, and final judge in most matters. The gentry lady spent most of her time, at least that spent in the presence of others, being a lady. Bluegrass society was highly competitive so great care had to be taken lest a social blunder affect family status. Because of the importance of social position, a great deal of attention was placed on family honor. Generation after generation of children were tied to family by the use of favorite names and of a mother's maiden name or another from her side of the family as a given name. That, too, was an antebellum practice.[13] In the Clay family, for example, there were so many Henrys that some were called Harry to distinguish them. Susan was named for her paternal grandmother and an aunt who had died as a young woman. Her brother Charley, born in 1899, was named for his father. The last two children were given names from the maternal family—Robert Pepper Clay for grandfather and uncle, Elizabeth Starling Clay for Elizabeth Pepper and her family.

Kentuckians were said to be high-spirited, generous, and hospitable, yet quick to take offense if family honor was questioned. Dueling was illegal, but men still fought and occasionally died in defense of family. Thirteen years before Susan's birth, an uncle, named Harry, died in a Louisville shoot-out over a three dollar loan and an insult to family honor.

Children learned the family history, their intricate relationships to other gentry families, and their obligation to their name in the leisure hours spent with parents and other relatives. Their formal education was received in private schools. Most gentry families still sent their children, particularly daughters, to private academies even though the public school system was improving. Though the twentieth century had dawned, education for a special class continued to reinforce traditional values. Male children were encouraged to develop masculine skills and not to be overly worried about academic excellence. Gentry daughters read romantic novels and poetry and learned to dance, serve tea, and participate in the light conversation that characterized such events. Their world was one of beauty and order, and every effort was made to protect them from ugliness and disorder as long as they were under their father's roof. Both sexes were taught that they would take their natural place of leadership in due time.

The training was put to full use in the fairy-tale social life that occupied much of the time of the young people. The older generation labored diligently to provide the young with social activities. Teas, receptions, card parties, dances, cotillions, and kermises provided weekly events for the children of central Kentucky's finest families. Such events were not entirely for the purpose of entertainment, however. They provided the means by which a kind of social sorting out occurred, and "proper" or "good" marriages were made. The right family connections, wealth, and social skill determined the most eligible of the season, and, if correspondence is any indication, the older generation expressed more concern about such matters than the younger.[14]

The older generation kept the ultimate goal in the minds of the young, but there was also a great deal of pleasure to be had, indeed a kind of seductive pleasure. The young men acted their most gentlemanly and young women enjoyed the attention that chivalry and their position on the pedestal of southern womanhood assured. Particularly for the women, it was the role to which virtually all their training applied. It was also the acting out of Camelot, and for a brief time the young women were more nearly the equals of their male suitors than they would ever be again. Moreover, the young absorbed values critical to the preservation of a way of life.

The social setting of the Bluegrass region into which Susan Clay was born looked to the past, but it was not devoid of change. In fact, she was born in the midst of the most significant change since the Civil War. Progressivism swept Lexington into the reform camp at the turn of the century. New money bought horse farms and changed the breeding and racing of thoroughbred horses from a gentleman's sport to a business. The old guard, resenting the intrusion at first, finally succumbed to the allure of wealth and incorporated the new residents into society.[15] And in the women's suffrage movement, Lexington provided national leaders in the persons of Laura Clay, a daughter of Cassius M. Clay, and Madeline McDowell Breckinridge, like Susan a great-granddaughter of Henry Clay. They led a group of "thorough-bred" women in pursuit of the vote and other reforms.[16]

Such a progressive posture, however, only slightly altered the attitudes about women or their social position. The suffragists themselves carefully fashioned their methods within the social context of the region. They even entertained Emmeline Pankhurst, the radical and sometimes violent English reformer, at a sedate tea at Ashland, the estate of Henry Clay, when she visited Lexington. Most women, one suspects, read the accounts of the "new woman" in magazines and on the society page of the newspaper but watched cautiously as events unfolded. Some doors were opened to brave young women, but the social values remained very traditional and very southern.[17]

The Peppers and the Clays had even stronger reasons to encourage a traditional set of values. Lexington and central Kentucky would change, albeit slowly and sometimes begrudgingly, but the two families into which Susan was born had deep roots in the gentry class and its values. Both families owned large Bluegrass farms and were known for the breeding of fine thoroughbred horses. Both families had illustrious heritages and the wealth, though there had been unfortunate reverses, to live very comfortably. And both families had been a part of the elite long enough that its manners and values were second nature to their members.

The Pepper family maintained their homes in Frankfort, the capital city overlooking the Kentucky River, but Mariah Pepper's father also owned land in three surrounding Bluegrass counties—Woodford, Scott, and Fayette. Robert Pepper Sr. had been a well-known and respected landowner and businessman for many years, operating one of the finest distilleries in Frankfort until fire destroyed it. Acceding to his wife's entreaties and to the changing attitudes about temperance, he decided not to rebuild it. He turned his energies instead to the breeding of trotting horses, and his stables became world renowned for such sires as Norval, Madrid, and Acolyte. His most famous sire was the champion Onward. Pepper advertised his stables as far away as Cape Town, South Africa, and Europeans and Arab sheiks shipped their mares to Frankfort to be bred to Pepper's stallions.[18]

The Peppers had no nationally recognized figures among their members, but they did trace their lineage back to solid families of Virginia, including those of several governors. Their position in the gentry was secure by reasons of breeding, wealth, and the social grace of their homes.

The Pepper homes took their character from Elizabeth Pepper. Despite the service of her relatives in the Union army, she epitomized socially the best of the southern lady. Like Catherine Clinton's plantation mistress, however, while appearing publicly as the kind, gracious, unflappable hostess, behind the scenes she organized the activities, staff, and finances of her homes with great efficiency. She welcomed everyone and exhibited to all the same kindness. The family noted with pride that the servants came when young and stayed until old because they loved and respected Mrs. Pepper. (There are no records of what the servants said.) She welcomed the younger guests and made them feel at ease just as she did her older friends. In the three years preceding Susan's birth she lost her husband, her only son, and a daughter yet bore her losses with the stoic resolve the stereotype attributes to all aristocratic southern women. In fact, she was so nearly the perfect example of the genteel southern woman that she served as the model for that character in Robert Burns Wilson's *Until the Day Break,* a novel published in New York in 1900.[19]

The Clays were equally secure as members of the Bluegrass gentry. They, too, raised thoroughbred horses, but they were better known for producing statesmen and soldiers. There had been several successful members of the family, though more perhaps in the eyes of their descendants than in reality. Yet central Kentucky honored none of its famous sons more than the Great Pacificator. Lexington and the region incorporated the Clay name into a definition of self. The grand tomb erected in Henry Clay's honor looked out over trees and buildings in the city's west end, and Ashland, the home of Henry and then James B. Clay, remained the most impressive structure on Lexington's east side. His law office, other Clay homes, and numerous memorials dotted the old city's streets. No matter where they turned, Clays could not escape their past.

If Henry Clay left a legacy to Lexington and central Kentucky, he left a large one to his family as well. Certainly to none was that legacy any keener, or perhaps more double-edged, than to the James B. Clay branch of the family, dominated in 1897 by the presence and the thinking of Susan's grandmother Susan Mariah Jacob Clay.

Like Elizabeth Pepper, Susan M. Clay maintained publicly the image of the southern woman. Much about her, however, supports the historians' debunking of the myth. Widowed in 1864, Mrs. Clay lived on a farm approximately five miles outside Lexington with two bachelor sons and a daughter. The two sons raised horses and tobacco on some of the richest land in Fayette County.[20] For their mother's pleasure, they also spent a great deal of time raising flowers in gardens surrounding the quaint English Tudor cottage. At the suggestion of the president of Kentucky College, later the University of Kentucky, they named the farm Balgowan, a Scottish word meaning "Land of Flowers." For years, however, there was something missing about the place for Mrs. Clay and her daughter Lucretia. They referred to Balgowan as "the Shanty."[21] It was no shanty, but it could not compare in fact or, more particularly, in their minds to the beloved Ashland, which Mrs. Clay had been forced to sell as a result of the financial chaos that followed the Civil War. To a degree, the Clays lived in the past when fame and fortune were greater.

Balgowan became a lovely museum of Old Kentucky and a memorial to Clay service to state and nation. Portraits of earlier Clays painted by Matthew Jouett, Oliver Frazer, and other locally famous artists lined the parlor. Henry Clay's license to practice law, carried in a saddlebag from Virginia in 1797, hung on one side of the mantle and a letter signed by Daniel Boone describing his surveying of wilderness Kentucky occupied the other side. Many of Henry Clay's papers were stored in an old trunk along with letters signed by George Washington, Thomas Jefferson, Aaron Burr, Zachary Taylor, James Buchanan, and other national figures. Other Clays reminded visitors of past service as well. A portrait of Jim Clay, the oldest son of James and Susan and a Confederate volunteer at age sixteen, hung on the wall. A crude Indian bridle, the gift of Geronimo to another son, Thomas Jacob Clay, hung above the mantle along with the field glasses that a third son, Harry Clay, had taken on the Howgate Expedition to the Arctic. Furniture saved from Ashland and the silver urns and candelabras given to Henry Clay by admirers filled the rooms. The family crafted a story about each item that emphasized Henry Clay's service and his popularity.

Throughout her childhood Susan would be reminded of her heritage wherever she turned.

But if the residents of Balgowan were as aristocratic as those of the Cliffs, they had not escaped tragedy, and their misfortunes tied them to southern traditions of conduct and demeanor. James Clay had been the rising star of the family before the Civil War. Before the age of forty-five he had served as chargé d'affaires in Lisbon, Portugal, inherited and rebuilt Ashland, served several terms in the U.S. House of Representatives, and refused President Buchanan's offer of the ministry to Prussia. An advocate of compromise in 1861, he nevertheless chose the South when those efforts failed. He would not live, however, to share the South's defeat. James Clay died of tuberculosis in January 1864 at the age of forty-seven.

Mrs. Clay's great expectations were crushed. She buried three children in the eighteen months before her husband's death, then lost Ashland as well as her share of her father's estate in the aftermath of the war. Moreover, she was convinced that her neighbors in a deeply divided Lexington enjoyed her misfortune. She bore her humiliation publicly with the nobility of spirit southern aristocratic women were credited with having by their very nature. Her children, however, felt the true impact of her losses. She taught them that it was a privilege to be a Clay and that they must accept the responsibility of being a member of their family and class. One faced tragedy and humiliation with confidence in one's breeding and place. Education in the manner of the southern elite provided both the means to withstand hardship and a justification of their father's political decisions. It was also the manner she had been taught from her own youth. If mean-spirited people watched the families of great men for minor indiscretions, and she was certain that they did, then the families of great men had to be the ultimate ladies and gentlemen. The sons and daughter of Susan M. Clay learned to be ever mindful of the image they presented.[22] They also learned that even though the "Clay star" might not be "in the ascendancy just now," Clay genes and proper attention to duty would soon restore the name to its rightful place of prominence.[23] If the Peppers were southern gentry because it suited their present station, the Clays practiced those values to honor the past and to recover family glory.

Both families considered it their obligation to instill their values and manner in Susan. The intensity of their efforts was enhanced because of the character of Susan's parents, Charles and Mariah Pepper Clay, and because of the circumstances of their early married lives. For the Peppers, Susan's birth brought reason to rejoice after a time filled with tragedy and sorrow. To the Clays, she represented the promise of a new generation. She was the first child born to the James Clay branch of the family since the Civil War.

Charles Clay, the last of James Clay's sons likely to produce a new generation, did not marry until he was thirty-nine years old. Born in 1857, he spent many years under his mother's tutelage. He was keenly aware of his duty as a Clay and a gentleman. Dignified and aristocratic in bearing, Charles dedicated himself as a young man to restoring the family prominence. He tried his hand at several jobs before receiving a commission in the U.S. Army in 1883. Promotions came slowly in a peacetime army even though he graduated from nearly every training school with honors; the Clays believed his lack of promotion resulted from the family's southern sympathies.[24] He assured his mother repeatedly that he was working diligently and conducting himself as a gentleman. By 1895, Mrs. Clay was reminding Charles of another family duty, its perpetuation. She had protested on several occasions when Charles or another son appeared to be falling in love, but with opportunities slipping by, she approved his courtship of Mariah Hensley Pepper.[25]

Charles Clay presented an impressive figure when he called on Miss Pepper in an army uniform tailored expressly for the occasion. Of slender build and medium height, Clay sported a thick mustache common to the age. The mustache and a military swagger added an air of manliness to an otherwise boyish appearance that belied his age. Even in an era when men were supposed to appear formal, Charles Clay seemed rather stiff. Ria Pepper thought so at first. She was twenty-six years old, quietly confident, and accustomed to the attention of young attractive men. Life had unfolded grandly for Mariah with very little effort on her part. Her parents had provided the wealth and the position to place her at the height of the Bluegrass social order, her education taught the skills, and nature created the beauty. And Ria Pepper was a beautiful young woman. Long, thick hair gathered behind her

Mariah Hensley Pepper, posing here shortly before her wedding, enjoyed a full social life. She had to be gently nudged by her mother into consenting to Lt. Charles D. Clay's request to call on her.

Lt. Charles D. Clay looked the part of the suave young military officer when he called on Mariah Pepper in 1895.

head framed a soft and inviting face. Her eyes were deep set and large, betraying the gentleness of her nature. She wore gracefully the elegant dresses that call immediately to mind images of the antebellum South.[26] She could easily have stepped into a pre–Civil War ball. On more than one occasion the local newspaper noted her presence at formal dances and parties, and she frequently had the honor of leading the "german," a processional dance that characterized such affairs. Her fame as a "Bluegrass belle" spread as far as Atlanta, Georgia; in an extremely large memory book filled with party favors, theater programs, and the like, she included an article from the *Atlanta Constitution* which called her a "star" of the central Kentucky social world.

Ria Pepper warmed slowly to Charles. They sat on the large wraparound porch at the Cliffs, walked together around the lawns and flower gardens, or played with one of an assortment of pets that called the Cliffs home. Ria was as skilled at breaking down masculine barriers as Charles was at erecting them. A proper soldierly image also proved impossible to maintain when Ria's pet monkey, Little Mike, insisted on jumping to his lap, sitting on his shoulder, or playfully swiping at his tie. Charles mellowed a bit each time he visited.[27] There was, beneath a carefully constructed surface formality, a degree of sensitivity and gentleness few who knew him would have suspected. Like Ria, he loved animals, and he could be remarkably gentle and engaging around young children. Duty, however, required the aloofness of a gentleman, and one saw but fleeting glimpses of that more sensitive side.

Charles proposed to Ria early in 1896 when he received orders assigning him to the Eleventh Infantry at Fort Apache, Arizona Territory. Propriety demanded a period of engagement and a carefully planned wedding so they set the wedding date for September and Charles reluctantly left for his new post.

They continued the courtship through letters. Ria gradually adopted the role of dependent and submissive female. She joked occasionally about the new freedom women were being promised, but she also assured him of the sense of security he gave her. She knew, she wrote, that he would be gentle and kind, protecting her and providing for her. He also assumed his role. Strong, decisive, and protective, Charles Clay took command. He made decisions about the wedding, for example, that one might assume he would have left to her.[28] He also began the duty of protecting her. Fearful of taking his refined bride to the wild and rugged frontier of Arizona, Clay secured a transfer back to the Seventeenth Infantry at Columbus, Ohio.

Married at Mrs. Pepper's home on September 8, 1896, they had hardly established a home when Ria discovered she was pregnant. It was a family decision that such a birth was too important to risk its occurrence on an army base.

Charles Clay remained in Columbus until after Susan's birth. He visited briefly on several occasions, but in early 1898 he received orders to go to Tampa, Florida, the staging area for the invasion of Cuba. With Charles away at war and Ria increasingly strained by concern for his safety, the Peppers and the Clays happily shared in the training of Susan Jacob Clay, the first of a new generation.

❦

CHAPTER TWO

Childhood

Ne'er so fair to me was girlhood
Ne'er was youth so perfect,
    joyous,—

—untitled poem

SUSAN CLAY WROTE THESE lines as an adolescent looking back on her childhood. Certainly, there was nostalgia in such reminiscences, but the description was not inappropriate. From the moment of her birth Susan was showered with attention and praise. Surrounded by servants who performed the mundane tasks and genteel adults who had both the time and the inclination to adore a child, Susan quickly learned to enjoy center stage. The adults instilled in her a degree of confidence and a belief in her potential by their encouragement and because of their style of life. She remained a member of a class that believed leadership its natural right. Refinement, leisure, beauty, and order characterized Susan's "perfect" world.

Susan Jacob Clay was welcomed into the world by her adoring public. At the Cliffs, relatives, servants, and guests vied for the chance to hold her and to praise her beauty. Mrs. Pepper immediately assigned a trusted longtime servant, Mary Jackson, to help Ria with Susan, but she found it difficult to do much. There were too many other willing hands. Ria wrote to Charles that frequently feelings were hurt when one person arrived a step sooner than others to answer Susan's cry. The elderly ladies who visited regularly commented, again according to Ria, on Susan's beauty and intelligence, and Ria's sisters and the other young women took her for walks on the lawns or to the large

Ria, Susan, and Mary Jackson enjoyed the lawns at "the Cliffs," the Peppers' summer home near Thorn Hill.

swing that sat under an oak tree near the house. Susan was affectionately called "la belle," the little lady of the Cliffs.[1]

The reaction at Balgowan was similar, though the relatives there saw less of baby Susan than they would have liked. Grandmother Clay, normally restrained, was delighted that the baby had been named for her and equally happy that Susan inherited the physical features of the Clays. She wrote to Charles that she saw intelligence in Susan's face and, on another occasion, that she knew Susan would grow into a fine lady. Mrs. Clay called her "Daddie's baby" and wrote letters inviting infant Susan to bring her mother for a visit. Her letters to Charles before and after such visits were filled with her own excitement.

Mrs. Clay wrote directly to Ria about the more practical matters of caring for her granddaughter. Although Elizabeth Pepper mildly chastised Ria for being too attentive, Grandmother Clay fretted about

Susan's health and urged Ria to watch for any sign of illness. With more than a hint of the stereotypical mother-in-law, Mrs. Clay wrote to Ria that Susan "seems to be predisposed to colds—I don't know where she gets this tendency—I never had a child to have croup."[2] She constantly reminded Ria how important Susan was to Charles as if that would add to her daughter-in-law's diligence. Later, when Susan had the croup again, the Clays brought a specially trained nurse from Louisville to stay with her until the condition improved.[3]

Lucretia, Charles's sister, also seemed to want to share the parenting role. Called Teetee because of her small stature, Lucretia Clay was a forceful woman. A genteel Victorian lady in public, within the family Teetee frequently said what she was thinking without the sugar coating. She had never married and, increasingly, as Mrs. Clay aged, saw to the operation of household affairs at Balgowan. In her spare time she participated in local organizations such as the Woman's Club of Central Kentucky, the Daughters of the American Revolution, and various Confederate women's groups. When the Spanish-American War broke out, she joined the Women's National War Relief Association and quickly contributed five dollars to the children's war relief fund so the name of Susan Jacob Clay would be at the top of the Honor Roll. She wrote to Charles, already in Tampa, Florida, as a part of the invasion force, and to Ria to inform them of their daughter's patriotism. She wrote frequently to Ria sharing hints on child rearing she had read or home remedies she had acquired from friends. On more than one occasion, however, she reminded her sister-in-law that Susan was a Clay and should be made aware of it whenever possible.[4]

Even the two bachelor brothers showed some excitement over the arrival of their niece despite their attempts to appear aloof. Tom Clay seemed to have more frequent business in Frankfort after Susan's birth and stopped by the Cliffs to make sure all was well. George, more spontaneous and fun-loving than most of the Clays, masked a keen interest with humor. In a letter to Ria, he suggested that Susan looked like her father but urged his sister-in-law not to tell him. Charles was, George Clay reasoned, already "puffed up" enough with his brass buttons and military braid. At Balgowan Susan became "Her Ladyship," a name decreed by her Aunt Teetee but accepted by all.[5]

The involvement of Charles Clay in the Spanish-American War and the dangers inherent to his participation certainly accentuated Susan's importance to the family, but for Charles and Ria she became the symbol of their marriage. Ria wrote almost daily, and Charles answered as often as his responsibilities allowed. Every letter contained long passages about Susan. Far less reserved when writing about his daughter, Charles wrote, "Sing her Daddy's song so she won't forget me."[6] Of course, Susan was too young and had seen too little of him to know her father, except for photographs Charles sent from Tampa and the mental picture Ria created for her. That image, however, was a strong one. The photographs pictured Charles in uniform, ramrod straight and very military. Ria Clay stressed Charles's gallantry, duty, and honor.[7] "Papa" was a noble soldier doing his duty to country even though he missed his family terribly. Ria read Charles's letters to Susan emphasizing, of course, his bravery and his love for his daughter. The image Ria drew for Susan was larger than life, one any man would have difficulty fulfilling in daily contact, but it was instilled deeply. When Charles sent new photographs to replace the battered ones, Ria reported that Susan, holding the pictures as high as she could, proclaimed "Two Papa, Two Papa" to everyone who came near.[8] The image of her father was so important that she kept one of the photographs throughout her life.

Ria also constructed an image of Susan for Charles and perhaps in her own mind as well. Ria proclaimed her daughter's beauty and brilliance from the time Susan was two weeks old. Indeed, Ria's existence, or at least her sanity, seemed to revolve around her daughter. Ria Clay was unprepared for what she faced in the years shortly after her marriage. She took pride in her husband's profession; gentry families considered the military a noble profession for their sons. But reality soon confronted the exaggerated images of gallantry, bravery, and patriotism she had learned from the romantic literature and the lore of Confederate heroism which had constituted her education. War seemed less noble when it threatened her husband. Ria Clay fought a continuous battle with her emotions, clinging to Susan as a living symbol of that marriage which was perfect except for his absence, and in her own mind made Susan the nearly perfect child. She was the "prettiest

smartest little girl . . . so jolly and dear." In another letter Ria proclaimed her daughter "bright, funny, and interesting." Everyone who
visited at the Pepper home noted Susan's brilliance, at least according
to Ria's letters.[9]

Ria Clay spent far more time with her daughter than was customary
for women of her class. She fed and bathed Susan on a regular basis
even though Mary Jackson was assigned the tasks and appeared willing to perform them. Ria took Susan for long walks both at the Cliffs
and in Frankfort when they returned to the city in the fall. She pointed
out flowers, brightly colored leaves, and other things of beauty, writing
gleefully to Charles each time Susan seemed to show interest. She
used every opportunity to stimulate her daughter's imagination, and
Susan's quick response pleased her immensely, encouraging her to do
more. She bragged in virtually every letter about Susan's latest feat.
She was drawing and rhyming words by the time she was two years
old.[10] Charles received the earliest efforts of his "artist daughter," a
group of stick people Ria interpreted as Susan, herself, and Papa, and
a signed letter before Susan was three years old. He, of course, sent
his words of delight and praise by return mail, Ria read them to Susan,
and more drawings were readied for the next letter. Susan's artistic
talents were enlisted early in the task of keeping her father's spirits
high. Ria made sure Susan knew how important her efforts were, the
Clays reiterated the message, and Papa's loving words received by mail
confirmed it. Lessons in noblesse oblige had begun.[14]

Susan Clay's early literary and artistic expressions, saved as evidence
of her intelligence, were just that. She was obviously intelligent and
quick. She also had the physical attributes that drew attention naturally. Her hair, blond and curly, hung about her face in ringlets, giving
her a devilish look. She had the features of the Clays—a thin nose,
high cheekbones, and a small mouth. Her blue eyes sparkled, even in
photographs, but flashed fire when she was angry, characteristics the
family liked to note that Henry Clay had possessed. Commenting on a
lawn party given her by Aunt Teetee in 1902, a Lexington newspaper
called her at age five "a child of rare beauty, with promise of being in
every way a lovely representative of her distinguished family."[12]

Constant attention and lavish praise created a confident and assertive little girl. Her mother indicated early that she had a mind of her

own. At age two Susan was "darling in her baby defiance," had "a fondness for bonnets and bows, and knowing which ones she prefers," and dominated any conversation.[13] That may not be unusual for small children, but it did not stop, nor did Ria or the two families attempt to limit her expression. That was not uncommon among families that practiced the values of the southern myth. Bertram Wyatt-Brown noted in his book *Southern Honor* that aggressiveness and self-confidence were encouraged in the children of the antebellum southern elite and that consequently discipline was very lax. Children of the leadership class needed confidence if they were to assume their role as adults. Girls, he argued, were treated the same as boys until the age of puberty, when their training to the role of submissive and demure women began.[14] George Clay indicated that little had changed in the Clay family a half-century later when he wrote to Ria in August 1897, shortly after Susan's birth, but he said it in purely Kentucky terms: "Give the little filly her head so she will have spirit."[15]

Susan developed plenty of spirit as a child because there was no one with the will or inclination to discipline her. If her father had been at home, things certainly would have been different, but Charles Clay's career kept him away from the family except for short periods until 1903. Ria, Susan, and, after June 1899, brother Charley, lived at Mrs. Pepper's homes in the presence of doting relatives. After 1902 the family could have been reunited except for decisions made by both Charles and Ria Clay. Charles retired from the army in 1902 and built the family home across the Versailles Road from Balgowan, but he soon determined that the income from his pension and the farm was insufficient to keep his family in the style he believed appropriate. As a result, he accepted a series of civilian assignments with the army which took him to four southern cities between 1903 and 1908.

Ria Clay could have taken her family to live with her husband in those years, and sporadically she did attempt to do so. For a variety of reasons, however, she inevitably returned to central Kentucky to live in her mother's house or at her new home. She did have a significant burden with her young family. Susan was six years old in 1903, Charley four, and Bob, the third child, was born just as Charles left for his first civilian assignment as commandant of Clemson College in South Carolina. A fourth child, Elizabeth, or Metzie, was born in 1904. Mrs. Pepper's servants were helpful with the duties required by such a young family. Ria also worried about educational instruction for Susan and Charley and medical care for all her children.

There was another reason Ria Clay remained in central Kentucky. It was probably the major reason she provided so little discipline for Susan as well. Ria Clay was a victim of her own upbringing, her husband's career, and male protectiveness. She had barely controlled her fears during the Spanish-American War. Charles had recognized those fears and protected her from the extent of his involvement. Indeed, his letters from Cuba gave the impression that he was a casual observer of the war rather than a participant.[16] When Clay returned from Cuba, however, a more honest account of his role surfaced slowly. The U.S. Army awarded Charles Clay a silver star for bravery under fire and promoted him to the rank of captain. Moreover, Ria heard her husband and his fellow officers tell harrowing stories about their experiences and lament the deaths of some fellow officers, men Ria had known.

Charles's next assignment accentuated the sense of helplessness Ria Clay felt. In late 1898, Charles was ordered to the Philippines as a part of the force sent to quell the insurrection against American rule. Ria's letters expressed a growing fatalism, and even Charles, initially, expressed his loneliness and lack of enthusiasm for war. Then, on March 25, 1899, Clay was seriously wounded in action at Banlac and once again became the protective husband. From the hospital he dictated a letter to Ria grossly understating the seriousness of his wound. He was more honest in a letter to his brothers but swore them to secrecy and continued to mislead Ria.[17]

Charles believed he was protecting his wife. She was expecting their second child, Charley, and Charles feared that the truth might produce such trauma as to endanger her and their baby. Army physicians urged him to have surgery in Manila, but Charles demanded to be shipped back to Lexington. Risking permanent paralysis, Charles did not have the bullet removed until July 1899, a month after the birth of his son.[18] As gallant as Charles Clay believed his actions to be, he did not protect his wife from the truth. Indeed, he seemed to relish telling the gruesome story once the danger had passed. He had remained on the battlefield for five hours after being wounded because others seemed to have a better chance of survival. Ria learned that Charles had feared for his own life. He had asked a fellow officer, Captain John Gregg, to carry news of his death to Ria should he die. She read a letter written by Captain Gregg to his sister describing the circumstances surrounding Clay's injury and the battlefield pessimism about his chances of survival. Another letter, written by the man who had carried Charles from the battlefield, left no doubt how serious they had considered the wound.[19] She heard the surgeons at Lexington's Good Samaritan Hospital discuss the danger of permanent paralysis. Finally, she saw the blood-stained uniform which Charles brought home to hang in the Clay home as a reminder of how close death had come.[20]

Male protectiveness, it seems, extended only to the point when danger was overcome. Charles Clay did not protect his wife from the truth; her knowledge of it was merely delayed, and thus she was denied the right to participate in decisions that could have a negative effect on her and those she loved. Ria Clay's sense of helplessness and insecurity increased significantly. Writing many years later to her youngest son, a West Point cadet, she expressed her resentment of the military. "I am weeping bitter tears as I write. I despise the Army—its requirements, its dangers, its utter unfairness and hypocrisy."[21] Charles returned to the employment of the army, but Ria chose to stay in central Kentucky, where her family and servants promised greater security.

Ria Clay also sought security in religion. Facing potentially life-threatening surgery to remove a tumor, in 1908, and again without her husband's presence, she sought comfort by converting from Episcopalianism, the Clays' church, to Christian Science. The religious congregation founded by Mary Baker Eddy promised a healing efficacy, and Ria Clay found solace in its assurances. Margery Fox argues that Christian Science provided a form of pious protest for late nineteenth-century women who felt powerless to affect their surroundings.[22] Ria Clay's conversion certainly seems to support that conclusion. It was one of the few strong decisions Ria made after her marriage. The Clays disapproved, but Charles seemed to know not to contest the decision too strongly. They reached an agreement of their own, one which further illustrates their southern values and Fox's argument. Susan and Elizabeth attended Christian Science meetings with their mother; the two sons remained nominally Episcopalian.

Susan and Charley posed for a picture to be sent to Papa. The Clays dressed the children in the style of the gentry.

With the exception of her conversion to Christian Science, Ria faced most things with increasing stoicism. She became extremely protective of her children, yet, at the same time, quite indulgent. She seemed to lack the energy as well as the inclination to discipline them. Strong-willed Susan experienced little rein on her spontaneity, a factor of considerable importance in the development of her character.

Susan's childhood, then, was not as perfect as her poem implied. And yet it was "joyous" because she was unaware of the imperfections. Families like the Clays and Peppers did not express unhappiness to their children. For example, Aunt Teetee said some very unkind things when Ria left the Episcopal Church. Forgetting that Henry Clay's father had been a Baptist minister persecuted by the Anglican Church in Virginia, she assumed Clays had been and would always be Episcopalian. Ria rarely went to Balgowan thereafter, but she said nothing to the children, and they were allowed to visit their aunt whenever they pleased.

The children did know their mother missed Papa, but she continued to portray him in epic proportions to them. In keeping with southern tradition, perhaps family tradition, his actions were presented in the most noble light. His wound symbolized his bravery, and his effort to protect Ria Clay and Charley entered the family's oral tradition as evidence of his gentlemanly self-sacrifice. By refusing surgery to remove the bullet, he had sacrificed his career for his family. No longer fighting a war, he continued to be portrayed by his wife as a gallant soldier absent from his family because he wanted to provide adequately for them. They knew how much he missed them and wrote to him regularly. He sent gifts at Christmas, wrote them notes, and joined them in the summers if they did not join him. Life would be perfect, Ria Clay implied, when Papa came home for good.

Susan's life appeared only slightly less perfect than if her father had been at home. Both the Clays and the Peppers sought to fill the void left by Charles's absence. Susan seemed comfortable listening to, or conversing with, the adults at Balgowan and Frankfort. She played games, usually of her own creation, or participated in other activities common to rural children with her two brothers and sister, a visiting cousin, or the servants' children. And in 1903, Susan and Charley began their formal education.

Virginia Tyler came to the farm each weekday to tutor Susan and Charley. Her instruction was anything but strenuous. Classes lasted only until noon and, unfortunately, Miss Virginia provided no more discipline than Ria Clay. Susan had learned to read when she was four years old, but Miss Virginia brought new books and new ideas. Susan talked at length about the stories, taking new directions based in her own imagination and Miss Virginia's suggestions. In the afternoons after her teacher had left, Susan often created her own character sketches or plays based on the books they explored. The timid governess had less success when she attempted to teach spelling or mathematics. Ideas gushed from Susan's mind; she had no time to check the proper spelling. Mathematics could not hold her attention at all. She had no patience for what she would later call the "colorless world of mathematics" and was inclined to distract Miss Virginia when she tried to teach it. The timid young tutor apparently received no help from Ria. The family version suggests that Susan's ability to lead Miss Virginia rather than be led by her was interpreted as another sign of her budding potential.

Miss Virginia left after lunch each day so the afternoons were spent at play. Susan's curiosity and sense of imagination made her the natural leader of the children. She also had the most forceful personality. Bob and Metzie, both much younger than Susan, idolized her in their youth. Charley was quieter, more pensive, and followed Susan's lead unless her spontaneity led her too far beyond the boundaries of reason. They made up games for themselves and the younger children. Mrs. Clay, though increasingly protective, allowed the children to do things most modern or urban mothers would reject as too dangerous. The boys were allowed to use rifles and pistols from a very early age, and even the girls were familiar with firearms.[23] All the children learned to ride horseback and explored the countryside on their ponies. Ria did not allow Susan to go unless Charley accompanied her, but together they rode to the creek, caught minnows and dragonflies, or created dams as rural children had done for centuries. They also rode down to Slickaway, the African American community where the family servants lived, frequently stopping to toss rocks in an old sinkhole on the farm before wandering back home. They were seemingly always welcome at Balgowan, and a leisurely ride placed them at Aunt Teetee's doorstep, where a pie or a cake, baked by the cooks, Aunt Matt or Millie Lawson, was ready to be sliced.[24]

At Balgowan they also played with Florence, Louis, and Boone, the children of Aunt Teetee's servants. Susan and Florence were about the same age so they made up stories for the younger children, sang songs, or taught them games. In the evenings, they played tag or hide and seek among the lilacs and locust trees that surrounded the house.[25] Occasionally, Aunt Matt and Millie Lawson allowed Susan and Florence to make cookies to share with all the children. That was about as close to a stove as Susan ever got. She never learned to cook or to do many other household chores. Nothing was ever said, but it was undoubtedly assumed that Susan Clay would always have servants to perform such chores.

In the wintertime, the children frequently gathered in the kitchen. Susan later recalled nostalgically the glow and pleasant aromas of that room. One suspects it was not the heat or the food alone that left such pleasant memories but the people there. Aunt Matt and Millie Lawson told stories as they worked and for as long as the children behaved. They could weave an interesting tale combining bits of local lore, the Bible, and their own experiences. Those stories contained a wealth of common sense, morality, and human decency that was passed to children, black and white, by the women who served.[26]

African American women played an important role in the education of the Clay children, as they did in many southern white families. Mary Jackson taught Susan Clay to read, kept her from danger as a child, and began to develop in her an awareness of right and wrong. As a young child, Susan ran to Mary when frightened because she was as indulgent and protective as Ria Clay. Mary Jackson was an early symbol of that secure world Susan learned to expect. Later, it was Millie Lawson who educated and befriended Susan. Susan learned to love and respect the family servants—Mary, Millie, Aunt Matt, Will, Green, and Abe. Elements of discrimination and paternalism certainly existed; it was the nature of that time and class. But there was also a love which was genuine, even if incomplete by modern standards. Millie Lawson named one of her daughters for Susan Clay and corresponded with her for years after there was any reason but fond memories for doing so.[27]

Susan spent most of her time from a very young age at her favorite preoccupation—reading. From the beginning she read about an idyllic world. Children's literature is supposed to trigger the imagination, but in that age, region, and class that purpose was even more pronounced. Susan easily escaped her world through the pages of a book. She read Annie Fellows Johnston's romantic tales of the Little Colonel, which glorified the old South and its values. She also read Harriet Beecher Stowe's *Uncle Tom's Cabin,* but it did not balance Johnston's stories because of the way Susan read. The excitement of flight and the noble struggle between good and evil captured Susan's attention rather than the tragedy Stowe intended. There is no evidence that she sensed the conflict of values such readings suggested or compared her Bluegrass world and its ways to that created by Stowe. It is equally certain that no one called such conflicts to her attention. Such comparisons were remarkably absent from the thought of white Kentuckians for at least another half-century.

Susan also read Dickens's *David Copperfield* until her copy fell apart, Thackeray, Scott, Barrie, and, later, Tolstoy from her father's leather-bound volumes. But her favorite reading was about King Arthur, Guinevere, and the fabulous court over which they reigned. Southerners had always preferred the highly romanticized accounts of medieval life. Mark Twain called it the "Sir Walter disease" because of southern appreciation of Sir Walter Scott.[28] Susan did not read critically but as if she could participate personally in that world. Many years later, she referred to the "colorful sins" of Guinevere as if her station and style absolved her of those transgressions. Her brother Charley read about soldiers, war, and exploring the Yukon; Susan dreamed of Camelot.

Ria Clay encouraged Susan's flights of fantasy. Perhaps subconsciously she envied her daughter's ability to escape reality, but there were other reasons as well. A sense of imagination and an idealistic view of the world were still considered essential assets for a proper young southern lady.[29] Despite the bankruptcy of the myth in her own life, Ria fulfilled her duty by preparing Susan for the world she believed, or hoped, her daughter would experience. The family said they knew what Susan was reading because she inevitably assumed the character of the heroine. She might appear for breakfast as Agnes of *David Copperfield* or Becky Sharpe. On another day it would be

Catherine Earnshaw. Her favorite character was the little Gypsy girl, Babby, created by James Barrie. Mrs. Clay even made a Gypsy costume which Susan wore when she was in a Babby mood.[30] She felt keenly the emotional ups and downs of the characters and acted out their responses or her own as if she were in their places. Such characters experienced pain, but it was temporary. In the end things were made right, and victory resulted from the characters' innate superiority and strength. Susan's youth was "filled with King Arthur and rainbows," but the lessons of her youth differed only in degree from those many other upper- and middle-class southern, and nonsouthern, girls of her era experienced.[31]

Susan's reading encouraged other forms of self-expression that brought her to the center of attention. Each book or story created independent ideas that spilled out as poems, stories, and plays. Notebooks filled with simple poems can be dated to the time Susan was six years old. Short stories are more difficult to date but appear to be the work of a child no older than ten. One of the earliest stories, "The Forgetmenots," borrowed the theme of King Arthur and his court but added a dash of southern honor and a happy ending.[32] Another short story borrowed from the Little Colonel.[33] Yet if the skills are those of a child, she nevertheless maintains an excitement and an air of suspense that does not allow readers to put her works down unfinished. More important, the stories indicate Susan's assimilation of the traditional values of family and community.

A story often became the basis of a play and an afternoon of activity for all the children. Susan inevitably directed and starred in the performance, her brothers, and occasionally a visiting cousin, providing the supporting cast. The best of such plays, or at least those producing the most excitement, were performed for Marm (the children's name for Mrs. Clay), the relatives, or servants called from their duties for the occasion. Relatives were frequently charged a nickel, but the servants were admitted free; noblesse oblige required the latter.[34]

The reviews of Susan's plays were almost always favorable. Occasionally, however, her creativity overcame common sense. Susan quickly seized a grand design but rarely considered the long-term consequences. When doing a play based on *Uncle Tom's Cabin,* for example, Susan decided that Bob, who was to portray Uncle Tom, should apply shoe polish to his hands and face. Charley tried to tell her the polish could not be washed off but to no avail. The idea seemed too perfect to worry about details. Susan's later remorse was as great as her initial excitement.[35] Ria Clay assigned Charley the unenviable task of containing Susan's sudden outbursts of genius. In the absence of her husband, she placed a great deal of responsibility on her oldest son. Traditional roles were as important in Charley's life as they were in Susan's. Calmer and more mature than Susan, Charley played a protective role long before he reached manhood. He called the expressions of Susan's troublesome "genius" her "luny experiments" and tried to convince her to contain her enthusiasm. When that failed, he tried to explain the circumstances to their mother.

Marm was often exasperated by her daughter's actions but rarely did more than mildly reprimand Susan. Susan tried to obey her mother's rules, but a new idea or even a field of wildflowers seemed inevitably to cause her to stray into forbidden territory.[36] Susan's early poems, stories, and plays also indicate the style she was absorbing. Her world was one of beauty, order, and great promise. She saw things in sweeping generalities and brilliant colors. Heroines overcame diversity because it was natural for them to do so, and every story, perhaps life itself, was summed up in the thought of happiness ever after.

The Clays and the Peppers apparently saw nothing amiss about Susan's education. In fact, within their homes, the families reinforced what she was learning. Modern historians have proven that the southern codes were more myth than reality, but they were also ideal. The myth was the standard all sought to attain, or at least were supposed to seek. A part of the myth was to hide the reality of shortcomings from outsiders and children. The Peppers and the Clays may not have always lived by the codes, but their violations were not discussed in the presence of Susan, her brothers, and sister. More important, the oral traditions placed events and family members in the best possible light.[37] Susan Clay learned her family heritage from proud heirs of a great tradition rather than from critical historians. And as a child she saw those around her living the ideal for her benefit.

The family members around Susan, and those about whom she heard stories, must have seemed as grand as the characters in the books she read. In fact, she did read about some of those people. Grandmother

Pepper epitomized the gracious southern woman. The children never saw her agitated or angry, and friends, servants, and her own children apparently adored her. She seemed to treat everyone, including the children, with the same quiet dignity, and people gravitated toward her homes because she created an air of hospitality in them. Susan read *Until the Day Break* and could easily pick from its pages the descriptions of the Cliffs, her grandmother, and her Aunt Lizzie. She read some of the novels of Kentucky writer John Fox, Jr., who visited the Pepper homes and who, she was told, had introduced her father and mother.[38]

Those who lived with or visited the Peppers exhibited their good breeding. The elderly ladies had known one another since they were girls. They had shared the happiness of weddings, births, and children's successes as well as the sorrows of death and loneliness. They all lived in the same area of the old town and possessed distinguished family heritages. They were also as much examples of a Victorian style as their homes were an architectural history of the city. Susan observed the conversationalists as she listened to them. Many years later, she remarked that Patty Burnley, a respected member of Elizabeth Pepper's circle of friends, could sit all afternoon without letting her back touch the chair. That was how a lady was supposed to sit in the early decades of the century. They, too, listened attentively as Susan recounted her own stories, and their kindly worded questions allowed her to elaborate, creating a richer treatment of themes or plots.

The younger group that came to the Pepper homes also included Susan in their conversations and activities. Numerous snapshots show Susan among fashionably dressed young men and women playing croquet, engaged in conversation, or walking about the lawn. Ria frequently informed Charles that Susan had been asked to go on a carriage ride or for a walk with some of the guests at the Cliffs.[39]

Susan grew particularly fond of one of her mother's sisters during her childhood. Lizzie Pepper was as much a lady in matters of dress and manners as any of the Pepper girls, but she had an independent streak. She enjoyed travel and the cultural activities more available in the large cities of the United States and in Europe. Though attractive and popular, she never met a man for whom she was willing to give up her freedom. She had refused a marriage proposal from Robert Burns

Wilson.[40] She traveled widely, but when she returned, she shared post-cards and photographs of exotic and romantic places with Susan. Lizzie explained to Susan the historical or literary background and her own enjoyment at experiencing each place. Lizzie's experiences blended naturally with the literature Susan read, and over the years, she too dreamed of seeing such places.[41]

Such influences cannot be quantified, but they should not be dismissed for that reason. They were experienced over and over until a style was absorbed rather than learned. At Frankfort, Susan was surrounded by ladies, old and young, and the experience undoubtedly helped form her definition of a lady. Their encouragement and praise enhanced her confidence, and she learned to dream of bigger worlds, though she had experienced little beyond the homes and farms of her relatives. At the same time, the style, values, and manners in those places looked back rather than forward. As Susan's poems and stories indicate, she internalized much that characterized those places.

When Susan visited the Clays, similar images of refined, cultured company prevailed. Grandmother Clay died in 1905, but Tom, George, and Teetee remained at Balgowan. Elderly unmarried cousins visited Teetee regularly, and each lived to virtual perfection the standards of the Victorian gentry. Uncle Tom and Uncle George also had friends who came to play whist and business associates who called to discuss the training of horses or thoroughbred racing. Charles Kerr, a distinguished judge and respected historian, visited frequently because of his friendship with Tom and George and because Aunt Teetee wrote biographical sketches of family members for his multivolume *History of Kentucky*. Colonel Richard M. Redd, a Lexington character in the best sense of the term, frequently rode over to Balgowan to chat with Tom and George Clay. A veteran of the Civil War, the Confederate army of course, Colonel Redd feared the young would forget the cause so he talked about it incessantly. He exaggerated the mannerisms of the southern gentleman; every lady deserved a grandiose tip of the hat. He also startled more than one new student at the University of Kentucky by racing his horse onto the campus, causing it to rear, then demonstrating the rebel yell for all within earshot.[42] Most Lexingtonians thought the colonel somewhat eccentric, but to the Clay children he was an engaging character who told marvelous stories the accuracy of

Balgowan, the home of Susan M., Teetee, Tom, and George Clay, appeared from the outside to be a simple cottage. Inside it was a museum dedicated to Clay service. The house was located near the site of the present Calumet Farm residence.

which was, at least for them, above question. The conduct of such men might differ considerably when they were in the company of ladies and when they were not. Uncle George, for example, was well known for his "spontaneous" actions when out of Teetee's sight. Around Susan and Aunt Teetee, however, the men behaved as perfect gentlemen.

Susan loved to go to Balgowan. Aunt Teetee and Uncle Tom always made Susan, Charley, Bob, and Metzie feel welcome. No longer young themselves, they seemed to gain energy from the children. Susan knew Uncle Tom would have something exciting to show them or a story to tell. In central Kentucky, "Captain Tom" was known for his integrity and his sense of dignity. The president of the Kentucky Racing Association, Tom Clay was frequently called on to settle disputes about the rules of racing because of his knowledge and his reputation for fair play.[43] With his brother's children, however, he was just Uncle Tom.

At age ten, Susan posed with her sister, Metzie.

Without ever saying anything to the effect, he seems to have wanted to provide the male role model absent from their lives. Though trained to be a physician, he had quit the practice of medicine to become an officer in the army and had fought in the Indian wars in the Southwest. He had a seemingly endless supply of stories about cavalrymen, Indians, and grand adventures.[44] Tom told the cavalry stories mostly with the boys in mind, but he had other stories that Susan could share. He challenged her sense of imagination with his own, and as she grew older, he encouraged her to help him create the stories that enthralled her brothers and sister. His stories all but replaced rules of behavior at

Balgowan. Thoroughbred horses could be dangerous, but he explained a better reason why Susan and Charley were not to go into the fields alone. The horses had little friends, the fairies of the fields, which were shy and would run away if startled. The horses would then be sad. As the years went by, Uncle Tom included Susan and then Charley in the game of adding to the story so the younger children would be safe.[45]

George Clay was a different sort of man. Described as high-spirited, he could have large mood changes. When in a good mood, he loved to tease Tom or joke about Charles's military bearing. He might dance around the room holding his coattails out behind him or tell a funny story about someone they all knew. George Clay possessed a biting wit, and he often exaggerated, humorously, the flaws he saw in others. He could also find humor within his own family. Aunt Teetee preferred to stress the nobility of the Clay character and their enlightened service to nation, but if the characters became, in her version, too saintly, George interjected a rendition that emphasized Clay idiosyncrasies. In a family that emphasized dignity, George made the children laugh and perhaps hid, at least in their childhood, the heavy sense of responsibility that went with the privilege of being a Clay. As Susan grew older she sensed that she and Uncle George had a lot in common. They were both high-spirited, a characteristic noted in many of the Clays, and thus they either had great fun together or they disagreed.[46] George Clay seems also to have sensed his niece's unique qualities. Susan loved to walk quietly in the woods and the fields, but Marm would never allow her to go alone. George took her with him when he checked the horses, stopping to watch the yearlings romp in the fields or listen to the birds sing in woods that had stood since frontier days. Susan later said they had a special bond, no less strong for being unspoken.[47]

To all outward appearances, George and Tom Clay were the masters at Balgowan. Control of the household, however, and probably a great deal more, rested in the hands of Lucretia Clay, Aunt Teetee. A slight sprig of a woman, she had the strong character and the Clay pride of her mother. She also inherited her mother's role as family historian and guardian of the Clay name. Angered by criticisms of Henry Clay, Mrs. Clay and Teetee had begun their own history of the great statesman in the 1880s. Teetee continued the process of "organizing" the vast collection of letters and papers Henry Clay had left to the family. Because they were overly protective of the family's reputation, there is some reason to believe that papers which projected the wrong image, could be "misunderstood," or might be used by jealous men against the family's good name were consigned to the fire by which she worked alone and late into the night.[48] She also found time to write religious tracts and a long, very Victorian novel centering around an estate that bears a remarkable resemblance to Ashland and characters very similar to members of her own family.[49]

Teetee provided a strong female role model for Susan, but she exercised that strength within the sphere of the southern woman. She could be extremely charming, but she guarded the Clay reputation vigorously and took it upon herself to enforce Clay values on other members of the family. Sometimes her concern was humorous and at others sad. She tried "to keep the boys [Tom and George] on the narrow road of good behavior" and was quick to tell them when they had strayed. When one of George Clay's fillies won a big race he ordered champagne for every woman in the grandstand. Teetee chastised him for being too enthusiastic and spontaneous. Occasionally, however, even she confused her Victorian values. Tom Clay discovered an Indian mound at Balgowan and began to excavate it. He triumphantly entered the house with several prizes only to discover his sister's righteous indignation. She demanded that everything be returned to its original state and with the children as her congregation conducted what may have been the first Episcopalian funeral service with a female in charge.[50] Throughout the episode, she was anything but submissive. Her staunch Episcopalianism had less humorous results when Ria joined the Christian Science church in Lexington.

Susan, of course, did not see this harsher side of Aunt Teetee. Neither Ria nor Teetee shared their disagreement with her. Susan saw a woman dominant in domestic affairs, active in women's groups, and hospitable to her nieces and nephews. She also learned at the feet of Aunt Teetee a glorious and exciting family history, an epic equal to many of those Susan read.

To enter Balgowan was to step back into history. The portraits hung about the walls and gifts to Henry Clay displayed throughout the house spoke clearly to his national importance. Aunt Teetee loved to tell the children stories of the past. She had a story for every occasion, and most of them emphasized a family trait that she hoped would become a characteristic of Susan, Charley, Bob, and Elizabeth. Again, they were not the accounts a professional historian would accept uncritically, but in family histories, reality serves the purpose of ideal, historical analogy encourages the virtues of present and future. Henry Clay was, of course, the major figure. She stressed his love of country and his great service as diplomat and compromiser. He would have been president of the United States, she declared, if it had not been for mistaken ideas spread by unscrupulous opponents. But "Grandfather" placed principle above success. In his own words, he would "rather be right than President."[51] Teetee emphasized those aspects of the family past that served her purposes: the needs of the future. She did not like Henry Clay's claim to have risen out of poverty, the "mill boy of the slashes." The Clays were descended from English nobility in Wales and had come to Virginia with Sir Walter Raleigh. She made heroes out of all the Clays. Henry's son Thomas Hart Clay served Abraham Lincoln as ambassador to Nicaragua and Honduras. She would have liked Thomas Hart better if he had served the Confederacy, but by being an ambassador he added to the family's prominence. He also epitomized another lesson. After the Civil War, when Grandmother Clay was having a difficult time financially, he had laid aside political differences to offer her and her children, including Susan's father, residence at Mansfield, his home. Clays were, Teetee taught, loyal to family above all else. It was a lesson repeated on many occasions.

Henry Clay Jr. was an example of gallantry. He had died in 1847 at the Battle of Buena Vista in defense of his country. Teetee proved her point by reading portions of a letter from General Zachary Taylor praising Henry Clay Jr.'s bravery.

Uncle George was inclined to interject his own less reverent accounts on such occasions, but there was a series of stories even he did not interrupt. Teetee talked about Grandmother Clay in terms as glorious as those of any romantic novel—how this daughter of Louisville's first millionaire had grown up in the beautiful social life of the antebellum era, how she had met and married James B. Clay, how she had furthered his career with her social skills, even impressing the Spanish grandees at the court of Lisbon. Teetee also told how Grandmother

Clay faced tragedy after 1861. James B. Clay had been humiliated in his own hometown when captured by Union forces. He had chosen exile rather than return to Lexington, but Susan M. Clay remained at Ashland with her children. Tragedy struck there too. Union forces camped on the lawns and disease invaded the dwelling. Death struck four times before the end of the war, and after it financial reversals forced her to sell Ashland. In the 1870s another son, John, died at the age of twenty-four, and in 1884 Harry Clay was killed in a Louisville gunfight. Susan M. Clay lost a husband, five children, an estate, and a sizable fortune in a period of twenty years, but she endured the tragedies with the inner strength of a Guinevere or the other noble characters of history or fiction. In her dignified way, she educated her sons, made a home for the youngest of her children, and preserved the grace and demeanor that had always characterized her. In the manner characteristic of oral traditions, the tragedy was secondary to the manner in which she had met adversity. Susan had known her grandmother long enough to carry an image of her. In Susan's lifetime Grandmother Clay had been confined to a huge wheeled chair, but she sat regally and not even a child could be unaware of the reverence in which she was held by her children. Susan M. Clay was the matriarch, a standard of strength and character.

Teetee told stories about her own generation too. The Indian bridle over the mantle was evidence of the respect the Indian chief Geronimo had felt for Uncle Tom. Ordered to guard Geronimo after his surrender, Tom Clay would have shot him if he had tried to escape, but when several of his fellow officers suggested killing Geronimo while they had the chance, Clay threatened to shoot them.[52] It was a matter of honor, and Clays were honorable men. The field glasses that rested near the bridle provided another tale of Clay honor. Uncle Harry Clay had taken them to the Arctic with the Howgate Expedition in 1881. He had remained in Greenland to join the Greely Expedition along with Dr. Octave Pavey, who was also going to join the Greely party as its physician. The story Teetee told contained elements of noblesse oblige, sacrifice, and honor. The Greenlanders had befriended the two men, but when a child fell ill Pavey refused to help the family. Clay begged the physician to look at the child, but he would not and the child died. Harry Clay wrote in his diary that he despised Pavey for his callousness and finally resigned his place with Admiral Adolphus W. Greely rather than be in the company of such a man. He told Greely it was a matter of honor. Aunt Teetee could prove how disappointed Admiral Greely was too. There was a letter from him to Uncle Harry expressing his regret but also his understanding.[53]

Aunt Teetee had a trunk full of letters signed by famous Americans. She liked to mention well-known people from the past such as John Quincy Adams, Albert Gallatin, and Aaron Burr. The very mention of their names seemed to say the Clays belonged in such circles.[54] Aunt Teetee did not open the trunk every time the children came, but occasionally she would find a letter from George Washington, Thomas Jefferson, or someone else the children had read about and, carefully placing it in their hands, allow them to hold it for a moment. Conversation on such occasions was reduced to a whisper approaching reverence.[55]

No child could escape the lessons of Balgowan. There were enough stories to last several childhoods, and Aunt Teetee rarely missed an opportunity to share them with her nieces and nephews. Susan learned the confidence derived from a famous heritage. She learned that it was a privilege to be a part of such a noble family. It was implied that she too had the potential to contribute on a grand scale because she shared the family bloodlines. To achieve success, she needed only to adhere to the values she was being taught—ladylike behavior, commitment to principle, a sense of noblesse oblige, and family loyalty—attributes that supposedly came naturally to Clays. Tragedy was also a part of life; it had cut short the careers of many promising Clays. But tragedy should not be feared; Clays had an innate strength that allowed them to endure with dignity.

Given all this, Susan could scarcely fail to believe in herself. The adults in her world adored her; the children looked up to her. She was constantly told of her potential, and some reason for praise was found in virtually her every action. Self-confident and poised, she believed strongly in her views of a near-perfect world because that in which she had been isolated for her first eleven years seemed ideal. The noble characters of literature whose moods she copied were matched by the noble figures of the Clay heritage and the genteel people of Balgowan and the Cliffs. Susan Clay was raised among people who saw their role in a particular way and practiced a certain style. It is little wonder that she adopted much of that view. She would later discover some of the less attractive or more demanding aspects of that world. At the age of eleven, she had many reasons to be happy and confident. Though she had seen little beyond the three homes in which she lived and visited, she had no fear of facing a broader world. She looked forward to continuing her education in Lexington, meeting other girls her age, taking a step into that broader world, and she, as well as her family, had no doubt she could compete. Childhood had been fair and joyous. The curious directions and absorbed contradictions which her training created in her would not become apparent for some years.

🌱

CHAPTER THREE

Youth

Listen! even the grass is filled with music,
Child-like, chuckling, dripping over—
We are close to the very lips of happiness!
—"Youth," *Poems by Susan Clay*

ELEVEN-YEAR-OLD SUSAN was becoming a young lady when her father returned home from Little Rock, Arkansas, and his last civilian assignment with the army in 1908. Physically mature for her age, Susan looked older than eleven, and, given her self-assurance and curiosity, she was ready to enter a new and different period of her youth.

At home, Millie and the other servants began to call her Miss Susan—a small but significant change that symbolized a rite of passage. It thrilled Susan that the much loved servants treated her as an adult. Her relationship with the servants' children also changed. Florence, Lewis, and Boone moved away and Millie's children, Mary Kate, Laura, and Sarah, became their playmates. But there was less time for play. Millie's daughters had to be trained to perform household duties. They were taught to iron the table linens and help with the light housework under Millie's direction. They also learned to serve for dinners, practicing with the family to be prepared when guests were present.[1] It was not a sudden or dramatic change but a process by which the children learned their place in the unchanging world of which they were to be a part.

Susan and Charley experienced changes too. Unhappy with the instruction Susan and Charley received from Miss Virginia's half days at the Clay home, Charles Clay decided they would attend school in

Lexington. After considerable research, conferences, and interviews, Charles chose a respected private school, the Miss Ella Williams' School, located on Lexington's North Broadway. Susan and Charley caught the interurban car at the front gate to the Clay farm each morning and rode it back from Lexington in the afternoons.

Miss Williams' School was considered at the time to provide an excellent educational opportunity.[2] The public schools in Lexington were improving, but many gentry families still sent their children to private academies. Miss Williams' School accepted both boys and girls, but it was most suited to girls, and the boys generally left before graduation.[3] Charley was there only a few years; he was then taught privately before his father sent him to Schadmann's near Washington, D.C., a school known for its preparation of young men for the entrance exams to West Point. Later, Bob refused to stay at Miss Williams' School even as long as Charley. There were not enough boys there to suit him so his father allowed him to attend public school, then a preparatory school in Lawrenceburg, Kentucky, before following his brother to Schadmann's and the U.S. Military Academy.

Adolescence came with a rush for Susan. The opportunity to participate in new things, explore new areas, and become involved in the social life of Lexington's gentry youth was exciting for her. She found her school interesting and challenging. For the first time she met girls near her own age whom she could see every day. Daily and formal instruction challenged her, and she thrived under a strong literature faculty. Susan's fellow students stimulated her curiosity and her teachers praised the stories and poetry she wrote, reinforcing the encouragement she had received from members of her family. She also had music lessons and studied French, which she had not experienced before.

Miss Williams' School also emphasized training in social skills. Though it was not a finishing school in the traditional sense, the young ladies received instruction in the manners and proper conduct required in Bluegrass society.[4] Such lessons were learned casually at first because the girls were young. They learned to dance, serve tea, and converse politely. They also studied the lives of great women such as Marie Antoinette and Mary, Queen of Scots, not for their historical role but as models of style and grace.[5] They learned similar lessons from daily

Susan sat with her sister at approximately fourteen years of age. Elizabeth admired her older sister throughout her life.

observation of Ella Williams and the other refined women who, like the residents of the Cliffs and Balgowan, taught by example.[6]

During the 1911–12 school term, Susan did not attend Miss Williams' School, but that year was one of the most important educational experiences of her youth. In the fall of 1911, she accompanied Grandmother Pepper and Aunt Lizzie on a trip to Fort McPherson, an army base just outside Atlanta, Georgia, where Susan's Aunt Pinnie lived. There were two major reasons for the trip. Aunt Pinnie's husband, Thomas Smith, and Frederick Goedecke, Aunt May's husband, were both officers in Charles's old unit, the Seventeenth Infantry, which was assigned to Fort McPherson. Aunt May had died in childbirth and, since her husband was a career soldier, Grandmother Pepper and another aunt, Laura, had assumed the responsibility for raising her child. The trip to Atlanta allowed the child, now a small boy, to visit his father for an extended period of time. The trip was also to help Pinnie, who was recovering from surgery. Unlike Ria, Pinnie followed her husband to his places of assignment, but in 1911 she needed assistance during her convalescence. Susan went along to help care for the Smith children. Under normal circumstances, Ria Clay probably would not have let Susan go, but Pinnie could not be refused. She had accompanied Charles Clay on the painful trip back from the Philippines in 1899, then retraced the long journey to be with her husband. Such loyalty to family required repayment in kind.

Atlanta provided a wide range of new activities for Susan. Her letters to her parents were filled with an excitement that was tempered only slightly by an effort to appear older and more cosmopolitan than she was. She enjoyed the daily walks, horseback riding, and games as much as the children they were intended to keep occupied. Once again Susan became the storyteller. The children enjoyed her stories so much, she wrote, that she had used all the old ones she had told her own brothers and sister and was frantically trying to make up more.[7]

Aunt Lizzie filled Susan's free time with other activities. Lizzie had shared with a younger Susan the visual images of her travels, but now she helped her experience the excitement and the cultural advantages of a major city firsthand. In Atlanta, Lizzie introduced Susan to the theater, concerts, readings, and the opera. Susan's letters described the performance of William Faversham in *The Fawn* and Julia Marlowe reading Shakespeare. She wrote ecstatically of Geraldine Farrar, Antonio Scotti, and the famous Enrico Caruso.[8] Geraldine Farrar would perform in Lexington several years later without a comment from Susan. In 1912, in Atlanta, everything appeared new and special to her.

Her letters reveal a young girl coming to a new level of maturity and pleased to be doing so. In her letter describing *The Fawn*, she spoke knowledgeably of the play as well as the "foolish conventionalities of humanity" it mocked. Susan still knew little of such things. In another letter, she encouraged her parents to see a film with two "popular little actresses" who were nearly twice her age.[9] She did have some reason to feel more grown up. Freer in Atlanta under the care of Aunt Lizzie than in Lexington, where her parents dictated her activities, Susan did things and saw things that would have provoked objections at home. She knew better than to relate some of her experiences to her father. She placed a description of a series of French plays Lizzie had taken her to see in a letter meant only for her mother.[10] There were other things about Atlanta Papa might have thought improper as well. Susan attended the post parties at which young officers met the eligible young ladies of Atlanta. She enjoyed herself immensely, primarily because she believed herself socially competitive with older girls. She wrote rather boastfully (but again only to her mother) that she was asked to dance as often as any of the other girls there.[11]

Susan also sharpened her tongue in Atlanta. Unfortunately, that was a prerequisite for a successful social life in Lexington as well. She described her competitors at the parties in great detail, barely hiding her pleasure at their shortcomings. She was appalled at their behavior and wrote with much amazement about the hopelessly outdated gowns worn by young ladies supposedly from the finest Atlanta families. She described one gown that seemed decidedly avant-garde. Susan's mock dismay scarcely covered her glee as she described it. The dress was "simply disgusting. . . . It was made of some soft clinging material and did not look a yard wide and to all outward appearances she looked decidedly minus underwear. When she danced you could see 'every little movement' sure enough."[12]

An older and more confident Susan Clay returned to Lexington in the spring of 1912. She promised her father that she would settle down to serious study, a promise she kept, but her enthusiasm probably

derived less from the promise than from the curiosity aroused by Atlanta.[13] Susan, the actress and playwright, had seen live examples of
what she had only dreamed before. She also entered Lexington's social
life with renewed confidence. Had she not been the belle of the ball in
Atlanta? She was ready to take Lexington by storm.

Susan immersed herself enthusiastically in her schoolwork. She
continued to study French and became fluent in the language. She
read voraciously again. In a small booklet she jotted down the titles of
books she was reading.[14] Her fascination with King Arthur and his court
continued. She read, for example, Geoffrey of Monmouth's *History of
the Kings of Britain,* and, to sharpen her reading skills in French, she
then read the French edition. She read Sir Thomas Malory's *Morte
d'Arthur,* William Morris's *Defense of Guinevere,* and Algernon
Swinburne's *Tristram of Lyonesse.* Her reading began to include much
more poetry as well, but, like her family, the teachers at the Miss Ella
Williams' School looked to men and to the past for their standards of
good poetry.[15] Susan read little modern poetry, and if there was any
material written by women, it was not recorded among those she liked
or was taught to respect. Matthew Arnold's *Death of Tristram* and
Tennyson's *Idylls of the King* were followed by readings in Milton,
Coleridge, and Wordsworth. The works of Thackeray, Scott, Tolstoy,
and many other great writers challenged her imagination and encouraged her to express her own ideas.

Occasionally those ideas got her in trouble. Apparently, the young
girl sensed that the works given to her by Mabel Lewis, her favorite
teacher, were the versions properly sanitized for young ladies. She read
them, but whenever possible she read the original texts as well. She
frequently forgot to "sanitize" her own reports. Moreover, her imagination and the curiosity characteristic of youth often led her to add
her own assumptions. A report written for Lewis on *Romeo and Juliet*
led to a hastily called conference between Williams, Lewis, and Susan's
mother.[16] The teachers praised Susan's writing, but they expressed grave
concern about some of the things she wrote and thought. Susan described a meeting between Romeo and Juliet far too explicitly, even
suggesting that Juliet might be with child. No proper young lady should
write or think such thoughts. The teachers suspected that Susan was

acquiring such ideas from the reading she was doing at home and suggested that Mrs. Clay screen everything her daughter read.[17]

Susan's intellectual curiosity often caused her teachers and her parents concern. She was a young woman now, and qualities that had been considered praiseworthy in childhood had to be curtailed in adolescence. Susan's inclination to blurt out a thought or to write too honestly jeopardized her reputation.[18] Charles Clay appeared to have noticed the problem first. Increasingly, other family members and teachers sought to subdue Susan's spontaneity. After 1912, teachers and family sought to balance brilliance and creativity with discipline. Of the four principles of the cult of true womanhood—purity, piety, submissiveness, and domesticity—at least the first three were alive and well at Miss Ella Williams' School and the home of Charles D. Clay.[19]

Mabel Lewis also sought to discipline Susan's writing by requiring her to revise her work. Susan expected her poems to come in flashes of insight, and she found much more enjoyment in writing a new poem than editing an old one. Lewis's influence can be seen in the poems contained in a small booklet dated from February 1913 to December 1914. In the manner of the time, Lewis taught by encouraging her students to read the great poets and to attempt to copy their style. One of the ten poems, entitled "Il Penseroso," obviously was written while Susan was studying Milton. Similarly, "A Sea Dream" attempted to capture the poetic rhythms of Coleridge's *Ancient Mariner*. For the first time, lines and words were marked out and new ones penciled in.[20]

Notes in the margins of the small booklet also indicate Mrs. Clay's influence on Susan's personality. Assertive, self-confident, and accustomed to praise, she reacted badly to criticism. Mabel Lewis read a poem by Susan entitled "Mammy's Voice" to her literary society, a group that met periodically at Transylvania College. The members were impressed with the poem and encouraged Lewis to convey their sentiments to the poet. Susan wrote beside the poem, "I am delighted and I benefit by praise more than criticism."[21] Such a reaction from a fifteen-year-old may not appear unusual. A second penciled note, however, indicates a stronger aversion to criticism. Susan submitted for publication a poem entitled "Lines to a Butterfly," but it was rejected. She wrote: "I sent this to St. Nicolas and was mentioned in the honor roll. Cold comfort! Never mind, I know I write better than Sophicles [*sic*] I sampled his tradgedies [*sic*] the other day."[22] Criticism in any form brought anger and defensiveness. To think her writing superior to that of Sophocles was the charming presumption of a teenaged girl who paid no attention to mundane matters such as spelling. Unfortunately, it went deeper than a teenaged presumption.

The poems "Mammy's Voice" and "Lines to a Butterfly" indicate a great deal about the instruction Susan received at school. "Mammy's Voice," praised by Lewis and her literary society, repeated the clichés and stereotypical images characteristic of southern, and, at the time perhaps national, attitudes regarding African Americans. Like Mary Jackson, the poetic mammy was delighted to care for a white child, the implication being that she was content with her existence, wanting nothing more than to serve. Such lessons were plentiful in Susan's education because they reflected the views of the community. In 1926, she would hear the same interpretations in history classes taught by professional historians at the University of Kentucky.[23] Other poems, including "Lines to a Butterfly," indicate other lessons. Overly sweet and melodramatic, her poems reflected and created the world of beauty and order young women were supposed to see. By encouraging such romantic images, home, society, and school effectively blinded many young women to all but their own experiences. A stanza from "Lines to a Butterfly" provides an example of the verse Susan was encouraged to write:

> How frailly beautiful thy
>   glinting wing!
> Riv'ling in radient [*sic*] hue
>   and irredescent [*sic*] grace
> The wondrous web which
>   fair Arachne wove,
> That luckless maid of
>   Hellen's ancient race.[24]

Though Susan's poetry improved significantly, she defined poetry throughout her life as beautiful expression regardless of the theme.

She also continued to seek the world of romance, beauty, and order promised her in youth.

The teachers at Miss Williams' School were less successful in teaching Susan the value of mathematics. She had the intelligence to succeed in any discipline but not the will. She would read poetry, novels, and history, study biology and geology, dabble at Greek and Russian as the mood struck her, but she despised the "colorless world of mathematics." Her father tried to help her, but the sessions inevitably led to a scene, with Susan dashing hysterically from the room. Concerned for her health, Captain and Mrs. Clay spoke to Ella Williams, and they decided to let Susan drop the study of mathematics.[25] Miss Williams believed Susan's natural intelligence would bring her back to it in time, but it was generally agreed that even if she did not, she would never have need of more than she had already mastered. The implication of social values is apparent. Susan would marry, her husband would handle financial matters, and she would never have to worry about such mundane concerns.[26]

Though unsuccessful in mathematics and hurt by the rejection of her poem, Susan experienced enough successes to offset such temporary inconveniences. In December 1913, the *Lexington Leader* published her short story "A Christmas Disappointment."[27] The local newspaper praised her adaptations of several plays for the Lexington stage, remarking that her potential as a writer was widely recognized in the community. She had reason to feel very good about her writing. Mabel Lewis shared her poems with others in Lexington, and adults in the community asked her to join their literary societies.

As at the Clay house, Susan's writings led to theatrical performances as well. Educational institutions and social clubs provided many opportunities for young people. Plays, variety shows, and musicals provided outlets for local talent. Private teachers also held recitals and the local press encouraged attendance. Lexington's newspapers mentioned several plays which Susan had written or edited and others in which she performed.[28] She sang and danced, portrayed the great ladies of history in "vignettes," or living portraits, and starred in plays.

Susan had been training all her life for such opportunities. She had a flare for the dramatic, the result no doubt of assuming the roles of heroines for so many years. She later said she saw herself as an actress in those years, playing the role for which she had been trained. Photographs in the family albums captured her in theatrical poses and in the costumes of the Queen of the Nile, Lillian Gish, or a poised southern lady. Although at times too theatrical, Susan carried herself with the confidence of an aristocrat. The long gowns and wide-brimmed sunbonnets accentuated her gracefulness, and her peers considered her a very attractive young woman. Whether posing in the garden at the Clay home, on a Lexington stage, or in a boat on the lake at Bluegrass Park on a sunny afternoon, Susan looked the part of the charming southern belle.

Beauty and talent were important in the social world of which Susan was a part. Lexington experienced the progressive movement, but that altered very little the traditional social life of the town.[29] From frontier days Lexington had portrayed itself as a progressive, modern city, yet serious studies frequently refer to it as parochial and isolated.[30] The windows of opportunity for women were opened in the early decades of the twentieth century but for the most part just wide enough to find a few examples to brag about. Indeed, many of the thoroughbred women active in the women's movement saw no inconsistency in their support of a traditional social scene for their sons and daughters.[31]

That scene was not unlike a grand play. The cotillions that brought the young together in a formal setting had been around since Mathurin Giron, a short, rotund Frenchman of pioneer days, opened the ballroom above his confectionery and hired Monsieur Xaupi to teach the elite to dance. Susan attended such formal dances throughout the social season, as well as other activities dispersed among them. Private parties and dances, formal dinners, and receptions brought smaller groups together. Teas and card parties provided the young women a chance to show additional social skills. There were also less formal occasions planned by social groups such as the Once a Week Dancing Club. One need only thumb through the social columns of the local press to comprehend the frequency and intensity of such gatherings.

Another important prerequisite to a successful social life among the Bluegrass gentry was a proper heritage. Among Lexington's elite, marriage (and that was the desired end of the flurry of social activity) was between two families as well as two individuals. The season's engagements were evaluated carefully, and contemptuous references were made to those who married beneath themselves. Such concerns were not unusual among the leadership class of small rural towns, but Lexington seemed more concerned with such matters than most. More than one young man or woman had his or her lineage dissected by the queen bees of society. Elizabeth Murphey Simpson, a friend of Susan's, later wrote a book entitled *The Enchanted Bluegrass* in which she labeled the concern more accurately. Kentucky's gentry was concerned with "pedigree."[32] Another Lexingtonian suggested that the concern stemmed from the attention paid to the breeding of horses, but in fact the concern with regard to humans may be older than the region's love of the horse. Susan's pedigree was above all but the pickiest of criticisms, but Lexington's elite tended to be exceedingly "picky." The Clays, not without cause, always believed Lexington's gentry took too much pleasure in family "idiosyncrasies." Lexington thought the Clays took too much pride in being Clays. No Clay, however, could be denied his or her place within the elite, idiosyncrasies and all.

For Susan, the social calendar provided merely another stage, and she intended to play the lead. At times she would have liked to discuss with a young man the latest book she was reading and the ideas that leaped to mind, but for once she disciplined herself. Conversation was supposed to be cheerful, humorous, and social, avoiding controversial topics. As Wyatt-Brown noted about an earlier time, a southern woman was not supposed to appear "too metaphysical." Such women did not make contented wives.[33] A description by Susan related to her own time indicates that little had changed since the mid-nineteenth century: "Fancy dazzling Tommie Jones with a flow of Greek or modern literature other than F. Scott Fitzgerald."[34] So instead of intellect Susan dazzled with wit, flashing eyes, and a ready smile.[35]

Susan had more than her share of beaux and collected memories of a time when she seemed in control of her "perfect" world. The pedestal of southern womanhood appeared ideal for Susan Clay. She seemed easily among the most eligible of central Kentucky's young women. In June 1914, Susan graduated from Miss Ella Williams' School in a class of ten young ladies. Williams knew them well and briefly characterized the strengths of each as she handed them a diploma. Pausing before

Susan, she said, "And Susan Clay? She can do anything she wants to do." Actually Miss Williams implied that in Susan's case, realization of potential was tied to personal discipline.[36] But the family, and Susan, heard what had been said for years. Doting relatives, parents, and teachers had long praised her potential. She was a poet, an artist, and a southern belle. Now it was time for potential to become reality—if it could in progressive Lexington.

✌

CHAPTER FOUR

Matilda, the Same Thing Has Happened to Me!

I stood
Driven deep in darkness
Chafed by the turbulence
Of bright, possible things.
                    —"The Pine Tree," SCS Papers

MANY OF LEXINGTON'S YOUNG WOMEN completed their education as Susan did in 1914 and waited for whatever came next. Most experienced the disappointment suggested by Judith M. Bordwick and Elizabeth Douvan in their essay "Ambivalence: The Socialization of Women." Encouraged to show their abilities during their school years, young women have traditionally confronted the reality of discrimination upon graduation.[1] In Susan's case the trauma was made worse by the confidence developed in her and the potential praised by those who knew her. Unfortunately, Susan's understanding of success and that of her parents, relatives, and teachers differed significantly. Susan dreamed of seeing the world and contributing to it as a writer or an artist. To the Clays success meant she had to limit her ambitions and, like the past three generations of Clay women, serve. The conflict created difficulties.[2]

Susan came slowly to a realization that she was discontented and slower yet to an understanding of its causes. Perhaps the discontent began as an uneasiness about some of the compromises expected of her as a young woman. Events that limited or confined her were offset by a seductive social life seen from the pedestal of southern womanhood.

She had been given so much that she felt guilty at times for being dissatisfied. Nevertheless, she felt confined by "darkness" and "chafed" by the potential that seemed restricted. Finally, she created an alternative. Her poetry became her means of self-expression as well as an avenue to understanding.

Her father's long-awaited return in 1908 had probably been an initial cause of discontent. Captain Clay, fifty years old in 1908, looked like a Kentucky colonel, though he would not have appreciated the comparison.[3] Like the women in Susan's life, Charles Clay projected a public image. He was very formal and dignified. He walked with a swagger acquired as a young military officer yet suitable to a nineteenth-century gentleman with a distinguished heritage. Such an image was dated by 1908, and many Lexington people thought him pompous. Charles Clay's values were also considered old-fashioned even in a community tied to tradition.

Aware of his responsibility to the Clay name and wedded to the values his mother had taught him, Charles Clay knew his role within the family, and that of his wife, his sons, and his daughters. In 1908 he took his "rightful" place as the head of the family, and he expected the children to know their places too. Susan and Charley would not distract him as easily as they had their mother. Papa also led the conversations that occurred each night after the dishes had been cleared by Millie and her children. Susan listened more often, and when she did speak, her father questioned her accounts and drew a rein on her spontaneity.[4]

Clay placed a great deal more importance on the "place" of his sons. He had dubbed his eldest son the "Charley of the future" at the time of his birth. He wanted his sons to be soldiers. No expense would be spared in preparing them for the U.S. Military Academy at West Point, which would give them the advantage within the army that he had not enjoyed.[5] He used the evening discussions to tell stories about his own career and the family which emphasized duty, loyalty, courage, and masculine virtues. The education of his daughters was different. They would attend school in Lexington. In the southern tradition, they would bring credit to the family by marrying well and sharing the success of their husbands and sons. But the girls could also learn from stories about duty and loyalty. The sacrifices made by his mother and other women in the family were recounted for their benefit.

Susan's reduced role was offset to some degree by the delight of having Papa home and the excitement of hearing accounts of his bravery firsthand. Similarly, Susan recognized her father's old-fashioned manners, but they seemed a novelty at first. Her letters from Atlanta in 1911 and 1912 indicate awareness of his values early on, but not a strong opposition to them. She described the French plays and the social life to her mother rather than offend her father's sense of propriety. The same attitude was apparent at home. After 1908, Clay ran a small thoroughbred breeding operation on the farm, but he was most discreet in discussing it in the presence of his daughters. He kept no stallions on the farm, shipping his mares away to be bred. When the mares were loaded on vans to be taken to the stallions for breeding, he told his daughters the mares were going to see their friends. For the girls, new foals appeared as if by magic. Charley and Bob were allowed to go to the barns during foaling season, but only on the condition that they say nothing to their sisters. Susan was not so naive as not to know what was occurring, but as Elizabeth Clay declared many years later, theirs had been "a far more beautiful and gracious world" in which ladies, or gentlemen in the presence of ladies, did not discuss the breeding of horses.

The installation of a telephone at the Clay home presented special problems, for other horsemen, unaware of Charles Clay's sensitivity, called him to discuss their business. Few such calls were received before a signal was arranged and Marm, Susan, and Metzie withdrew from the parlor into the dining room closing the large doors behind them. As their father grew older and increasingly hard of hearing, he shouted into the telephone, but no one told him that his voice carried beyond the hall and through the doors.[6] The charade continued for many years. Susan appreciated that part of her father's gentlemanly refinement.

Other of her father's activities were less appreciated. His return to the family coincided with and perhaps precipitated the beginning of Susan's training as a lady. Though she anticipated the gaiety and attention of a brilliant social life, there were additional demands. The

Susan and Charley rode their horses on the Clay farm. Both were excellent riders. Susan formed a close friendship with her brother during adolescence.

spontaneity and creativity for which she formerly had been praised seemed to cause her father displeasure, which at times led to criticism of her. He expressed concern about her activities, her conduct, her very thoughts.

The question of young men raised a whole new interpretation of family history for Susan. Marriages were the major reason for the orchestrated social life Susan entered shortly after her return from Atlanta, and marriages were as much a joining of families as individuals. Consequently, the utmost care had to be shown to any potential relationship. The slightest hint of scandal, a history of poor health, or too modest means in the family of a boy Susan seemed to like led to long family discussions. Even the brothers felt the scrutiny of relatives. At the age of fourteen, Charley began to go horseback riding with a young woman. The family, including uncles and aunt, forced him to stop seeing the girl because there had been mental health problems in an earlier generation of her family.[7] They did this, of course, despite the fact that several of Henry Clay's sons had suffered from severe mental depression. Young men came to visit Susan and, later, Metzie, but they quickly sensed the concern of Mr. and Mrs. Clay and many chose not to return.[8] Susan and Metzie became convinced that no man would ever suit the family.[9]

Susan increasingly felt the heavy burden of her family heritage, as do descendants of many great men. Moreover, for Susan it seemed unnecessarily burdensome as well as premature. Her family was too tied to the past, unaware of a more modern view. Susan also received the double message that Carolyn G. Heilbrun in *Reinventing Womanhood* has noted was sent by many mothers to their daughters: succeed, but not so much as to jeopardize "feminine allure."[10] The entire family gave that message to Susan.

The realization of her restriction may also have been triggered by the freedom she experienced in Atlanta. Certainly, she recognized some of her father's sensitivities. She also implied the limitations, real and imagined, of small towns like Lexington and recognized that her Aunt Lizzie's views and actions were less traditional. It is unfortunate that Susan did not write more about her Aunt Lizzie because it is impossible to gauge the effect Elizabeth Pepper had on her. Certainly, Susan respected her aunt and envied her ability to travel. When the family pressured Lizzie about her refusal to marry or her frequent traveling, she often said, "I'll do as I please." According to Elizabeth Blanford, Susan adopted the phrase as her own when her family scolded

some action she took. That implies some influence, though Susan
certainly continued to do as Charles and Ria Clay pleased in most
matters.

Aunt Lizzie also became involved in the local suffrage movement
while Susan was in her teens. There is little hard evidence that the
suffrage movement influenced Susan, but she certainly did not live in
a vacuum. The movement found strong leadership among central
Kentucky's elite, including Susan's family. Aunt Lizzie represented the
Pepper branch. Laura, Mary, Anne, and Sallie Clay, daughters of the
abolitionist Cassius M. Clay, were distant cousins. Madeline McDowell
Breckinridge, leader of state and national suffrage organizations as
well as other reform efforts, was, like Susan, a great-granddaughter of
Henry Clay. She was also the wife of Desha Breckinridge, editor of the
Lexington newspaper and a close friend of Charles Clay. Margaret
Ripley Wolfe noted that kinship and class ties became a "blessing rather
than a bane" for southern advocates of suffrage.[11] That was certainly
true in the Clay household. No reference to the suffrage movement
can be found in the Clay correspondence, but that absence can be
interpreted as a positive rather than a negative. Susan may not have
been free to participate, but neither was the movement subject to the
criticism it most certainly would have received had family as well as
close friends not been leading it. Susan clipped articles and pictures
about the movement from newspapers and magazines to save in her
scrapbooks. Like many women, she watched cautiously, but hopefully,
from the sidelines, fearing the consequences of participation or just
not yet feeling comfortable being involved.[12]

A lack of political involvement did not mean an absence of new,
perhaps even modern ideas. Certainly, her poems indicate a break with
the traditions her father preferred she observe. An early prose poem,
"To Flame the Unknown," left unanswered questions. She pondered
man's fascination with fire in the poem. Noting that different people
defined flame differently—the scientist as the burning of gases, the
poet as passion, primitive tribes as God—she questioned man's ability
to devise a single definition. The poem perhaps expressed her uneasiness with many of the simplistic answers teachers and parents expected
her to accept without question. In the Clays' world there were no unanswered questions. In that world that looked to the past—the Clay

home, Miss Williams' School, and much of Lexington, Kentucky, and the South—young girls were supposed to write happy verses and leave deeper philosophical issues to men.[13]

In another early, symbolic poem, "The Butterfly," Susan pondered the death of a beautiful but frail creature at the hand of man.[14] The butterfly, near death, lit upon the hand of a young boy, who closed the hand, killing it. She asked poetically if he perpetuated death out of "youthful sympathy," to end the creature's suffering, or because "a madness seized thy thought," a callous example of power.[15] Though melodramatic and naive, the poem nevertheless spoke to the questions she wanted to ask and to discuss but was not free to do so. She learned by experience not to share such poems. Some early poems she apparently did show her parents because several contain critical marginal notes in her father's handwriting. One short poem beautifully described the colors of autumn leaves but concluded with a somber statement about autumn bringing consciousness of ending. Her father expressed his disappointment that the beautiful description ended so sadly.[16] His rebuke added to her doubts. Her ideas evoked concern instead of the praise she had been taught to expect. Increasingly, she left certain poems hidden in her room, poems that stated more obviously her sense of confinement.

In a short story Susan criticized community and family values more openly. The *Lexington Leader* published "A Christmas Disappointment" just before the holiday in 1913. In a single line she summed up her frustration with requirements forced on young women. "No one seems to realize that beneath our little blue calico outsides we have individual souls."[17] The comment was surrounded by less forceful remarks and attributed to a fictional character, but its meaning is evident. In her story, a sixteen-year-old orphan girl, named Susan, recounts an experience from her childhood. Led to expect that Santa Claus would fulfill her special wish if she followed the rules, she experienced disappointment on Christmas morning when her wish was not granted. She criticized herself for expecting too much; she should have expected to be treated no differently from everyone else. It was, as events were to prove, the story of Susan Clay. Susan did not want to think and act like the other girls. She had hoped for too much and on the doorstep of adulthood found the promise was a lie. The pedestal of the southern lady brought attention, beauty, and refinement, but it required her to suppress her own thoughts.

Realization of the causes of her discontent occurred more rapidly after her graduation from Miss Williams' School. In a dilemma common to American women, Susan was, in a sense, all dressed up with no place to go. She encountered the mixed messages a changing society sent to young women. Her traditional upbringing and community values promised success if she played the role of the lady, but newspapers and magazines carried the story of a more modern woman—the Gibson girl, the suffragist, and, later, the flapper. Susan had been praised for educational and social successes necessary for both routes to success. Upon graduation, she confronted the realities of her world. Professions were closed to her, and subtle pressures were placed on her to curb her ambitions and to accept a traditional role.[18] For Susan Clay, the limitations were severe because of the era and family values, the ambitions greater because she was the great-granddaughter of Henry Clay. Moreover, she was at a disadvantage because personal strengths necessary to overcome the external pressures were poorly developed at least in part as the result of her upbringing, and other "virtues," such as family loyalty, held her to her place.[19]

In Lexington, young women of her class had three major options in the period when Susan reached maturity. Some were allowed to go away to continue their education and to enter careers traditionally closed to women. Their lives indicate that change was occurring. In Lexington, however, they were the exception rather than the rule. Others accepted the only professional positions open to them in the Lexington of the 1920s, teacher or bank teller, but employers, families, and the community expected them to resign when they married. (The same requirement held true in Sinclair Lewis's Gopher Prairie, Minnesota.) The remainder, the overwhelming majority, remained in their fathers' homes until their particular knight in shining armor swept them off their feet and into marriage. Indeed, many of those who were allowed to go away to college returned to marry a proper young central Kentucky man and to settle into the same social setting.[20]

The Clays allowed Susan to continue her schooling, but she had to remain in Lexington. When Ella Williams closed her school that fall and accepted the position of dean of Sayre College, Susan followed her there. In March 1915, Williams died suddenly. Susan left Sayre and enrolled at Transylvania College. There, tragedy, of a sort, struck again. Susan had fallen in love that fall, but the relationship ended as abruptly as it began. The young man never said why, and Susan, deeply hurt, withdrew from school. Though precipitated by the death of Miss Williams and the broken love affair, her decision to leave school with no place to go resulted from the weight of the confinement she experienced. She wrote, "I stood / Driven deep in darkness / Chafed by the turbulence / Of bright, possible things."[21] Those "bright, possible things" seemed beyond her grasp in 1915.

The crisis revealed another aspect of Susan's sense of confinement. Lexington society could be extremely cruel. Gossip provided the major entertainment, and a joke or cruel comment at the expense of the Clay family and its members was more than a figment of Grandmother Clay's imagination. Susan felt the criticism and the scorn. Then she began to doubt herself. She explained her feelings six years later, in an article, "Apology of a Small Town Poetess," published in the *New York Times*. Again, it was a fictional Susan, a small-town poetess like the author, who described a failed romance. The questions she asked were not unusual although she would not have believed it at the time. What had she done, she asked, to make the young man lose interest? Had a jealous girl said something to make him dislike her? Were her erstwhile friends talking about her behind her back and enjoying her humiliation? Susan stated in the article that she felt like the "popular star who had been hissed [from the stage]." For the first time, Susan's internalization of the more negative aspects of the family saga are apparent. The Clays had long believed that coarser men resented their good fortune at having been born to such a distinguished family. The family believed that Lexington's elite had enjoyed seeing Susan M. Clay lose Ashland and they now resented Susan's beauty, talent, and popularity. That was the price one paid for being a member of a great family.[22] Susan learned that family lesson, but the pain seemed more intense and less noble than that borne by her great-grandfather Henry Clay or her grandmother.

Such events might have had less impact if she had not been, at the same time, confronting her own helplessness against the limitations upon her. Her parents might allow her to attend Sayre or Transylvania, but they would not let her leave Lexington. Because of the cost of educating Charley and Bob, there was no money to send Susan away to school. The priorities were clearly and openly stated. The boys were told repeatedly that if anything should happen to their father, they would be responsible for the well-being of their mother and sisters. There was another reason Susan could not go away. Ria Clay simply would not hear of it. She would have kept her sons close to her, too, if not for her husband's plans to send them to West Point. Even so, she wrote frequently to Charley and Bob expressing an exaggerated concern for their safety. She gave Charley advice about his health and his studies and encouraged Bob, even as a plebe at West Point, not to run or exercise too strenuously. She imagined every sort of danger, and the boys were cautious about telling her of their activities.[23] Their caution was of little avail; she found something in virtually every letter to enhance her fear. Her control of the girls was more successful. Charles's plans for them could easily be fulfilled in Lexington. She had no intention of letting them out of her sight.

Nor was Susan free to take a job in Lexington. Despite the suffrage movement, there were few real changes in Lexington.[24] Madeline McDowell Breckinridge used her husband's newspaper to support the cause, but a rival paper continued as late as 1917 to quote discriminatory quips such as, "The test of true womanhood is more in the quality of her pancakes than the etherealism of her thought."[25] Change came even more slowly to the home of Charles and Ria Clay. Susan might mimic the independence of her Aunt Lizzie, but no Clay woman had ever worked outside the home. The family history contained a moral for all occasions, and Susan heard new ones to illustrate why she should remain in her father's home. Henry Clay's wife, Lucretia, had rarely joined him in Washington. She remained at home and, according to the family, operated the plantation. Henry Clay left her money to provide for family and plantation each time he left for Washington, but when he returned, the family argued, she gave it back with a profit. Historians raise questions about that account, crediting overseers rather than Lucretia Clay, but this spoke to Susan of the role a woman could play within the context of Clay values.[26] Susan M. Clay had served her father-in-law as amanuensis and furthered her husband's career with her social graces. She had been a strong woman, but her strength had been exercised within the accepted sphere of woman. Aunt Teetee cared for her mother and brothers, and Susan's own mother had provided a home while Papa was away. A Clay woman simply did not work outside the home. Her parents urged her to be patient. Some young man would propose marriage in time.

Several young men did propose marriage, but even that option seemed closed to Susan Clay after 1915. None of Lexington's young men approached, in her mind, Lancelot, Romeo, or Robert Browning. Susan had lived too long in the romantic world of her dreams. Or was it that she refused to accept less in a man than she wanted? Susan sought someone to share her interests, to discuss in some depth and with a degree of equality the art and literature she enjoyed. Most of the young men she met were interested in business, horses, and tobacco or law. As her poem "To Elizabeth" implied, she wanted to exhibit the lasting beauty of a star; she believed most Lexington men wanted their wives to be flowers. Her concept of beauty involved depth as well as physical brilliance.[27]

Susan dealt, however, not only with her own requirements but those of her family. Charles and Ria Clay inevitably found flaws in young men who called. In such an atmosphere and mood, Susan grew uncomfortable, frustrated, and eventually angry. She argued with her father, but he and Mrs. Clay refused to bend. Charles Clay had been warned by his own mother to marry carefully.[28] He would be no less insistent about his own children. Thinking herself helpless, carrying the burden of her past, Susan became melancholy, stayed in her room, and at one point threatened to take her own life.[29] From 1915 to 1919 there were only signs of despair. Susan passed the time wandering aimlessly about the farm, sitting amid the flower gardens at Balgowan or alone in her room drawing and writing. She later called the time her "cloudy period."

Susan's creative efforts at that time reflect the melancholy she experienced. She seemed dangerously close to sinking into the debilitating depression that had characterized the Clays for three generations. Her drawings were extremely somber. Her poems rarely mentioned individuals, but her paintings were generally mood sketches of people. Self-portraits were characterized by a fixed stare as if she was trying to escape the reality of her existence. Sketches of her sister or brothers

Susan's artistic ability included cartoon characters as well as people. These drawings were probably inspired by her friendship with Wyncie King.

Susan sketched her brother Bob deeply engrossed in a book. Most of her sketches captured somber moods.

created the same moods or pictured them sleeping as if that was a form of escape. Static landscapes were done in dark hues of green and gray. In her paintings, leaves hang limply and even the air seems hot and heavy. One senses silence and inertia as if time stands still.[30]

The poems she wrote in those years denote a young woman's sense of confinement and the desire to know freedom. Many of the poems written during the years between 1915 and 1922 were published in 1923 in a small volume entitled *Poems by Susan Clay*. They show that though Susan Clay lived in the twentieth century, the values of her father's home were decidedly nineteenth century. A four-line poem, "The Firefly," suggests the theme of containment versus freedom in imagery derived from the memories of her rural Kentucky childhood.

> The sky and valley hold me close tonight
>   like cupped hands,—
> But I shall crawl to the verge of them
> And lift my wings to you.[31]

The same theme characterized the poem "The Butterfly." In a six-line piece called "The Inland Sea," Susan Clay is a small body of water contained by mountains.

> This little deep, blue sea
> Hovered with cloudy dreams,
> Looks upward always,
> —wistful . . . silent,—
> At the tall knees
> Of the mountains.[32]

In her early work Susan expressed her sense of confinement primarily in physical terms. Heaven, stars, and clouds represented freedom as she looked up from her place. In one poem, freedom was a soaring eagle and the "pale dove-colored rim of Earth / Expands to him."[33] It was the earth which confined humanity.

In "Poppies," first published in *Town and Country Magazine* but also included in *Poems*, she again used the theme of earth's confinement, and the yearning for freedom was contained in the imagery of trees with long fingers feeling the stars.

> Let us kneel and watch their gray stalks
> Waver upward like lines of smoke;
> Light and slender as Joss-sticks
> Lit with a bit of blossom.
> Look, I balance one aslant
> Like a peace-pipe with a glowing bowl!
> Should we lie among them
> Half asleep—
> They would be a thicket of young trees
> Feeling the stars with curious, thin fingers.[34]

In "A Sea Dream," she struggled against the confinement of a sea-blown mist.[35] The poem "To—" spoke of mental confinement when she wrote:

> You, who alone, knew how to push apart
> The stiff brown stalks that clutched here in my mind,
> Coarse-stemmed, and harsh and strong,
> Driving me mad for colour,—I whose heart
> Beat low to their dull subtleties so long.[36]

Poems like "To—" reflect the youthful naiveté and romanticism of their author, though she has moved significantly from the tortured expressions demanded by her teachers. One can easily trace the maturing of the poet by following such themes that she repeated over and over again. Those "stiff brown stalks" were earth clutching at her, restricting her efforts to be free. Interestingly, she referred to the dull subtleties that held her down. Her training had been subtle for the most part—like that experienced by many women, so subtle that focus was difficult—and it was the belief in the traditional image of woman, held to and taught by her family and community, that held her to place. Sandra Gilbert and Susan Gubar found the theme characteristic of many nineteenth-century women poets. They argue that

Companies used the fencing along the interurban line to stencil epigraphs and advertisements. Susan and several friends took snapshots before phrases they thought suited them. "Never Excelled" seems particularly appropriate. Susan was never excelled in her youth; she was wondering if the phrase might also be her epitaph.

nineteenth-century women often felt imprisoned by their circumstances and expressed those feelings in spatial imagery of confinement and freedom. They go on to say, "Literally, women, like Dickinson, Brontë and Rosetti were imprisoned in their homes, their fathers' houses: indeed, almost all nineteenth century women were in some sense imprisoned in men's houses." Susan Clay wrote in the twentieth century, but the influence of old values and restrictions remained.[37] She, too, was a poet, a woman, imprisoned in men's houses.

Susan spoke more directly to her frustration in the concluding lines of a poem titled "Void." She used the imagery of night and day to describe her life as one of unending boredom.

> Night is only the narrow edge
> Between two stupid sides of a page

Unnoticed in turning.
And dawn
A monotonous voice
Somewhere in the midst of a sentence
About duty and waiting.[38]

Duty, family, waiting, propriety. The poem notes the problems in lines no longer stylized or clichéd but simple and honest. Susan Clay had become aware of the forces that restricted her. On a single sheet of lined notebook paper she graphically tied her present discontent to the past. She had visited Balgowan and stopped at a locust tree where years earlier Uncle Tom had attached a doll's face beneath a wedge-shaped fungus common to such trees. They had called the face Matilda, and it had been the subject of countless stories suggested by Uncle Tom and embellished by the children. It had been a symbol of childhood joy, but now the face was nearly covered by the fungus, and Susan wrote:

When I found her canopy had completely overgrown her face and she was imprisoned forever . . . I whispered against the spot where she had gone under, "Matilda, the same thing has happened to me."[39]

CHAPTER FIVE

✻

Escape

You, who alone, knew how to push apart
The stiff brown stalks that clutched here in
　my mind
　　　　　　　　—"To—," *Poems by Susan Clay*

CHARLES AND RIA CLAY recognized their daughter's melancholy. There
were too many examples in the Clay family for them not to recognize
it. They were inclined, however, to explain it in worn-out clichés more
appropriate to the nineteenth-century cult of true womanhood. Susan
had always had a flair for the dramatic. Her moods were those of Babby
or Becky Sharpe, Catherine Earnshaw or Agnes; such ups and downs
were normal behavior in teenaged girls. Or the Clays attributed Susan's
melancholy to her high spirit; that quality had justified many of her
actions. Because she was creative, they reasoned, she was also overly
sensitive—Susan Over-do, her mother called her. Ria Clay suspected
that all would be set right when Susan married, but she never saw the
inconsistency between that thought and her own actions any time a
man called on her daughter.[1]

　　After World War I, the Clays did not have the seductive social life of
Lexington to mask Susan's discontent. They moved to Louisville in
1917 when Charles Clay rejoined the army. By the time they returned
to Lexington, many of Susan's friends had left Lexington to take positions in cities that allowed women greater opportunities. Moreover,
within Lexington, the social scene had changed; as in so many places,
the gaiety of the prewar era could not be restored.

Though it was not immediately apparent, Susan was also changing. Slowly she began to creep out of her despondency and self-pity and to take the first tenuous steps that led to open rebellion. There were several reasons for the change, but one of the most important was her poetry. High-spirited and romantic, Susan Clay seemed incapable of being analytical or rational until she sat down to write. In the process of choosing words and phrases that expressed both beauty and meaning, she achieved understanding. In that process, she not only articulated the forces that confined her but gained the resolution to act against them. Her poetry, then, both provoked and explains her actions.

The poems that can be dated after 1915 reflect the evolution of her thought. Earlier works implied confinement and freedom indirectly through spatial imagery. After 1915 her poems explained her unhappiness more specifically. Her tone increasingly mirrored that of the 1920s—sarcastic, irreverent, and sometimes glib. She increasingly attacked the icons of Clay and southern values. In a poem entitled "Portrait" she criticized the Clay family. Susan's sister, Elizabeth, recalled in later years the warmth and security of sitting around winter fires at Balgowan surrounded by the portraits of famous men, hearing the stories of gallant exploits and noble service. No doubt Susan as a child had felt similarly, but by 1919 she found the same scene laden with lessons of confinement and tradition. In "Portrait" she attacks the "family wisdom" that limited her opportunities.

> The head of this agéd mandarin is like a
>   tea-pot
> Soaking, in the warm fluidity of thought,
> All the written wisdom of his race.
>
> Each twisted symbol is an ancient rolled-up
>   word,
> A pinch of tea leaves, dry and enigmatical,
> Uncurling, with an acrid fragrance,
> The mummied dreams of distant dynasties.

> The mind of this learnéd mandarin is like
>   black tea
> That has grown bitter, steeping knowledge.[2]

The significance of the poem escaped the Clays. They thought Susan
was writing about Chinese warlords.[3] The title only hints at the fact
that she was criticizing her own family. Statements in her 1921 *New
York Times* article, "Apology of a Small Town Poetess," however, iden-
tify the real subject of the poem. In the article, she wrote of a family
"mummified by tradition" and" thoroughly satisfied because it is old,"
a family where to be young "and to want something new is to be in
exceedingly bad odor."[4] Not only are the themes of old wisdom and
patriarchy the same, but the similarity between the line "The mummied
dreams of distant dynasties" found in the poem and the reference in
the article to a family "mummified by tradition" seem more than coincidental. Susan obviously resented family obligations and traditions.

Other poems attacked different aspects of Clay values. In "To Elizabeth" she mocked the image of the young southern lady. The poem
was about one of her friends, a young lady who epitomized the values
and the behavior taught by the Lexington gentry. Elizabeth was the
social butterfly stealing from life "some little tatter of happiness." She
loved parties and exuded charm and affection to many men. But it was
a charade. Elizabeth's beauty was physical. "One could not gather stars
from you, but flowers." She was a showpiece, a public image: she had
no intellectual depth. Taking a stab at another pillar of family and
community, the church, Susan wrote, "You must be accepted unrea-
sonably, enthusiastically, like religion, through a sort of returning necessity."[5]

At times, Susan Clay could be analytical. She critiqued the weak
image of southern women with sharp, ripping phrases and concluded
the poem with an attack on the society that made young women such
shallow images, used them, then forgot them:

> Careless, improvident with love, because too
>   much has been given you.
> You cannot grow bright in the ardor of
>   others like iron in flame;

> They will burn you as hard and dry
> As clay in a potter's oven.[6]

Susan Clay made her most provocative attack in an openly erotic poem entitled "Ideals." She focused on religion and her society's emphasis on physical beauty. To write such suggestive verse was as unacceptable as being irreverent, but to be irreverent by combining eroticism and mockery of religion directly affronted both family and community. "Ideals" turned the concept of the virgin birth upside down. Instead of God going to a virgin, a woman, the lowliest of women, takes advantage of God.

> Beauty is a strange woman,
> A bold woman,
> With disordered hair
> And bleeding feet.
> She is seeking Divinity
> With the thoughts of a harlot
> And insatiable eyes.
>
> She is the bearer of flame
> Trying to tear itself
> With beating wings
> From the clutch of her torch;
> The mother of fierce, miserable children
> Born from her blasphemous kiss
> On God's unknowing lips.[7]

"Ideals" is an extremely shocking poem for a daughter of the Bluegrass gentry to write. Susan had discovered what the "stiff, brown stalks" were that clutched at her mind. She no longer longed for color but demanded it. Poem after poem lashed out at the walls, or the values, "That make the sensitive places of spirit / Ache like the angles of a close-confined body."[8]

The strength derived from writing about her discontent led to actions to alleviate it. Her parents allowed her to visit Aunt Pinnie Smith in Washington, D.C., during the winter of 1919–20. Indicative of the widening gulf between Susan and her parents, she was shocked when they agreed to the trip and then suspicious of their intentions. In Lexington she believed no man would suit her parents, but in 1919 she feared that they agreed to the trip hoping she would meet a proper young military officer. Her younger sister later had a similar experience and suspicion.[9]

Susan had other things on her mind. Shortly after arriving in Washington, she enrolled in classes to learn typing and shorthand. She also began to search for a job and accepted one as a stenographer. Susan's poetry showed the influence of the new spirit of the 1920s. Now her actions followed suit. She planned to remain in Washington and become the young professional woman she had read about.

Unfortunately, Susan had not counted on her mother's wariness. Alert to the slightest hint of aberrant behavior, Ria Clay sensed that something was afoot. Susan, a victim of her own excitement, said too much in her letters, and Mrs. Clay began her attempts to deflect Susan's plans. At first she merely encouraged Susan to return home; she had been away a long time. When Susan's intentions became clearer, Marm became more direct. She argued that Susan did not need to take a position of employment; Colonel Clay could care for his family's needs. If Susan took a job, Lexington would think the Clays near bankruptcy. When that plea did not accomplish her purpose, she informed Susan that it was improper for an unmarried woman to live away from home. Susan, apparently, remained unmoved. Then, Ria Clay, herself so much a product of family loyalty, resorted to guilt. She expressed to Susan her own loneliness and her sense of failure as a mother. Indirectly, she was implying that Susan was violating one of the standards of the southern woman, loyalty to and sacrifice for family, though that responsibility has not been limited to women of the South. "I have been wondering and thinking lately, trying to come to some conclusion of what my precious Susan expects and wishes to do—Do you want to live away from me? This thought makes me sick at heart. I dare not think such a thing."[10]

Susan was nearly twenty-two years old, and her misery at home was apparent even to her mother. For nearly three years she had been suffocated by lack of direction or opportunity and her own self-pity before resolving to act. Mrs. Clay deposited the burden of the past upon her and Susan's resolve crumbled. By spring, she was back in her parents' home. Susan's failed resolve is difficult to explain. Indeed, no simple explanation may be sufficient. In the very act of writing her parents, revealing her plans, she may have wanted them to bring her back. She seems to have been poorly equipped to be a typist. She was of the class that made decisions rather than recorded them. Her sister later found herself miserable in a clerical job at the Metropolitan Museum of Art in New York because of that same family image. Susan also faced the adjustment young persons leaving home for the first time in any era find they must make. Yet her mother's entreaties had not fallen on insensitive ears. Mrs. Clay's pleading letters struck a responsive chord, producing the sense of guilt they were intended to create. Guilt was a major component of southern training. Sinclair Lewis's "village virus" certainly seems to apply as well. Within Susan there were elements of two worlds. Her modern side yearned for freedom; her traditions encouraged a return to the comfort of the small town. Even as she complained poetically about duty, waiting, and mummified values, her father's house provided security.[11]

Her decision indicates another characteristic of her thought—one that remained with her throughout her life. She was inclined to react to the weight of emotion at a given moment without anticipating the long-range effect. She forgot her own misery when her mother's was so immediate and poignantly expressed. It would not be the last time Susan would make such a mistake. She had held freedom within her grasp and let it slip away.

Susan resumed her vigil from her father's home, but it did not take long for her to realize her mistake. She slipped into depression again, feeling trapped this time by her own decisions. Colonel and Mrs. Clay used the same tired explanations. Ironically, of all the family members, Teetee Clay understood best what Susan was feeling. Susan might dream of faraway places, of great art and literature, but she was enough the product of her upbringing to dream also of marriage and family.[12] Yet her Prince Charming had not appeared; she wondered perhaps if he ever would. Teetee had had similar experiences over fifty years earlier. She had been engaged to a young man in Racine, Wisconsin, shortly after the Civil War, but for reasons known only to her the engagement had been broken. She found solace in service to family,

Ever the "starlet," Susan posed with one of the family pets. Lovers of animals, the Clays always had several dogs and cats and befriended other animals that seemed to need their help.

mother, brothers, and community. Like Susan, she put her dreams on paper, a long novel in which the fictional Teetee overcame the obstacles to enjoy a "happily ever after" marriage.[13]

Teetee seemed determined that Susan would not suffer her fate. She argued that Susan would not find a husband on her father's Versailles Road farm or among the flower gardens at Balgowan. She told Susan to quit working all the time; "you are too young and attractive for this." Teetee urged her niece to stop being so critical of those around her. She was "too tense" and needed to look for the good in others.[14]

Action followed advice. Teetee dragged Susan to meetings of the Woman's Club, the Daughters of the American Revolution, and the United Daughters of the Confederacy. To be sure, no men attended such meetings, but the network of women who did were the means in Teetee's world by which eligible men might be found. Ironically, Teetee was facilitating a phenomenon common to the 1920s. Winning the right to vote proved a double-edged sword for women. Certainly it opened the means to political involvement, but that came slowly. Victory also caused the women's movement to lose focus.[15] In her carefully researched study *The Torchbearers,* Karen Blair argues that cultural organizations, like the Lexington Woman's Club, became the means by which women influenced their communities in positive ways. Additionally, she argues that women who were not inclined to be politically active found service to the community in keeping with their traditional values and increased their own confidence levels simultaneously. In this way a second, less political level of change developed and broadened the women's movement.[16]

Susan Clay participated in several such groups throughout the 1920s. She attended meetings with her aunt, joined poetry societies and writers' clubs, and took occasional classes at the University of Kentucky. Such activities proved critical to her sanity. They also, as Blair argues, provided a pathway to renewed confidence, though the path was neither smooth nor straight.

One such event proved in time the means by which she escaped her father's house. In March 1921, the University Arts Department and the Woman's Club jointly sponsored an exhibit of approximately one hundred paintings chosen (by the Milch Galleries of New York City) to

exemplify the best of American art. The exhibit was accompanied by
the director of the project, a naturalized American, originally from the
city of Riga in Latvia. He had selected the paintings and was prepared
to speak authoritatively on the collection. His message was the same in
Akron, Kansas City, Louisville, or Chicago: American art was better
than Americans realized. In Springfield, Ohio, he explained one of the
major reasons he welcomed the assignment: "Strange as it may seem
that a Russian should be engaged in Americanization work, yet it often
takes an outsider to see the real worth of anything great or wonderful."[17]

William Sawitzky delivered his message well. In fact, he sold himself to his audiences before he offered the product. Advance material
was generally published in the leading newspapers of the city. The
newspapers carried a simulated interview with him along with a photograph. His Russian background was emphasized in the stern set of
the eyes and mouth; he looked like a man who knew what he was
talking about. Additional interviews, published after the exhibition
opened, presented a different side of William Sawitzky. He was not
only knowledgeable about art, but, knowing how interested Americans
were in Russian affairs in those years immediately after the Bolshevik
revolution, he volunteered to speak to groups about the upheaval. He
discussed topics in a calculated manner. He casually mentioned his
poor English and Russian accent and that both embarrassed his wife.
Actually his English was superb, and he had that hint of accent that
Americans found charming. His speeches were such a blend of authority, light humor, and pleasantry that he could say things that might
have caused others difficulty. The Red Scare had ended only within
the last year, but Sawitzky stated his opinion that a revolution was the
only way to bring Russia into the twentieth century. Newspaper accounts indicate no objection to his views but did note that audiences
listened intently as he detailed the circumstances surrounding the death
of his brother at the hands of the Bolsheviks.[18]

Sawitzky had become a citizen of the United States in 1917 and
served in the New Jersey state military reserve. He had offered his
services to the Intelligence Department and was accepted because of
his language skills—he spoke English, French, Russian, and German.[19]
His talents, ease of manner, charm, and obvious gentility led to instant

popularity. Descended from the Russian noble class, he had not lost the bearing of nobility. Furthermore, he had added to it the aristocracy of the intellectual community. He could speak as knowledgeably about literature and music as about art and politics and was considered easy to talk to, gentle, and serene in his demeanor.[20] Moreover, he was as attentive to the conversation of a woman as a man and subtly encouraged others to express their thoughts. Women, particularly, found him extremely charming.

This combination of strength, knowledge, and sensitivity appealed to Susan Clay. He discussed with her art, the England of Arthur and Guinevere, or literature "other than F. Scott Fitzgerald." He shared Susan's love of animals, particularly birds. As a young man, Susan learned, Sawitzky had participated in an ornithological expedition to Persia and Afghanistan.[21] He visited the Clay home and walked with Susan to Balgowan to evaluate the family portraits. She poured out her soul to him as she had done to no one except perhaps her brother Charley. No one will ever know the substance of their conversations, but an undated letter, written on his "last night in Lexington," indicates that they shared deep confidences. He wrote, "And to have a young woman of your intellect and pride come and confide in me, meant more to me than I am in a position to explain." The subject of their conversations and their depth are apparent in the conclusion of his letter: "Don't let the others tame you. Keep forever your fire and hunger! Never throw yourself away!! Always remember the words of Polonius. . . . And this above all things, to thine own self be true!"[22]

The relationship developed rapidly despite the fact that Sawitzky was married. One individual present at the time of their introduction later claimed they fell in love at first sight.[23] Hindsight usually has perfect vision, but intimacy did develop quickly. His letter indicated only her sharing of deep concerns with him, but she loved him and that love gave her strength to stand on her own. Sawitzky was not only a sign of rebellion but a catalyst for it.

The new strength became apparent first in her poetry. New love poems expressed excitement and, more important, hope. The naively romantic quality of her adolescent poems is evident again. In a poem entitled "Passion," she wrote:

Someone is throwing over me
Bright rings of sensation.
They shake down to my ankles in quick,
    vivid hoops
Like a game of quoits.
I have no strength to step out of them.[24]

She learned quickly that caution was required in the expression of such thoughts. She penned several short poems which she left in view of her parents. An untitled piece read

Because I can neither see
Nor hear you
I write your name, carefully,
Over and over
That you may be in some way
Tangible to me.[25]

In Charles Clay's unmistakable hand, a note beneath it read, "I wish I knew who he was." On the reverse page, beneath another poem he wrote, "I wish I knew who he was, again." Above that poem Susan had either blacked out a poem or merely turned the pencil so as to sharpen it by rubbing it against the page. The colonel revealed his curiosity, or suspiciousness, in an accompanying note: "You made a very good job of obliterating this one. I tried to read it but failed."[26] Marm also noticed her new spirit and suspected its cause in a general sense. She chose to remain silent at least for the moment.

The new confidence sparked action as well. She wrote to a friend, Helen Bullitt Lowry, who had moved to New York to take a position with the *New York Times,* and sent some of her poetry. Armed with a favorable response and Helen Lowry's offer to introduce her to some publishers and editors, Susan told her parents that she wanted to go to New York.[27] Expecting opposition, she had the answer to any question about finances. She had inherited a diamond ring from Grandmother Clay which was too matronly for an unmarried woman in her early twenties. A jeweler had appraised its value at five hundred dollars, a sum, the twenty-four-year-old Susan argued, that would easily cover the cost of her trip. Reluctantly, and only after arranging suitable chaperonage, the Clays consented.[28]

As in Atlanta a decade earlier, the urban milieu sparked a fever pitch of enthusiasm in Susan. As promised, Helen Lowry introduced her to editors and writers of the *New York Times*. Susan also met artists, actors, and poets with uninhibited and stimulating personalities. She saw Sawitzky again and renewed her acquaintance with Hortense Flexner, a poet from Louisville who lived in New York. Susan enjoyed a freedom of expression she had not felt in Lexington and commented in a letter that Henry Brock, an editor of the *Times,* conceded that "he came out worsted in [their] conversation."[29] The lifestyles were equally free. They might dine and dance at a distinguished restaurant or decide at midnight to eat at a quaint cafe in the Bohemian quarter of the city. Brock jokingly referred to her poetic "hot stuff" and "saw possibilities of an original personality in me." Susan also met Witter Bynner, the president of the Poetry Society of America, who praised her poetry and gave her letters of introduction. She accompanied Bynner and Brock to a party at the studio of Oscar Cesare, "a big, lovable childish Swede. . . one of the real geniuses."[30] She also met friends from Kentucky. Charles Herz, Frank Breckinridge, and Susan attended several plays together and went to the Biltmore Hotel for tea and dancing.[31]

Intoxicated by such heady freedom, Susan wrote to her mother describing without reservation all that she was experiencing. She had begun a letter on July 2, "I can't understand why you don't write me. You don't seem to care after all whether I am having a good time or not."[32] She was to learn quickly how much her mother cared. On July 12, Ria Clay sent a letter that indicates perhaps as nothing else the restrictiveness of the Clay home and community.

> Your interesting letter telling me of the interesting people you have been meeting through Helen Lowrey [sic] came yesterday after six days of anxious waiting. Now Susan I am much afraid that you are infringing on your rights and your reputation in going around with the childish Swede and the editor etc. *unchaperoned.* You must keep faith and do not ease your conscience by doing doubtful things and then mentioning them casually.

I do hope that you find a publisher for your poetry and your prose, but keep your dignity and remember "noblesse oblige" (if this is the way you spell it) and do not abuse the blessings that God has given you.

Remember that the fashionable Twentieth Century girl is a godless girl and an unfaithful creature, to self, parents and pretty near everything in life.[33]

Ria Clay not only knew how to spell *noblesse oblige,* she knew what it meant for a Clay of central Kentucky, particularly an unmarried twenty-four-year-old female.

Susan, duly subdued or more cautious, returned to Lexington after nearly a month in New York. Her uncharacteristic serenity is perhaps explained by the fact that she did not plan to stay long. Ready to try independence again, she had secured a position as a reporter and feature writer for the daily *Louisville Herald.* There seemed to be a breakthrough in family attitudes that summer. In one week of August, Susan left the Clay home for Louisville; Lieutenant Charles D. Clay Jr. left for assignment at Fort Snelling, Minnesota; and Bob began his first week at West Point. The children, except for Metzie, were grown. Susan discarded the long, flowing dresses and traditional broad-brimmed hat for a simple, dark suit and a conservative hat. She looked like the young professional woman of the 1920s.[34]

In Louisville, Susan wrote for the society section of the paper, and her writing style indicates a high level of confidence. Susan Clay was certainly no 1920s flapper, but that was the image her writing portrayed. Some of her columns, however, were so inane as to make virtually no sense, though that may have resulted as much from her editor's changes as from her enthusiasm.[35] The most persistent trend of her column was to satirize the values of her society, particularly as they related to women's roles. Even her titles seem intended to show contempt. The article in the September 25, 1921, issue was entitled "Aha! Milady's Nerves Are Soothed Through Esthetic Window Dressing."[36] By mid-October Susan's articles were striking hard at convention. The October 16, 1921, column was about the coming out of Louisville's debutantes. She referred to them as the season's "Buds," noting that there were very few of them. She explained, "Really, they have been plucked so ruthlessly in recent months that only a scant handful are showing a desperate 'self-determination' to bloom at all hazards." She referred to the seven girls participating in the events as "the seven wise virgins who have resolved to be old-fashioned . . . for after all isn't that what they have been growing up for?" She concluded the piece by implying that the girls and their mothers were foolishly caught up in a social scene that had little merit. Her references to the carefully planned social occasions, the orchestrated coquetry, and the pretentiousness came dangerously close to losing its veil of satire.

A week later Susan penned another feminist satire. The racing season was in full swing, and her subject was women at the race track. The article was entitled "It's the Most Surprising Thing My Dear—The Way They Act; Why, Even Grandma Gets a 'Kick.'" In mock horror she wrote of how women of all classes of society were openly placing wagers at the betting windows. What was the state of morality when women old enough to be grandmothers were openly enjoying themselves at the track?[37] She was contemptuous of conservative values and seemed by her use of language to seek controversy.

A third article attacked the convention of motherhood. She suggested that women should acquire pet dogs instead of children. More modern areas of the country had adopted the practice because dogs more readily reflected the personalities of their owners. That was, after all, the real purpose of having children. Additionally, dogs were more reliable than children and far less trouble.[38]

Susan Clay, the daughter of the Bluegrass gentry, was certainly acting, and writing, in a most unaristocratic fashion. She seemed to be intentionally trying to shut herself off from her own class, mimicking the behavior of those modern women who took chances and challenged traditional views.[39]

There were reasons for her self-confidence and sense of freedom. She believed she was escaping the confinement of Lexington and the Clay home. First, she appeared to be breaking into the world of literature. Her "Apology of a Small Town Poetess" appeared in the *New York Times* on December 13, 1921. She also learned that *Town and Country Magazine,* a prestigious publication aimed at the elite, would purchase several of her poems, and Alfred Kreymborg expressed interest in others for a collection he was editing.[40] Finally, she felt free and in control of her life for a special reason. Susan Clay believed that she would soon become Mrs. William Sawitzky.

CHAPTER SIX

❦

Romance

Who could know
That my love for you
Is coloured with ruby and emerald?
—"Secret," SCS Papers

IN LATE DECEMBER 1921, Susan Clay resigned her position with the *Louisville Herald* and returned to her father's home. This time, however, her return appears to have been a calculated decision on her part. She had not been happy as a journalist. Her editor too frequently deleted literary references from her work. Additionally, in a interview for the *Herald,* the writer Edna Ferber argued that journalism would not help her become a poet or a short story writer.[1] Moreover, the interest being shown in her poems justified in her mind greater concentration on her writing. At any rate, she did not plan to stay in her father's house for long. William Sawitzky had started divorce proceedings.[2]

William Sawitzky, or Vassili, as Susan called him, made an immediate difference in her life. In her notebooks, she jotted down random notes expressing thoughts of love, Vassili, or concern over discovery of those thoughts. The greatest change occurred in her poetry. Suddenly, Susan became more like her gentry peers than she had ever been. If its cause had been different, even her father would have approved the change in her poems. Her new verses were light, pretty, and romantic. She was "close to the very lips of happiness," one poem proclaimed. Thinking of Sawitzky, she wrote a poem she titled "Message":

As a dove folds its cry in its throat
I called you.
As a gentian speaks with shut lips
I whispered your name:

And through the thin walls of my heart
Beloved, you heard.[3]

Susan's love had to remain a secret from her family.

Who could know
That my love for you
Is coloured with ruby and emerald?

For it goes with humming-bird wariness
Beating its wings into grey mist.[4]

Poetically, her love came "Through the rain! / Through the silver stalks
of rain"[5] to add color to her drab existence in her father's house. In
"Parsifal," she proclaimed her excitement:

The thirst that I have to drink your soul,
  O beloved,
Is like the lust of a drunkard
For the wine in the cup of Christ.[6]

Susan convinced herself that destiny had brought them together.
"You and I looked upward at one star. / Though the shoulder of the
world was thick between us, / And at this apex our eyes met."[7] Their
intellectual intimacy developed quickly. They shared much, and understanding came so easily that all obstacles were rationalized away.
Sawitzky shared with her the problems of his marriage. He had married the only daughter of a well-to-do family in 1915. According to
Sawitzky, that was the chief reason the marriage was not happy. Although his income averaged approximately six thousand dollars per
year, it was not enough to keep his wife happy. The couple had a son in

1916 and a daughter in 1918, but the marriage, he claimed, had been finished in all but name long before his trip to Lexington.[8]

Susan and Vassili corresponded regularly after her return from New York. Few of those letters are extant for Susan feared, with good reason, that her family would misunderstand. There is evidence, however, of that correspondence. A letter in late 1921 from Hortense Flexner King[9] referred to information she had received about Susan from Sawitzky and implied that there was a regular correspondence between them. Additionally, Susan told Sawitzky much later that her mother had grown concerned about their correspondence, demanded to read the letters, and expressed displeasure about their "friendship."[10]

The issue grew more tense when Colonel Clay became involved. Sawitzky planned to visit Susan in late November 1922. Sawitzky was a married man, nearly eighteen years older than Susan, and a foreigner. Charles Clay had objected to his daughter's suitors for much less reason. He swore that he would shoot Sawitzky if he attempted to see Susan. This time, however, Susan refused to concede to her father. Elizabeth Clay recalled years later very heated discussions between Susan and her father.[11]

Once again, traditional values stymied Susan's hard-won strength and resolve. On November 23, 1922, tragedy struck the Clay family as harsh a blow as could be delivered. Late in the evening the Clays received a telephone call from a representative of the U.S. Army at Fort Snelling, Minnesota. Charles Donald Clay Jr. was dead.

Charles was the pride and hope of the Clay family. The oldest son, he bore the weight of the generations. In physique and personality, the twenty-three-year-old Charley epitomized the best of the Clay family. His father had called him "Charley of the future" since his birth; his mother had assigned him the task of protecting his sisters. The family preached duty and honor to him until he found it virtually impossible to distinguish between discretion and valor. Charley was the champion of the underdog, the defender of the defenseless, and the burden of family duty rested heavily on his shoulders.[12]

Fulfilling his father's dream, Charley entered West Point just before America's entry into World War I. According to the family account, he wanted to resign so he could fight (as Clays had done in every American

The pride of his father, Charles D. Clay Jr. attended West Point for one year. He later joined the regular army as a lieutenant.

war), but his father refused. Taking matters into his own hands, he intentionally accumulated enough demerits to be asked to leave, but by the time he was officially detached from West Point, the war had ended.[13] Disappointed, he returned to Lexington and entered the University of Kentucky. In 1921 the army offered commissions as first and second lieutenants based on a written exam, and Charley scored high enough to be commissioned a first lieutenant, thus redeeming himself in the eyes of his father. By November 1922, he was stationed at Fort Snelling, Minnesota, and the Clays believed all was going well. Then came news of his death.

The most difficult task that sad evening was telling Ria Clay. Colonel Clay and Susan waited at the front gate to meet Mrs. Clay, who had been in Lexington shopping. With them waited Helen Rogers, a Christian Science practitioner. Charles Clay had granted a begrudging tolerance to the practice of Christian Science by his wife and daughters, but on that night in 1922 he was quite willing to ask for the help of its practitioners. Nevertheless, Elizabeth Clay recalled years later hearing her mother's haunting scream from nearly a quarter of a mile away. Susan and Metzie stayed by their mother's side for days, reading to her from Christian Science literature selections suggested by Rogers and other Christian Science friends. Ria Clay's grief was so deep that they worried about her life and her sanity.

The colonel grieved too, but he expressed it as a southern male and a Clay was supposed to, by hiding it. He handled his grief by filling time with action. A board of inquiry at Fort Snelling stated that Charley had been unhappy in the weeks before the incident and that he had been drinking heavily. Without further investigation, the board declared his death a suicide. Charley's death was hard enough to take, but the collective decision of the family was that suicide was out of the question.[14] Colonel Charles Clay had another war to fight, one in defense of his son's honor. There was evidence to support the Clay contention that Charley had not killed himself. His letters to the family from Fort Snelling had been filled with enthusiasm. He enjoyed his unit and was particularly pleased with his sergeant, a veteran soldier, who, Charley said, knew how to handle men. He had also established a satisfying social life through the web of Lexington connections that meant so much at the time. He renewed acquaintances with the Foster family of St. Paul and Lexington, who treated him like a son.[15] Moreover, Colonel Clay did not believe that a young man contemplating suicide would have purchased Christmas presents and planned a trip home to see his family. Clay traveled to Washington, D.C., to call in favors from old army acquaintances. He spoke to General R. C. Davis and showed him Charley's letters to his mother. He also saw General George Duncan, another personal friend, to ask for a more thorough investigation. Meanwhile, Colonel Clay received additional information to support his argument. A Minnesota businessman, traveling through Kentucky, stopped by the Clay home at the request of Charley's friends to tell Colonel Clay that an effort was being made to cover up the details of Charley's death. Later, in a letter, the colonel received more details. The pistol involved in Charley's death was not the one issued to him, and there was evidence that the body had been moved to corroborate the army's account of the incident. Charley's friends believed the commander of the base was attempting to protect his own career by covering up the murder of one of his officers.[16]

On March 8, 1923, Colonel Clay received a telegram stating that the secretary of war had ordered the board at Fort Snelling to reconvene to make an additional investigation.[17] Clay went to Fort Snelling for the hearings, and, under questioning, several young officers changed their testimonies. Additional information revealed that Charley's life had been threatened by another soldier. On April 24, 1923, the board overturned the original findings and declared that Lieutenant Charles Clay had died in the line of duty under undetermined circumstances and "not of his own willful misconduct."[18]

No one was ever charged with the murder of Charley Clay. One suspect deserted his unit and fled to Canada, but the army did not seek his extradition.[19] Still, the primary goal had been achieved. The Clay family never truly learned to accept the death of Charley, but they did learn to live with it once the verdict of suicide had been removed.

At home, the primary concern was for Ria Clay. She clung to her daughters as though to let them out of her sight would mean losing them as she had lost Charley. The entire family sought to console her. Bob, an eighteen-year-old plebe, had his own grief to bear as well as

Elizabeth as an adult

Robert Pepper Clay graduated from West Point. A soldier "from the day he was born," his sisters said, he served with distinction in World War II and retired with the rank of colonel.

the trials of a first-year student at West Point, but his letters to his mother reflected a sensitivity far beyond his years. At home, Susan and Metzie grieved for their mother as much as for Charley. Like many families, the Clays could fight with each other, but they were as one in the face of tragedy.

Ria Clay required much of her daughters in that period. They dared not leave her and conceded to her every whim. She made unreasonable demands, perhaps the worst an insistence on reading William Sawitzky's letters. Her approach was more civil than that of Charles Clay, and it was more effective. As she had done when Susan sought to stay in Washington, Mrs. Clay used guilt, pity, and family loyalty to force from Susan an unfair promise. Not only did she want to read Sawitzky's letters, but she exacted from Susan a promise not to write to Sawitzky or to see or speak to him when he came to Lexington. It was a selfless, if rash, promise indicative of the degree to which Susan had internalized family values, but at that moment each of the Clays would have promised Marm virtually anything.

The impact of Susan's decision was felt immediately. Sawitzky was virtually on his way to Lexington to see Susan at the time it was made. True to her promise, she refused to see him even to explain the situation. Sawitzky, unfamiliar with southern values, was completely dumbfounded. He went to Susan's friend Elizabeth Murphey Simpson, who tried to explain to him the special nature of the Clay family and the immediate circumstances. Sawitzky returned to New York without seeing Susan or attempting to change her mind.[20]

Susan busied herself with the task of consoling her mother and sought to create a life for herself within the context of traditional family and community. They attended Christian Science lectures and read and talked about articles in the *Science Journal*. Occasionally, they went into Lexington to eat lunch and shop. Beneath the surface calm, members of the family attempted to deal with the grief each felt. Susan continued to see old friends. She sought to put Vassili in the back of her mind and, as if to assure herself, dated other men, but they were little more than friends or escorts.

Susan also continued to attend cultural events in Lexington and enrolled part-time at the University of Kentucky.[21] She became involved in a group called the Scribbler's Club, an informal literary society composed of students and faculty members. She found there the stimulating conversation she had not believed possible in Lexington as well as the encouragement she needed to seek publication of her poems. Granville Terrell, a university professor associated with the group, urged her to publish, apologizing in advance if his letter seemed too forward. True "lovers of talent," he wrote, would welcome her poetic "genius."[22]

The encouragement of the Scribblers did lead to publication. She published first in the *Kentucky Kernel,* the student newspaper, and won several prizes. Ironically, it was Carol Sax, through whom she had met Sawitzky, who introduced her to the publisher of her book of poems. At Sax's invitation, Ralph Fletcher Seymour brought a collection of etchings to exhibit in Lexington. Susan showed him the sights of Lexington and the countryside; her mother wrote peevishly to Bob that Susan had caught a cold walking in the rain with Seymour without her rubbers.[23] The relationship did not become anything more than a professional one despite Mrs. Clay's fears. In December 1923, he published *Poems by Susan Clay,* a collection of twenty-six short poems written between 1917 and 1923.

Susan dedicated nearly four years to her mother. They were not easy years. Mrs. Clay's deepest grief passed, but she was no less demanding, and Susan's efforts to placate her mother seemed only to perpetuate the problem. Susan tried to make a life of her own again through clubs, poetry societies, and her own poetry, but Marm made it difficult. She criticized Susan's friends, calling them a "not choice circle" in a letter to Bob. She resented Susan's efforts to leave her side even for a moment. When the publication of her poems gave Susan the chance to travel, Ria Clay objected and criticized her for wanting to go. She called her poetry "dark and dreary—desperate and to me somewhat sacrilegious." She wrote Bob that she wished there was a school for women like West Point. Susan and Metzie needed discipline and character.[24]

Given Susan's sacrifice for the principle of family loyalty and Mrs. Clay's constant criticism, it is little wonder that Susan suffered serious depression again. Even the success of her poetry and favorable reviews of it could not lift her spirits. She was nearly twenty-nine years old, and happiness seemed as far away as ever. Her desire to attain a measure of freedom had not disappeared, however, and she came slowly to realize she had sacrificed her one chance at happiness. In August 1926, Susan Clay wrote to William Sawitzky.

The letter was not easy to compose. She had to wonder if his feelings had changed over time. Susan wrote many drafts before the letter satisfied her. Only a draft version remains, and in it, words, phrases, and sentences are marked through, with revisions and revisions of revisions added. Susan wrote that she wanted to explain why she had refused to see or communicate with him in the months following the death of her brother. She had believed that she was doing the right thing at the time, but "I have become skeptical of my own best intuitions." Vassili, "a man of wide experience with persons and places," probably had understood the situation better than she had:

> You met my parents and relatives and could see no doubt that they live by standards and prejudices that are inadequate for the broad reaches of this age. Not only this narrowness and intolerance, but poverty, too, has segregated us until we seem to live within an enchanted circle of loneliness [last two words marked through]. We of this generation are like the animals of Galopagus who have become strange and separate and have lost the sense of the defensive through isolation. We are too blunderingly naive and the world bewilders and hurts us.
>
> A year before you came to Lexington the last time, my brother, who was a young field artillery officer, was found dead in his room with a pistol wound through his head. It was pronounced suicide though we never knew surely.
>
> You could never imagine the horrible effect this had on my mother. Her grief was so dreadful and so near insanity, that in my pity for her I promised her anything however unreasonable. As you know, she thought my frank fondness for you improper because you are a married man, and as time went on this was one of several things her morbid thought fastened upon. She insisted on reading your letters, misunderstood it all, and made me swear that should you ever come here again, I would refuse to see and talk to you and to give no explanation. Mother's temperament, I imagine is like that of your Czarina—absorbed, sensitive and given over to religious fervour distorted by superstition. I came to hold back my thoughts like bated breath in her presence for fear of hurting her more. Now I feel for many reasons that this was useless and wrong.[25]

Susan admitted her need for his advice and said that she still felt close to him despite the lack of communication. As the letter becomes most intimate, a page ends and there is no more. Nevertheless, it contains a great deal of important information. The assessment of the Clay family indicates her acceptance of the oral traditions. Yet her longing for freedom is apparent too. The letter itself is indication of a resolve to take control of her life, even if the means she contemplated seem traditional.

Sawitzky was in Europe when Susan wrote to him. He had left the employment of the Milch Galleries to establish his own business buying and selling artwork, evaluating paintings for prospective buyers or seeking buyers for those wishing to sell paintings. The trip kept him in Europe for nearly a year while Susan's letter followed him from city to city. He did not receive it until after he returned to New York. Divorced since late 1923, Sawitzky did not hesitate for a moment. He wrote back on October 9, 1926, to let her know he had received her letter only that day because of his trip to Europe. He expressed his delight and promised to write a more lengthy letter immediately.[26] In the second letter Sawitzky claimed that Susan's refusal to see or talk to him in November 1923 had left him dumbfounded and hurt. He knew nothing of the difficulties the family had experienced at the time of Charley's death nor, he claimed, had he sensed the hostility of Susan's parents. He apologized for his failure to understand the values of central Kentucky and immediately showed how little he really did understand them. He asked Susan if the fact that he was now divorced from his wife would "put a different light on me in the eyes of your mother." He spoke openly about his marriage as if he were trying to give her information to use in the debate that might take place at the Clay home. His marriage had been uncongenial in every way. Indeed, the "inner separation" had already taken place when he met Susan in 1921. "I was no longer married in the deeper and real sense of the word."[27] He was, he said, truly sorry that her parents had suffered because of him, and he understood and supported her desire to abide by their wishes. That was, of course, the obligation of any child to parents. At the same time, children and parents must realize that the right of self-determination "is the most sacred thing the individual human heart and soul have." Paying homage to her religious nature, he argued that to deny or violate that right was "to speak in the vernacular of religious people, a sin against the Holy Ghost." He quoted Polonius to her again and suggested that when out of concern for others he had failed to be true to himself, it had inevitably led to an unhealthy situation.[28]

Sawitzky then changed his approach, again in a manner that appealed to Susan's sensitivities. He apologized further for his delay in writing but explained that her letter had not reached him because of his busy schedule in Europe, where he had visited seventeen countries. He had flown from London to Paris and from Copenhagen to Hamburg. He described in graphic detail the beauties of that part of Europe. The Baltic and the Danish Islands were particularly beautiful, he wrote, when seen from an airplane eight thousand feet in the air. He described a bullfight in Barcelona and told her of his photographs of the crater at Vesuvius. "The world is so wide and beautiful, and just waiting to be discovered and loved again and again. It is so very wrong to sit in a corner and be save [sic] because life is not always gentle and likes to play us dirty tricks."[29] He could not have appealed to Susan Clay's longings or fears more effectively. She had been sitting too long in her own little corner—Lexington, Kentucky.

Again he changed his approach. Knowing she loved intrigue, he asked if her parents would censor their correspondence. He then added: "I was political editor in Russia when we had 'preventative censorship' and I had enough of it."[30] William Sawitzky certainly knew what he wanted. As later evidence will show, he loved Susan Clay very deeply, but, as she had suggested in her letter, he was familiar with the ways of the world and of people. He knew that the one thing that stood in the way of his happiness was Susan's sense of what was proper. She might chafe at the restrictions of her family and community, but like many women of that time, she had internalized a portion of the very paternalistic restrictions she struggled against.[31] Susan Clay might long intellectually for freedom, but in practice she still worried about the impact on her family and on her reputation within the central Kentucky community. Sawitzky summed it up accurately in a letter of December 23, 1926, when he wrote, "please, for once forget the 27 [sic] little white fences of your New England forbears [sic]."[32] In fact, Susan's "forbears" came from Virginia, but Vassili was speaking of moral ancestors rather than literal ones. His ally, however, was her desire to discover that wide and wonderful world of which he was a part and to share with someone the love of art and culture she found so restricted in Lexington society. She dreamed of Atlanta, Washington, and New York. William Sawitzky offered her even more.

By April 1927, Sawitzky was ready to press matters further. He planned a business trip to Cincinnati and Louisville and wrote to Susan on April 14 that he wanted to stop in Lexington to see her.[33] She must have telegraphed him immediately because he answered some communication from her three days later. In that letter, he reassured her of his intentions, speaking of the "invisible bond" between them. Sawitzky urged her to pick a place for them to meet but added, "I have never forgotten our walk in the open and I wish I could meet you somewhere away from the crowd and alone with the sky and trees."[34]

Susan's fear of interference from her father now became apparent in Sawitzky's responses. He wrote again three days later agreeing to follow her suggestions "and make it as convenient and safe for you as I possibly can." Susan had warned him to avoid a "Mr. S." at the Lafayette Hotel, where he would stay. Apparently, "Mr. S." knew Colonel Clay because Vassili remarked that he was aware of how provincial Lexington was. He agreed not only to stay instead at the "antiquated" Phoenix Hotel but to take his meals in his room to avoid being seen. It is, he continued, "a nuisance that people and circumstances make life more complicated than it already is. However, it isn't our fault and if chess has to be played, let's play chess."[35]

After nearly six years apart, Vassili and Susan secretly met on Tuesday, April 26, 1927, in the woods behind Ashland, the Clay family estate. What was said is unknown, but Sawitzky's first letter after that meeting was addressed to "My Precious." He carefully addressed it to the residence of Mrs. J. D. Clinkenbeard, Susan's friend and Christian Science practitioner, so the letter would not be opened and read by the Clays. Finally, Vassili and Susan began the intricate plot that would lead to their becoming husband and wife. In that short time together, they had decided to marry secretly and leave Lexington before her family learned of it.[36]

Sawitzky wasted no time in beginning the preparations. On the morning after their meeting, he was in Covington, Kentucky, consulting with the county clerk about state marriage requirements. He reported to Susan in an April 27 letter that there would be no difficulties. All that the state required was for them to give their names and ages and "armed with the license, the ceremony can be performed, in the presence of two witnesses, by any justice of the peace." Vassili's relief was apparent in the tone of his letter. He also reminded her that she had promised to measure the circumference of her finger so he could purchase the ring. The letter next turned to the question of discovery. "There is only one thing we should not overlook entirely. Is there a possibility of the county clerk or the justice being a friend or an acquaintance of your family or relatives? If so, he may take it into his head to delay action and to put in a telephone call which could ruin the whole situation." If there was a shadow of such a possibility, Vassili suggested that they go to Frankfort or Paris, another small town near Lexington. Again aware of Susan's sensitivities, he suggested Louisville as an even better alternative, but only if "you can see your way clear to take a train . . . for Louisville." He had already checked train schedules and written to ask friends to serve as witnesses if Susan agreed to his plans. Again he returned to his fears of discovery. "Please give your opinion on all this and give the fact a thought that the nosiness or narrow mind of a small town official may prove to be a disastrous complication. And as the conditions are: We cannot afford to take such a chance."[37] Vassili closed the letter with expressions of his happiness.

> I am still like in a dream and can hardly believe that a vision and a faint hope which I have carried in my heart for years, is about to become reality. The hope was so faint, that I have never given it much previous thought, and only in your letter of last August I found an undercurrent of interest which set me to thinking. Still, I didn't believe it possible and dismissed it. However, it kept on coming back and grew into a deep longing to see you and to hear your voice. And when I finally saw you yesterday, the whole world seemed full of redbud trees and meadow larks![38]

Susan was as happy as Vassili, but at this point her fears and her social upbringing made her a realist. She wrote two letters on April 28. Although there were ministers who would not marry them because Sawitzky had been divorced, she believed it would be "more dignified" to be married in Lexington by a minister. There was one minister in town who might marry them "without any foolish exactions." He had officiated at the wedding of Mrs. Clinkenbeard's daughter, who was a divorcee.[39] Mrs. Clinkenbeard also agreed to serve as a witness, but this would require a slight change in Vassili's plan. Since Mrs. Clinkenbeard was leaving town on Friday, May 6, Susan suggested that Vassili come to Lexington on Wednesday and that the marriage take place at 1:00 P.M. Thursday, May 5. Showing her own fears of discovery, she suggested that Vassili address his letters to Mrs. Clinkenbeard. If Susan's name was on the letter, it might be placed in the family's postal box even if addressed otherwise.[40]

The second letter contained much of the same information except that she now informed Vassili that she could not find a minister to marry them. By "some trick of chance, all the unprejudiced ones will be out of town when we want them." It was of little consequence, she stated; she had wanted to be married by a minister only out of respect for her mother. She had located a justice of the peace in the same building where they would obtain the marriage license. She would plan to spend the night of May 4–5 with Mrs. Clinkenbeard, telling her mother that she would be staying several days. Then Vassili could meet her there before they went to get the license.[41]

Sawitzky had left Cincinnati for Dayton and consequently received the second letter before the registered one caught up with him. Communication would continue to be a problem. They were plotting and writing at such a furious pace that they often lost track of what had been said and which letters had been read before the current one was written. Nevertheless, they anticipated each other's questions more often than not. Sawitzky accepted Susan's change of the marriage date but then returned immediately to the question of secrecy. He intended to check every detail for fear of some miscalculation. He had looked at the train schedules again. If they married in the morning, they would have to wait for the 2:20 P.M. train from Lexington to Cincinnati. He suggested that "it may be safer" to drive to Paris after the wedding and catch the train there at 3:05 P.M. "As you know the local situation ever so much better than I do, I will follow your lead. Only: don't let us take any unnecessary chances, a small slip has often lead [sic] to regrettable consequences."[42] He further suggested that Susan bring no luggage; they could purchase the necessary clothing in Cincinnati or Dayton. Vassili was obviously concerned. There is no way to know what Susan had told him about the situation at home, but the letters suggest that he wanted to take no chances of a confrontation with the colonel. At the same time, he remained sensitive to Susan's desires. He suggested that they could be married by a justice of the peace in Lexington, then find a minister in Dayton whose views were "broad enough" to give them a religious wedding. Susan agreed to all his plans except driving to Paris. It was, she said, an "unattractive little place" to spend even an afternoon so she suggested that they take the omnibus to Cincinnati after the ceremony.[43]

The plans, then, were finally set. Sawitzky would arrive in Lexington on Wednesday night, meet Susan the next morning, and they would go to the courthouse for a license and then be married. Once the plans were made, they exchanged a series of letters more like those between lovers. Susan wrote on May 2 that she was in a special world. She had never expected to find such happiness; if Vassili had any faults, she wrote, she could not see them and would at any rate "probably make fetishes of them . . . for I love every detail that contributes in any way to the making of you."[44] Vassili, somewhat more subdued by age and experience, wrote: "Only a week ago we didn't know what a world of happiness, peace and beauty life had in store for us. The thought of you and that you are giving me your heart, your life and your fullest faith, moves me as nothing ever has moved me before. Life has taught me many things and it has, above all, given me a sense of values. So I am hoping that I will always be worthy of your love and confidence."[45]

The wedding went as so intricately planned. The émigré Russian, a man of the world and a divorced man, had stolen the colonel's daughter—with her full cooperation.

❦

CHAPTER SEVEN

After the Wedding

As a gentian speaks with shut lips
I whispered your name:
And through the thin walls of my heart
Beloved, you heard.

—"Message," SCS Papers

SUSAN AND VASSILI LEFT Lexington for Dayton, Ohio, immediately after the ceremony, the first stop on their journey to New York. They had encountered none of the "interferences" both had so greatly feared, and Susan was as much the blushing bride as any nineteen- or twenty-year-old who had experienced a traditional wedding and send-off by friends. But she was nearly thirty years old, and at the Clay home the tears would not be those of happiness. In Dayton they visited with Vassili's friends, and he proudly introduced his new wife. She found them to be highly intelligent people and was both fascinated and stimulated by their conversation.[1] Sawitzky's friends were undoubtedly cultured, urbane people like himself, but Susan's accounts of their brilliance probably had far more to do with their being his friends than with any critical assessment of their intellect. In truth, Susan found anything and everything associated with Sawitzky superior to all she had known before. On May 7, two days after their marriage, Susan and Vassili wrote separate notes to her parents. The two letters form an interesting contrast. Susan's note was particularly characteristic. She was first the blushing bride—idealistic, romantic, certain of everlasting happiness.

Susan and Vassili sat for a picture shortly after their marriage. This photograph seems to capture the serenity that marriage provided for Susan.

> Dearest Mamma, surely you cannot object to our marriage when I tell you it has given me perfect happiness. Vassili and I have for each other a complete devotion and understanding, and our love penetrates so deeply into our spiritual backgrounds, that we could not fail to be lastingly happy. We seem to have almost identical preferences and dislikes so we can go in and out of each other's minds without disagreeable surprises. He is courteous with me and has my complete trust.[2]

The frustration Susan had hidden in her poetry, however, now became more overt. Both Vassili and the decisive action of elopement enhanced her confidence. Quickly, she took the offensive against any arguments from home by stating not only that the marriage was a good one but that she could not and would not live without Vassili. As to the elopement she wrote, "I am sorry that I had to marry without your knowledge, but you must blame yourself for it." She compared the love she shared with Vassili to that of Robert and Elizabeth Barrett Browning. Both couples had eloped for fear of parental interference, but as time would tell, Colonel Charles Clay, though paternalistic, was no Mr. Barrett. There was also in the letter the Susan Clay of the "27 white picket fences" and of her moral forebears. It was the genteel Bluegrass lady who appended the following paragraph to her letter: "We have just ordered engraved announcements of our marriage, of course, in your's and Papa's name. . . . I will address the ones I particularly want sent and mail them to you to send from home as this is a more dignified way of doing it."

Vassili's note was far less aggressive in tone. He had, he noted, "laid myself open to severe doubts regarding my integrity and my sense of social responsibilities" by marrying Susan without "formally asking you for her hand." He diplomatically explained their decision to elope but asked for the Clays' forgiveness if it was wrong. Like Susan, he stressed the similarities of their thoughts and preferences, and he emphasized his love for her: "May I say that Susan has my whole heart, all my faith, loyalty and devotion, and every bit of my goodwill? She is the culmination of my life-long dream of a wife, sweetheart and helpmate, a dream which is finally coming true. Susan is my taste more than any other human being." Perhaps forgetting momentarily that he had addressed the note to Colonel Clay as well as to Mrs. Clay, he waxed philosophical: "In short: we both feel that we are deeply congenial and that—even before we knew of each others existence—we had hitched our wagons to the same star." He closed the letter by thanking them for "having such a daughter," promising to do all in his power to make her happy, and asking for their parental blessing.[4]

Vassili's letter apparently eased Ria Clay's concerns. She wired the couple immediately, with reserved but conciliatory remarks, and invited them to spend a few days at the Clay home before going to New York. Vassili answered Mrs. Clay on May 11, claiming that business responsibilities would keep them from paying the requested visit, but promised that he would present himself to the family at a later time. Apparently, Ria Clay had also expressed some concern over his nationality. Vassili explained in his letter that though his father was Russian, his mother was from a Yorkshire family and her mother had been a native of Scotland. He expressed his hope that this lineage would make him acceptable but then added diplomatically that he was sure that Colonel and Mrs. Clay would agree that one was either a decent person or one was not, nationality having little to do with it.[5]

Such well-written notes might appease Ria Clay, who was willing to be appeased rather than lose her daughter.[6] Nevertheless, she had probably overstepped her authority by inviting them to pay a visit, for the colonel was not so easily placated. On May 11, he wrote a long letter to Sawitzky. Sawitzky destroyed it, but the contents can be reconstructed from Sawitzky's lengthy response three days later.[7] The two letters constituted a frank exchange of views between two proud men. Sawitzky's values had been instilled a world apart, but they were very similar to those of the colonel. He felt a strong responsibility to protect his wife. That duty, and his pride, again not unlike that of Charles Clay, probably led him to destroy Clay's letter without showing it to Susan.

The twenty-page response that Sawitzky mailed on May 14 indicates that the colonel's letter contained harsh words. He thanked Colonel Clay for a "very frank and straight forward expression of your opinion, in spite of the fact that it isn't complimentary to me." The colonel wanted to know the answers to a series of questions. First, why had Sawitzky not come to ask for Susan's hand in marriage? Sawitzky's answer indicates that the question was probably stated in a much less neutral manner. He responded, "First of all let me say that I have always acted in the open and that anything that has the appearance of being underhanded is distasteful to me. I personally would have preferred to go to your home and talk matters over with Mrs. Clay and yourself." He went on to say that he had enough Scottish blood in him to enjoy a good argument and when necessary a fight for a good cause. If his Scottish blood was insufficient, his Russian blood did not lack for spirit or gameness either. He did not allude, however, to the colonel's earlier threat to shoot him.

Sawitzky concentrated his argument on a subject in which the two men shared common interests if not always the same view. He argued that Susan's state of mind was such that a trying scene between himself and Colonel Clay would have caused her irreparable harm. Vassili's language at this point was not that used to charm Mrs. Clay; he was communicating with the colonel. The letter also reveals Sawitzky's assessment of Susan and her "poetic nature." He wrote:

You are basing your opinion mainly on the moral and social side of the question and you are overlooking—if I may express myself frankly—the psychological side of it. You have been searching the heart and mind of your daughter with the eyes of a loving father, which doubtless are deep and just, but which cannot have the sensitive intuition and understanding of the eyes of a lover. No young woman on earth can open her heart to her parents the way she opens it to the man she loves. . . . For this reason I feel at liberty to say that I found Susan to be in a precarious state of mind. You are a soldier and in your life you have dealt mostly with realities and facts. A higher power has willed that you should have a daughter whose mind lives in a world of emotion and imagination more than any other way. Susan is a poetess and an artist, which often in the opinion of the differently constituted and more materialistic person is something odd, something to be mentioned only with a kind of pitying smile. I do not share this opinion. I think that poets and artists are the milestones on the road of human culture. They are in their emotions, ever so much deeper and more sensitive than other people, they suffer immeasurably from the ugliness and brutality of life, they are so easily misunderstood and more easily hurt. In other words, they have to pay a heavy price for their divine gift, which is to express what so many of us feel but are unable to say. . . . You may be inclined to think that I am exaggerating, but I am afraid you did not realize quite clearly enough that Susan's spirit was slowly breaking under the adversities of conditions. After a talk that lasted for over three hours I found that Susan didn't have the strength to confront a discussion of the case at home, that everything in her shrank from the possibilities of outside interference. So you see, I had to choose between two alternatives—either to disregard conventionalities and public opinion, or to expose the beloved one to raw hurts and pains which could have scarred her oversensitive nature beyond repair. Of the two evils I chose what I am convinced was the smaller one. I acted with no other aim in view than to do the best for the sake of her inner life.[9]

Vassili was under no illusions that he could convince the colonel of the correctness of his actions and said so. Nevertheless, he continued to answer the questions raised in Colonel Clay's letter. Yes, they intended to have their marriage sanctified by a minister, and no, he was not of the Greek-Catholic faith but a Protestant. Riga, the "Boston" of Russia, was one of the centers of the Protestant Reformation and at one time the headquarters of Gustavus Adolphus, the champion of Martin Luther. His former wife and children had no financial claims on him, and he was able to provide comfortably for Susan. He gave the colonel a brief accounting of his earnings since coming to America. He had not carried life insurance but would now do so. Colonel Clay objected to the disparity in their ages, and Vassili did not disagree, although he used the opportunity to mention his clean living and good health.

The colonel was also less than subtle in objecting to the fact that Sawitzky was Russian. He would have preferred to see his daughter marry "a native American with American ideals." Sawitzky patiently detailed his "antecedents and my pedigree." He emphasized his hostility to Bolsheviks and, perhaps overstating matters in his own defense, claimed that his family was as well known in Riga as were the Clays in Kentucky. In closing his twenty-page response, Sawitzky turned diplomatically to the one thing upon which they were certain to agree, their love for Susan.

My dear Colonel Clay, the one thing that is nearest to my heart, as it is yours, is Susan's happiness. May I therefore suggest that we try and forget the things that were not what we had hoped they would be. Every living day we have something to forget and something to learn. Please do not feel that you have been beaten and that you have to surrender. Please remember that since time immemorial lovers have defied conventions when they didn't see another way out. It is the old conflict between two generations, between the interests of society and the interest of the individual. Of course, it hurts when it strikes home and I think it quite possible that if I was in your place I would have written a letter very similar to the one you wrote me. But now since it is water over the dam, lets [sic] get together in a spirit of understanding and good will and turn our faces to the future.

Susan is everything I expected her to be, and more. The only shadow over our young married life is that we have hurt where we didn't want to hurt. Won't you be kind enough to send her a loving word?[10]

Vassili's long letter was not without effect. It indicated that he was ready to assume the role of guardian and defender, the role the colonel expected of fathers and husbands. Colonel Clay did not respond to the letter, but Mrs. Clay was pleased that Vassili had made the effort. Then, too, Susan and Vassili were seeking to follow social protocol. The announcements of their marriage arrived in Kentucky, and Mrs. Clay mailed them as Susan's letter had suggested. A brief announcement, as vaguely written as possible, was sent to the *Lexington Herald*. The *Herald*, in turn, apparently did its homework and sent an announcement for publication in the *New York Times*. The announcement made particular mention of the fact the couple had eloped and the disparity in their ages.[11] Indeed, Lexington seemed to enjoy the Clays' embarrassment.

The colonel might never fully forgive Sawitzky for the circumstances surrounding the marriage, but time would show him the serenity marriage brought to his daughter and for that he gave Sawitzky a begrudging respect. Sawitzky, too, was a man of honor and pride. He would not soon forget the harshness of the colonel's letter. Nevertheless, both Clay and Sawitzky were gentlemen bound by codes of conduct as demanding, if not as restrictive, as those governing women. It would be improper to act out their resentments in the presence of "their" women. Most important, they both loved Susan. Later, in 1932, with the Depression growing worse, the colonel invited Vassili to bring Susan to live with them until the economic hardships ended. Vassili allowed Susan to decline the invitation. He would visit in the Clay home, but on most occasions he managed to have pressing business when Susan came to Kentucky for a visit. At other times, he would stay at the Lafayette Hotel. In the summer of 1929, the couple lived in Lexington, but they rented an apartment in town even though the Clay home could easily have accommodated them.

Relations between Sawitzky and his father-in-law, then, were correct and at times even cordial. The women of the family wanted to believe that all was normal and that the two men had resolved all differences. That they did believe it indicates the success of the efforts of both men.[12] In fact, their pride was too great to allow them to forget the past; the duties of a gentleman were too deeply ingrained for them to relive it openly.

Sawitzky expended most of his efforts where he thought he had the greatest chances of success—winning over Mrs. Clay. He wrote notes to her regularly, exuding the charm of which he was exceedingly capable. In almost every note he thanked her for having such a wonderful daughter. In a manner more like one old friend writing to another, he spoke of a July vacation on Cape Cod, the wealthy and respected friends with whom they stayed, and the ease with which Susan was adjusting to her new life. He casually mentioned that the members of his family in Europe had sent their congratulations and expressed their eagerness to meet Susan. His friends and relations here were equally elated and had "taken her [Susan] completely into their hearts." Indeed, he wrote, "All in all: everything looks bright and there is no reason to worry about anything."[13] Susan also kept a steady flow of letters heading toward Kentucky telling breathlessly of her new life. She entered into the task of rearranging Vassili's apartment with the excitement of a new bride. "I find to my great satisfaction," she wrote to her mother, "that Vassili not only needed a wife, but all of her accessory accomplishments—I mean all the little details that make things comfortable, and that women seem to realize intuitively when they become responsible for half the happiness of a home. You can't imagine what fun I am having."[14]

She described her new home as if it was a palace. Actually, Sawitzky's entire apartment was smaller than Susan's old room at home in Kentucky. The apartment consisted of one room and a bath, but a wrought iron divider separated a bedroom area from a sitting room. Vassili's collection of books filled floor-to-ceiling cases standing against most of the available wall space and made the room even smaller. Several paintings, which Susan described as "pleasant," and a collection of Russian icons provided an artistic touch. There were no kitchen facilities, but that was of no consequence. In 1927, money was no object; they could take their meals in restaurants. Moreover, Susan Clay did not know how to cook.

At any rate, they did not plan to stay long in the apartment. Vassili had already begun to make plans to combine business with pleasure in a leisurely tour of Europe. Susan, of course, was ecstatic at that idea. Her new world broke around her with remarkable speed. Married in May, she experienced New York and the New England states in June and July, and then went off to Europe for six months. Her marriage was proving to be all she had hoped it would be. Not only did she love and enjoy Vassili, but the union allowed her to reach for the freedom of a larger world which she had previously sought only through her poetry. She was the drunkard of her poem "Parsifal," intoxicated by all that she saw.

Her first letters to the family revealed her enthusiasm. She described her surroundings in great detail and with obvious glee. Their trip through Ohio introduced her to a new landscape and plants she had never seen. She sent sprigs, leaves, and blades of grass to her family. Her description of Lake Erie showed the ecstasy she was experiencing as well as the sensuality with which she could write: "I saw Lake Erie for the first time and it was gorgeous. The water was like a heavy silver skin, with a muscular movement undulating beneath it as if it responded voluptuously to the stroking of the wind. I will never forget my first sight of it."[15] In July, they visited New England, and Susan's letters described Cape Cod and its natural beauty. Frequently, they became so busy in their pleasure that Susan had no time to write. She sent postcards in place of letters, apologizing for not writing but filling every available space with prose descriptions as vivid as the pictures themselves.

But that was merely a beginning. They sailed for Europe in late July 1927 aboard the SS *Statendam*. Vassili and Susan made London their headquarters for the first four months of their trip. Vassili dealt with business matters each morning and Susan read from John Richard Green's *Universal History*. In the afternoons they explored the city or drove into the rural areas to see Roman ruins and historical or literary sites or to walk in the meadows and enjoy the things of nature they both loved.

Susan's letters to her mother contained long treatises on English history or pleasant descriptions of their experiences. Letters jumped excitedly from one topic to another and then to a third, disjointed yet with vivid descriptions. Susan described a sprig of heather or a bit of fern, then enclosed a sample within the letter, certain it would interest her parents as much as it did her.[16] She wrote of Cornwall, which led to a recounting of the legends of King Arthur, Guinevere, and the castle Tintagel. They spent several hours there, and Susan climbed to the top of the hill behind the castle ruin to a tiny enclosure where once a chapel had stood. As in the days of her youth, Susan was again the heroine, this time Guinevere, and she imagined, ironically perhaps, the lady praying "not to be delivered but absolved from her colorful sins with Lancelot."[17]

Later letters gave long accounts of her trips to Westminster Abbey, a place so enthralling to her, "so exquisite to the senses," that she was on two occasions almost locked inside overnight "with Edward the Confessor." The memory was enough to inspire seven pages of comments on early Danish and Anglo-Saxon kings of England. Even the indulgent Vassili became disgruntled. Her letters were "too filled with King Arthur and rainbows and not enough about the practical side of our trip to such a father and mother."[18] Susan confessed that he was probably right but knew her parents would forgive her because "these anecdotes and emblems are all so fascinating to me."[19]

It was not just the history but everything that fascinated Susan. Her description of London's fog is a ready example:

> Everything has been covered with the famous London fog, which at times becomes so heavy that even the rooms are misty with it in spite of keeping the windows closed. London fogs are different from any other kind, being a mixture of soft coal with the moisture laden air into a texture so heavy you feel it could almost be folded. Someone estimated that 72 tons of soot were suspended over London one evening; and you can well believe it when you see the hundreds of huge chimneys crowded with chimney pots all shapes and sizes like earthenware jars on a pantryshelf. Of course the ugly old city looks its best this way, especially at night. There is a certain massive majesty about it, and the mist is like the huge, wistful soul of its past risen out of a grave which modern London covers like a tombstone. The lights spread and blot through the moisture until they seem to have opened like great flowers.[20]

Susan also sent snapshots taken by Vassili showing her feeding the pigeons at St. James or the deer in a park or looking at a historical monument.[21]

They remained in London much longer than originally planned. Vassili suffered a serious attack of influenza, which left him too weak for activities of business or vacation. By December, however, he had regained his strength sufficiently and they moved on to Genoa, Italy. They spent much of December at Sante Margherita Ligure, a tiny village about an hour from Genoa. Susan loved the Mediterranean Sea, which she could view endlessly from their rooms, and wrote long, descriptive letters, painting in vivid colors all that she saw. At one point in her description she slipped into a rare political statement describing Benito Mussolini's followers in terms he perhaps would not have appreciated:

> In the street was a changing and picturesque throng, romantic looking muscular bodied soldiers in swaying olive green capes and felt hats with a gaily upturned feather, old women in black shawls with shoulders like the boles of trees, and shrewd unhappy faces, lovely girls unfortunately too smartly dressed, Franciscan monks with bare feet in sandals and knotted cords about their waists, and black-shirted Facisti big and little for it seems Mussolini has organized them in assorted sizes from two feet high upwards. These piccolo Facisti are filled with dignity and self-importance and look very cunning marching by in their tiny black shirts. Mussolini's scowl is stenciled in black on the side of every public building and his immense energy seems all pervading.[22]

Then it was on to Venice and finally to Paris. Susan's ecstasy seemed unlimited. She had drawn a mental picture of each place they visited from her earlier reading. She was delighted when the scenes were as she had imagined them and equally delighted when they were different.[23]

Many of Susan's letters contained snapshots showing her serenity and happiness, which she carefully emphasized in her remarks. Marm's letters had begun to ask some questions with an agenda of her own. Ria Clay seemed to imply that once the excitement had worn off, Susan would return to her senses and to the Clay home. Susan addressed her mother's concerns obliquely. In fact, she had begun to miss her home although not for the reasons implied by her mother. Though she had longed to escape the bonds of central Kentucky and her family, the roots went far deeper than she realized. She began to feel the first pangs of homesickness. She seemed to miss little things the most. She asked her mother to include in her letters news of the family pets and daily activities of family and servants. She shared her mental images of what the weather must be like back home as the seasons progressed. Kentucky writers have traditionally been drawn back to the land of their birth for inspiration. For Susan it was that and more.

Vassili and Susan had barely settled into a new apartment back in New York before she was planning a trip to Kentucky. Initially, Susan wrote as if she and Vassili would make the trip, but as the date of departure grew closer, Vassili used his business as an excuse to remain in New York. Consequently, Susan made the trip alone, arriving on April 7, 1928, for her first visit since the marriage eleven months before.[24] Susan was so excited to be home that even Vassili's absence did not dampen her spirits. The family talked into the early hours of the morning, asking questions so fast that answers went unheard. The first days were wasted in hurt feelings from words said without thought, questions asked, and answers given, too bluntly.[25] That was the nature of the Clays. Within a short time those difficulties passed, apologies were made, and more productive discussions were undertaken.

Fortunately, Susan saved her most important news until calm prevailed. Her delay is partially explained by the special nature of her news and perhaps because Susan feared the reaction. Ria Clay continued to harbor concerns about Susan's happiness. If Marm had not been convinced, Susan could only fear the worst from her father. Now Susan announced that she was going to have a baby. To her surprise, the family responded favorably. Even the uncles of Balgowan expressed their excitement. Susan did not specifically mention her father's reaction, but that in itself perhaps indicates that he softened a bit at the thought of being a grandfather. Susan basked in a warm glow of home and family, receiving the spiritual nourishment that, despite rebellion, disagreement, and frustration, she required and the family provided.[26]

Family members were not the only central Kentuckians anxious to see the recently married Susan. Arriving shortly behind her was the first wave of Lexington's young female brigade, eager for the latest "news" of the proper young lady who had run away, or so it was rumored, with a Polish Jew.[27] Elizabeth Simpson, the subject of Susan's poem "To Elizabeth, "arrived on my very heels" to ask a few prying questions.[28] Susan was not taken by surprise. She did not like the games of Bluegrass society, but she knew how they were played. The picture of naive excitement and enthusiasm expected of a new bride, she gave no satisfaction to her old friend's curiosity. There was no mock naiveté in her letter to Vassili. Fannie Redd was giving her a dinner party on Tuesday evening, and she planned "to make the natives stare in my pearl colored dress."[29]

Fannie Redd's dinner was given on April 10, and Elizabeth Simpson had a tea for her on April 12 at Avon Farm. It was actually more a reception than a tea, given the number of guests. It seemed all of Lexington wanted to observe, firsthand, the young woman who had defied the "mandarins" of the Clay family. Susan enjoyed the attention and the notoriety attached to one who ignored convention. She was particularly pleased when people who had known Vassili spoke highly of him. She wrote ecstatically when Frances Jewell McVey, the wife of the university president and queen bee of Lexington's social set, spoke of Vassili as both brilliant and attractive. McVey even invited her to lunch so they could talk of Vassili to their hearts' content.[30]

The social whirl was terribly exciting, but Susan soon tired of it. She apologized to Vassili for the "harum-scarum way" she had written. People had been so nice to her that they had upset her calculations. Not only had she failed to write regularly, she had hardly been out to walk in the yard, much less in the fields. Susan had come to Kentucky to see her parents and the land from which she gained her strength. She wrote, "I would like to finish out the two weeks, for Kentucky is so lovely and poignantly familiar with flickers curtsying and calling on the locust trees and robins scratching in the freshly plowed garden."[31]

Susan also recognized once again the pettiness of Kentucky society. Her letters to Vassili recalled the causes of the frustrations with her community that she first felt as a young woman. Vassili had asked her to try to sell some Russian icons he had purchased for resale. He was unaware of Kentucky society, and Susan in her desire to be involved in every aspect of Vassili's life, momentarily forgot. Her memory was jarred by Elizabeth Simpson. When the subject of selling icons was broached, her friend quickly warned Susan that people would think she needed money to get back to New York. Susan wrote Vassili, "When I am away from Lexington I forget in some measure the shallowness of people's interests and conversation, and their eternal personal criticism. But in the last few days I have heard enough to forcibly freshen my memory." Susan was both hurt and angered by such petty cruelties. "I love Kentucky so,—its rocks, and trees and fields, but people here disgust me beyond measure. My only desire is to stay here at home until I come back to you."[32] She was particularly annoyed by what she interpreted as the parochial response to a young Englishman, John Rothenstein, who was teaching in the university art department. She found him to be very pleasant, though people in Lexington criticized his "English voice and too fashionable knickers,—people here are such asses."[33]

Undoubtedly, Susan's response had much to do with memories of cruel remarks aimed at her and her family. She was the guest of honor at dinners, luncheons, and teas virtually every day of her visit and repeatedly mentioned how nice people were to her. As the trip grew longer, she stated that in one way all the attention was an annoyance because "I care so little for human beings (excepting you and a few others) and so much for the out of doors."[34]

Susan's life was, in these few months after their marriage, inextricably bound to Vassili's. Susan needed her family, but she needed Vassili more. Like her mother, she easily made the transition to adoring and trusting wife.[35] Vassili calmed her ever-sensitive reactions. He exhibited a calmness that encouraged the debate of ideas.[36] Susan never lost the tendency to become animated in debate, but during the years of their marriage she was not as shrill in argument as she had been. She found comfort in his presence and adored him for it.

Sawitzky was equally devoted to Susan. In January, while still in Europe, he had written to Mrs. Clay more in the tone of father than husband. "And as for Susan, please rest assured that I have acquired the habits of an English governess, telling her to put on this warm thing and that warm thing, to button up her coat, not to forget her gloves, etc. etc."[37] Susan basked in his protectiveness. When she traveled to Lexington in the spring, he wrote of his relief when he learned of her safe arrival and in another letter cautioned her to borrow a heavier coat if the weather turned bad. Susan returned his concern in full measure. When he complained about the cleaning woman's failure to appear, she threatened to come home immediately. Vassili quickly assured her that he had done some cleaning and all was well. After that, he was cautious in mentioning problems so that Susan would not feel that she was shirking her duties. He learned not to tell her that he missed her but relayed the hopes of their pet finches and even "Domie," the automobile, that she would return soon. A feather fallen from tail or wing became a gift to be enclosed with Vassili's letters.[38]

Susan left Lexington on April 24. Eager to be helpful to Vassili, she had learned of some paintings in Louisville, possibly the work of Gilbert Stuart, and, armed with his instructions, she hoped to do the preliminary evaluations. She also felt freer to seek buyers for the icons there. Concluding her business, she then took the train for New York for a reunion with her husband.

Susan was happy with her world. The sense of suffocation she felt in her father's home no longer impinged upon her love for its residents. The pettiness of Lexington's gentry frustrated her because it reminded her of the past, but it was less personal now and she knew she would not be confined by it. She wrote to Vassili that she was "feeling so amiable with them all for a change. I kissed all my interminable cousins." She could now accept the eccentricities of family and community because she was free of them. She was also returning to her husband. She had, as she had noted before their marriage, either found no weaknesses in him or made fetishes of them. Indeed, she gave him a control over her life she had refused to family and community. Sawitzky combined the best of her traditional and modern images. Her pregnancy was the capstone of it all. It fulfilled her duty as woman and wife and was the ultimate unity of their spirits. It assured her parents' acceptance of her marriage and justified her decision to take charge of her life.

๚

CHAPTER EIGHT

The Making of a Poet

I will listen to saints and prophets.
I will sit at the feet of wisdom
But I will reserve O God
The right to wonder.

—untitled, SCS Papers

RETURNING TO NEW YORK, Susan rejoined her husband and awaited the birth of the child they would adore. Then, two weeks later, she suffered a miscarriage. The loss of the child nearly destroyed her fragile nature. It did destroy the delicate balance between her traditional and modern selves. That loss drew her back to her past and, as contradictory as it may seem, away from it. The traditional Susan saw the loss as a personal failure. To lose the child was to fail as wife, woman, and mother. She felt guilt and shame. She turned more obediently to her husband, seeking his protective care, and, as if the miscarriage was a punishment, regretted and repented her rebellion against family and tradition. She sought solace in the practice of religion "enthusiastically" and "out of necessity." The other side of Susan recalled her anticipation at the thought of her child and the love that had grown as it had matured within her. That side could not accept the guilt her traditional side assumed was hers. That side reserved the right to wonder.

She began to ask questions, ones no southern lady was supposed to think, much less articulate. She pondered the spiritual and physical act of love that created the child and her mental and physical feelings in pregnancy, subjects no woman was supposed to write about. She probed the meaning of death, a topic too morbid for Bluegrass gentry ladies. She questioned the role of God in her pain, certainly not unique to her but generally considered too philosophical for a woman of her breeding and in conflict with the teachings of her church. In the process, she created poems of beautiful expression and haunting meaning that are valuable as poetry and as a record of woman's struggle between traditional training and the right to self-expression. In time, her poetry would evolve from the conflict between confinement and freedom in women to the restrictions felt by all humankind.

To describe a traditional Susan and a modern Susan is, however, somewhat misleading. Generally speaking, she continued in public to seek the stereotypical feminine pose.[1] Her study was the special place where she was comfortable asking the questions that plagued her. Even there, however, she sometimes felt guilt. Sometimes within the same poem traditional values and modern expression blended.[2]

Vassili took the responsibility for writing to Colonel and Mrs. Clay on May 6, 1928, explaining the loss of the child. He wrote cautiously on such a delicate subject. His letter was "the bearer of sad news: Our hopes to have a baby this coming fall will not be fulfilled." Susan had noticed "certain suspicious signs" on Saturday afternoon, May 5. They called their doctor, and on Sunday afternoon she was taken in an ambulance to a private hospital of highest reputation. At 6:00 P.M., the doctor performed "the necessary minor surgery." Vassili sought to assure Mrs. Clay that, despite their disappointment, there was no cause for concern. He then sought to explain the loss. His own traditional views, and perhaps those of the medical community, were apparent.

> What caused the unfortunate occurrence is difficult to know. I have cautioned Susan repeatedly to be very careful and I am sure she hasn't done anything for which she would have to blame herself. The doctor expresses the opinion that Susan, while normal and healthy, is more delicate than the majority of women and that for this reason she will have to be exceedingly careful during the first few months of a certain condition.[3]

Susan wrote a brief note to her mother two days later. She tried to reassure her mother that they would try again to have a child, but she shut off any further discussion of the miscarriage. At the end of the note she wrote, "As to the sorrow of it, it is deep, but it can't be helped and it does no good to speak of it."[4] As far as can be determined, she did not speak of it again to her mother or other members of the family. Marm was so fearful for Susan's health that she begged them not to try to have another child. Vassili and Susan declared it their decision, but apparently they shared her concern. They would have no children.

The surface calm belied the mental turmoil and anguish Susan experienced. She turned in every direction frantically seeking relief, understanding, and peace. Husband, family, and Christian Science provided support but were insufficient. So, slowly, she sought to work through this crisis, as she did all others, in her own mind and poetry.

Susan had not written poetry in the first year of her marriage. Instead, she had occupied herself with the chores of being Sawitzky's wife and writing long, descriptive prose poems about the things she saw in Europe. She had put the best of her two worlds together. The miscarriage tore them apart, and she needed her alternative again. From 1928 to 1933 she fashioned poems from her tortured thoughts.

The questions raised as a result of the miscarriage became the basis of her mature poetry, and the evolution indicates the struggle between tradition and the right of expression. The imagery of confinement remained a strong factor in her poetry, but she probed more universal themes in search of freedom. She still thought it existed in heavens and stars, but she also sought freedom through the power of her own mind and thought. Freedom would come with understanding of the forces, some human, some cosmic, that confined her. Susan wanted intellectual control of the formidable and unseen forces that seemed to want to destroy her. It was more than that, however. Susan Clay Sawitzky was no systematic student of philosophy; she was a survivor. She used concepts that helped her understand the issues faced by "everyman." Her poetry of that period is a statement of the grief process experienced by women and men who suffer significant loss. Consequently, the themes are sometimes inconsistent both with her actions and within the body of her poetry. More centrally to her, poetry provided the means to express thoughts her traditional upbringing did not allow her and to discover explanations of the events which would help her face the future.

Initially, she questioned her ability or desire to survive her unborn child.

> I hold the mirror of life
> Before the mirror of death,
> And look into a future
> Of endless and terrifying corridors.[5]

The statement, later entitled "Fear of Forever," appeared frequently in her journals between 1928 and 1933, the period of her most intense struggle. It appeared also in later times of crisis.

Thoughts spilled randomly from her pen in the ensuing months. Expressions of hopelessness indicated her fragile spirit.

> Each line of life is so essential
> The loosening of one small stitch
> Would cause the whole of Spirit to unravel.[6]

It was not merely her spirit that was unraveling, but the idyllic view of life and the world around her she had acquired in her youth. She had been taught that Clay women, aristocratic women, the women of literature, had an internal strength that rose to the surface in times of crisis. She was unable to tap that reservoir in herself. She penned a question—"What is the opening to spirit?"—and noted her "loneness" in her search for the answer.

> We feed upon each other
> And in this cannibal craving
> There is no nourishment.[7]

Anguish and confusion continued as the base of her writing, but in time new emotions began to appear. The first of these was anger.

> I am the log
> That holds the enraged flame
> By the blade of its wing.
> Turn upon me

Indignant One
Tear my flesh
With beak and claw.[8]

The poem "Petition to Jehovah I" significantly bridges the stage of self-pity and a desire to find the opening to spirit:

Jehovah,—not God thou,
But the upflying likeness of the brain,—
I know when thou has drained the purple dusk wine
From deep stained valleys,
For I too, have tasted these shadows
Bubbling with stars.

I know when I am in the way of thine anger
But I beg as drunkard to drunkard one boon:
Six days shalt thou labor to give me pain,
But the seventh—give death,
(And a faint, still knowledge of death,
Like a sleeper who feels sleep is sweet.)

O Jehovah, what rest like this?
To remember only—there was much to forget,—
And to taste the long Sabbath of unbeing.[9]

As Susan taunts Jehovah to end her pain, both the fear of forever and the anger are apparent. But reason is appearing alongside emotion. The God of Christian Science was not responsible for pain; she felt pain because she refused to see it as unreal. The subtlety was lost on Susan in 1928, but she was aware of the teachings of her faith and blamed Jehovah, "not God thou," but an Old Testament version, perhaps her father's God. The distinction indicates that her mind was contemplating more than her emotions. She realized that she was treading dangerous ground. To pose such questions about death and to taunt God, even as Jehovah, were both outside her faith and heretical for the southern lady. She noted her dilemma in its proper context—the struggle between traditional values and the need to know. In the poem "Gift" she summarized the dilemma appropriately:

> I feel the clutch of roots
> In dull grey mist of mud,
> But miles within me
> Lies the ooze of cloud,
> And in the night the sharp-edged, time crushed stars
> Sink to their height in me,
> Settling like sand across a floorless deep.[10]

"The clutch of roots"—tradition, community, heritage, family—could not contain the desire to know, and, as in the poetry of her youth, she looked to the heavens, clouds, and stars for relief.

The myth of the southern lady remained; she felt guilty for thinking some of the thoughts that raced through and out of her mind, but she could not contain them. In "Inference," she asked:

> And I—
> With groping and driven spirit
> Helpless as cloud,
> Should I not guess at currents fierce and holy
> Sweeping me on
> In ways both swift and still?[11]

It was a dilemma she faced throughout her life. She justified her right to think by crediting God with creating it. The Almighty

> . . . grants eternal charters of new freedom
> That man may go exploring at his will,—
> Grooving his own ellipses
> On tranquil planes of mind.[12]

Her planes of mind were not always tranquil, and her traditional side led to guilt even as she exercised the freedom to explore new ideas. In youth she had fought efforts to make her think like all the other girls, but she was never certain that her thoughts were acceptable. In one of her poems she defined death as a kind of sleep in which the sleeper was "contented—unthinking."[13] In another she said she was inclined to think too much.[14]

Susan Clay Sawitzky faced a dilemma experienced by many people. Would she find answers through the power of her own mind or through submission to the teachings of her church? Southern lady or no, Susan had never been comfortable with submission, yet she could not escape the sense of guilt for her failure to submit. Unlike her mother, Susan had grown up in Christian Science. She had attended Science readings, read the journal, and talked with the spiritual guides, called practitioners. Mrs. Clinkenbeard, a practitioner and friend, had helped when she eloped with Sawitzky. She knew Mary Baker Eddy's teachings about the power of mind over body. It is little wonder that she sought answers through thought. But she continued to struggle with the conflict between the power of the Deity and that of her own mind, between the spirit and the body. She scribbled notes in her journals throughout the 1930s lamenting on the one hand the "hard-headedness" that interfered with her religious faith and on the other her dependence on Christian Science.[15] She sought the advice of practitioners and copied passages from *Science and Health* in her journals.[16] Yet the conflict remained unresolved. She also wrote in her journal:

> Between the sweet spirit of my mind
>   And of my body
> I am strung like a star—
> Held as by two stretched threads
> Of irresistible longing.[17]

Finally she made a pact with God. The terms were definitely hers.

> I will listen to saints and prophets
> I will sit at the feet of wisdom
> But I will reserve O God
> The right to wonder.[18]

Susan's traditional values often crept into the study where she wrote, becoming pronounced at later times, but she thought and wrote more freely there. At least in her study she could find a sense of balance between the conflicting forces. She pondered her miscarriage in frank, feminist terms and, in moving yet analytical poems of mother's love, wondered about the source and the fate of her child. Her thoughts led her to ponder "life's two great mysteries—death and God" and provided a relative, and temporary, acceptance of her own fate.

The poems about her unborn child are among the most moving pieces she wrote. In "Unfinished One," she began traditionally by asking the question women are inclined to ask of themselves: What have I done to you in ignorance? Vassili had raised the issue in his letter to Mrs. Clay and implied that her physician had considered it as well.

> O little soul
> injured and incomplete,
> Stuck round with flesh:
> O half aroused and blinded one,
> What have I done to you in ignorance?
>
> We, looking past each other,
> Clutching each through each,
> Feeling no more the intervening walls;
> Seeking like bees
> The sacred, deep-set honey,
> The smothered glowing coal that sears and heals
> The crying of the flesh:
> We drew you to us in a swift vortex
> Our bodies fluid in love.
>
> What mist of drowsy sense
> Medusa thin and pale,
> What opalescent heaviness
> Is this my love about you
> In bubbled folds of dream?
>
> Could I have rounded you
> In earth, to cope with earth,
> To understand the baseness of the gift

And all its humble, helpless tenderness,
The blundering loss of you
Had hurt you less.[19]

The second stanza is not traditional nor was it acceptable subject matter for the "woman poet" of her time or for many years thereafter. In it
she boldly proclaims the physical act of conception. The stanza is a
defiant statement expressing the beauty and sanctity of the experience. She then returns to the pregnancy, her desire to nurture, and the
"blundering loss."

Perhaps her best poem about her child was "Lullaby." The title implies a traditional, motherly approach, but in 1928 the descriptions
were anything but traditional. She blends an appeal to the reader's
emotions with descriptions of pregnancy and miscarriage that are
frankly Darwinian.

That day a tide rose warm and measureless
Out of the deep,
And Life lay dim over a loosened world:
Then sinking, left me like a sea cast pool
Holding you close,—a lowly clump of being.

I soothed you in gentle brine,
I cupped a cradle softly in my flesh.
My blood went round you hushed
With pulsing step;
I fed you with the singing of my heart,
And no one heard but you.
It was a time when all the simple ones
Of water and earth became my child.
It was the mother of cleft, creeping things,—
Cold fingered, weedy lunged,
That strain the thick, archaic slime for breath,
And held my arms to little helpless bodies
Matted with hair.
I told the knotted rosary of time
For you were all in holy pantomime,

The children of all else
Though not yet child.

How safe I thought you in this wet foot print
Of ebbing sea.
And then the flood returned,—the buoyant flood—
And you were gone,
Broken, small fragment of eternal dream.
But like the sh-h-h of pebbles swinging softly,
I tend you still,
Holding beneath my heart its emptiness.[20]

After describing the child in the womb, cradled in mother's flesh, fed by the joy and elation of its mother, she turns to an analytical account, describing the development of the child in her womb in evolutionary terms. The two approaches blend in the final stanza. The first four lines are statements of physical occurrence; the last four speak of eternal dream and mother's mournful holding to the thought of one who was not to be.

"The Flight" contains the same blending of romantic moods with references to subjects considered inappropriate at the time. It also extended the concept of reality beyond the grave.

You came to me as quietly
As a star,
Spirit unhurt by birth;
Rapid as light,
Like light unmoving,—
Leaning out of your orbit
Bending a new path toward me;
Feeling the pull of me
Swung steep about your side.

I saw you against the earth brightness
Whiter than noon,
Making its mid-day dusk.
You seemed englobed against a pale sky,

Nucleated with darkness,
Holding an alien seed
Misted in light.

You gazed at me with wondering, stern eyes,
—Perceiving, not interpreting me,—
As bird flown downward from the North
Looks first at man,
Across the barriers of its innocence;—
Fearless, and Arctic mild;
And in this look
Of him I love,
(Before his blood and bone
Inherited)
I knew you for my child.

So you approached me
Flooding full my face.
And then some doubt,
Some vague unreadiness,
Loosened you from me:
And icy tracks of space
Feel still your burning feet
Unshod with flesh.[21]

Her child, however, is not confined to the grave. In addition to the
influence of Christian Science, Susan Clay had read Tennyson, Blake,
and Whitman, and she had studied classical philosophy at the University of Kentucky. In "The Flight" she introduces a neo-Platonic interpretation of life and death to her philosophy and poetry. Her child had
come as if from some distant star and then returned to "icy tracks of
space." Birth was the process of adding flesh to a preexisting soul. The
theme is also present in "Leonids," one of the last of her poems dealing directly with the loss of her child.

Tonight, where our roads cross in the sky
You will pass, wild band of little children;

Orphaned from what you were, and known no more:
Unclaimed by mortal name or destiny.
  What suddenly lights your beings as you run,
—Soundless as fireflies as they streak the grass,—
To see the earth go by?
I look at you and wonder which is my child
Whom, lest he answer,
I can never call.[22]

The same theme is apparent in poems written about her brother Charley. She had suppressed her grief at his loss in 1922 out of concern for her mother. Her child's death raised questions from the past, and her treatment of them revealed her maturing thought. In 1923, she had written one poem about his death. The title, "Bewilderment," probably said more about her state of mind than about the poem itself.

I bring you red roses, Beloved;
They will make a little blaze in the blue
    weather
That you may remember how warm youth
    was.
But there is only a long mound,
  A cruel, still mound that lies
As a misunderstanding between us.
Soon there will be a stone
To daze me with finality of set words
Like a priest.

Can you feel where I stroke the grass
Like a coverlet over you?
For I know where your lips are—
Under here;
(There is a little childlike, oval hole
Between them when you sleep;)
And your brows like the quick stroke
Of a bough on the white sky.
Farther down here are your hands;

The clasp of Death
Has bruised them with blue shadows.

O there is a child in my heart, expectant
    Wistful,
Because of her ceaseless faith in finding you
    here
In this strange place,—
I hurry faster and faster,
As impassioned to reach you, in spite of my
    frozen thoughts,
As an eager current of Spring water
Under the ice.[23]

By 1929, her style was more analytical. In a poem originally titled "Bewilderment—To Charley," then just "To Charley," she probes her own mind and the nature of death.

This star that rocks above me
In the wind
You are a dream detached
From him who dreams:
A moment of the past
Beheld by love.
Your light falls toward me still
From emptiness,
A lonely leaf
Drifting through time.

Where has he gone
Who shed you from him
Like a leaf,—
Like a feather from his wing?
On what rich darkness
Burns his wondering breast?
What years yet must I live
To see him now?[24]

There are significant problems with the poem from a literary perspective. Most important here is the apparent mixing of pronouns. She compares Charley to a star, seeing its light, or his impact, long after the source is gone. Then she speaks directly to him. "You are a dream detached" and "Who shed you from him," but between the two references she speaks of him in the third person, "Where has he gone?" Nevertheless, the poem asks the questions she wished to pose. Where was Charley? Did God "shed" Charley from him? When would she be reunited with him? Her answer to where Charley was has changed, too. He was no longer in a grave, separated from her by a mound of earth. He was a dream, a light, a leaf. He was free.

A second poem dealt more specifically with her personal loss. In "A Coat," the memory of her brother is recalled by an old coat that retained a faint aroma of him.

> In the sweet, dark hollows of these sleeves,
> In the folds of these sleeves,
> In this rubbed collar,—you cling.
> The faint odor of you is here,
> In its creases your young movements.
> Yours only, like the lines in your hands.
>
> How can the scent of you, the look of you be here
> And you not here?
> My brother, my friend, deeper than I knew.[25]

In "A Coat" death also brings greater understanding. It is death that makes her aware of their closeness and her dependence on him. Throughout their youth she had appeared to be the dominant child, but Charley had been a steadying force for Susan, for all the children in the family, and for the first time she realized his importance to her. The most important aspect of the poems about her brother in relation to the development of her thought is his release from the grave. He exists in another form. The question is when, not if, she will see him again. Susan expands upon that theme in the poems in which she sought to define death. It is in those poems that the greatest influence of Christian Science can be seen. Not only had Mary Baker Eddy, the

founder of Christian Science, placed great importance on the mind as
the means to finding peace, she had, perhaps because of her own illnesses, written a great deal about death. Although man had not reached
the spiritual maturity to escape mortality, she defined death as more of
a transition than an ending. Death was, she argued, an illusion; life
was real. She thus sought to weaken the power of death over her own
thought and that of her followers so the search for spiritual maturity
could proceed.[26]

Although Susan's thinking paralleled that of Eddy, she had to find
understanding in her own way. Her early poems are characterized by
confusion and hazy image.

> Sometimes I see the dead look in at me
> Holding me with their eyes,—
> And I move as though harnessed with heavy water
> As a boat moves
> Pressing its breast-bone against pulling,
>   V-shaped thongs.
>
> My body to them is as substanceless as theirs to me.
> We pass through each other
> As ripples pass through opposing ripples,
> Without touch, without altering form:
> So life and death enter each other unknowing,
> In a sorcery of cross wavelets
> Woven dizzily over the sunken, ultimate deep.
>
> I too, am dead if these are dead,
> And if I live, they live.
> Like moving water severed as it grows
> Incessantly from rim to rim,
> Pushed from the edge of nowhere
> To splinter on the rocky lips of death,—
> We meet and slip beyond, and leave no trace,
> Phantom dissolved in phantom . . .
> Fleet moment . . . Without end.[27]

Susan rarely dated her poems, but this appears to have been one of the earlier ones because her definition lacks the clarity of other poems. Being is "woven dizzily" over a "sunken, ultimate deep" as if it defied reason or comprehension. People leave no trace but dissolve as if a spot on time eternal.

   "The Alienated" also treats the impact of the dead on the living but in much clearer focus. It is the living who are alienated. Interestingly, it is freedom, that force so elusive to Susan Clay Sawitzky, from which humanity is alienated. The purity of death is the means of achieving that freedom.

> Through cold, dividing window panes of change
> You peer,
> O wistful dead,
> Pushing your eager faces close:
> Your soundless moth words flutter
> Against the invisible, chill wall.
>
> You come
> With soft, insistent clamor,
> Seeping like flakes of snow into our lives
> Through loose, unguarded cracks of consciousness.
> You are the white swirl of snow
> That stands within the threshold
> Of a closed door.
>
> There is freshness thrust into a world
> Of thoughts too thickly breathed,
> But I am unacclimated to freedom
> And stifled
> With the purity of death.[28]

Other brief poems continued the theme of death as gentleness, as peace, as the return of flesh to the soft bosom of earth. In two poems, she reversed the normal imagery of life and death. In "Spring Melting," life is frozen and death a warming.

Death will grow slowly gentle
Like a thawing field,
A great relaxed whiteness, worn and sunken,
Touched by the long, blue fingers of spring.

And we, contented,—unthinking,
Under this sleep,
Shall feel about us the cool, relenting tears
Wept softly from the white eye-lids of snow.[29]

In "Belief" she wrote,

I cannot lie in that great hush forever,
Hard as the clods of a Winter field
With ice swollen tight in its vein.
I know that death will relax at last
Like a rough hand fallen asleep.[30]

She was slowly robbing death of the fear and pain humanity felt in relation to it. Death freed human beings from the fear and pain of life, but it could not destroy. The soul, spirit, or mind,—the essence of humanity—returned to its source. She could, then, confront the grave without fear. In terms as vivid as those of James Joyce she consigned flesh to earth and freed the soul to wander the universe.

Earth, you smell of many bodies,
Amorous, . . . nostalgic smell!
An old, creased garment reeking the close trace
Of gone identity,
The clinging shadow of all parted things.

Hound-like I draw in the scent.
No direction points down the wind,
It is everywhere, the clue,—and leads nowhere:
This fragrance from you as I bend close;
Odor of rest,—odor of homogeneity,
Something eager, magnetic, that draws me down,
A drowsiness,—a will to creep in and sleep.

You, the rich residue of those gone down,
Of dark forms unforming,
Losing their intactness:
Bulbs softening, blackening, after many Springs
Have pulled out all their scented leaves and blooms;
Forest logs wrapped in their heavy years
Drenched once more to the ancient, unmoved sapling,
Riddled with shaking green leaf flame,
And peeping fungi
Squeezed out of sodden fissures;
Worn bits of fur and feathers
Like grey lint matted and flattened,
—Once from some high bough fallen hot and limp,
Claws curling, coagulating, open eyes,—
Seeking now under fall of leaves and rain.

Let me lie too, where the moist, healing ointment
May touch my lips and hands and all my willing flesh:
Let me feel rain, the sweet digestive juice,
Loosening me, building me into the vast body wall.
Let me go down into the lower places of sleep
In company of disintegrating things,
Part of all forest deeps holding the roots cold claws,
Part of bogs with their black, primordial brewing,
Part of all gardens feeling the crunch of spades,
Part of fields corded and coiled like heavy rope
By the winding plough in Spring, . . .
A shadow freed in darkness.[31]

The poem was titled "The Return." Many years later, it became a part of a much longer poem, "Equivocal Answer," which encompasses life and death. Though she broadened the poem to include all humanity instead of herself alone, the years destroyed none of the eerie familiarity with the reality of physical decay.

In the early 1930s she carried her definition of death to its ultimate form. She had always found solace in nature, observing the seasons and the regenerative process with the eye of an artist and poet. She began to read Hindu philosophy in 1931, not in depth or critically, but she took from it that which appealed to her and justified the direction her thought was already taking. In a long unpublished poem, "Corn," written around 1933, she compared humanity to the yearly rejuvenation of the plant world.

> I must be born perpetually, again and again,
> Knowing periods of death
> And periods of necessity
> For breaking death.[32]

In a second poem entitled "Re-creation" the concept of reincarnation was again evident. It was also linked to her belief that mind is the essence of humanity, earthly existence small and confining.

> I have gone in and down,
> I have made myself small;
> I have shut myself in inertia
> To stare upon one desire.
> I am hugeness drawn in,
> I am nebula contracted,
> I am veins run back
> To the well of a heart,—
> I am the craving focus of an eye
> That gathers the sun of the brain
> As into a funnel.
> I am prayer in the center of silence
> Blooming inward
> With petals bound.
> I am the withdrawn,
> The self-obsessed,
> I am the new nucleus
> Of wasted things:
> I am death.
> And when I unfold the freshness of my rays
> I am birth.[33]

Finally, she went back to one of her first random thoughts after the miscarriage. She had written in her journal,

> Forever, I am at the moment of birth and death
> For life is only a thread run through two holes.

By 1933, she had replaced the word *run* with *circling*. Life is a thread, circling perpetually between birth and death. She was so pleased with the concept that a collection of poems prepared for publication in the late 1930s was titled "The Circling Thread." Susan thus robbed death of its finality. It was merely one part of a circle, birth leading to death and out of death new life.

The consideration of death led naturally to consideration of the forces that directed the affairs of humankind. She had difficulty with the concept of a nurturing and omnipotent God in light of the pain she experienced. As a young woman she had accepted religion much as she described in "To Elizabeth," out of a vague sense that one was supposed to accept it. She had even used it as a means of attacking family and society. Like her mother, however, the conflict between myth and reality made the issue more intensely personal. In the depths of her grief, Susan felt abandoned by God. She proclaimed God a "lonely" or "unknowing" Deity, one who sits in "unreflecting black-ness" looking at a world "That is, and is not His." God seemed to provide no answers for her so she declared him "Absorbed and Mortal—deaf." If God is in control, let Him prove it by destroying her, she taunts in "Petition to Jehovah I," hoping Jehovah's power is real yet not completely believing it either.

Susan Clay Sawitzky, like most of those who asked such questions, never found answers that were completely satisfying. She vacillated between the thoughts of a skeptic and more traditional expressions of God. Emotionally, the teachings of Christian Science were impor-tant to her, and that added to her dilemma, reinforcing her sense of guilt over her thoughts and doubts. To Christian Scientists, pain is, at base, the result of a lack of an understanding of God. God is spiritual, and humanity must struggle to emphasize that portion of itself which is like God. Her pain and "loneness" were the results of her own shortcomings. Yet, as she searched her own motives and actions, she found no cause for personal blame and defiantly refused to accept it. Her pain was real to her; she had desperately wanted her child and had consciously done nothing to hurt it, and her love for her husband, the source of that child, was pure and spiritual.

The struggle revolved around the conflict between her view of herself and the requirements of the traditional woman. At times Susan Clay Sawitzky interpreted the loss of her child as punishment for her rebellion against family and community values; at other times she was almost angry at the thought that society blamed her. Consequently, her public life and her poetry were in contradiction; even individual poems contained antithetical strains of thought. In one poem she wrote,

> When man is unused of God
> He rusts in the scabbard of himself.[34]

In others, she questioned the omnipotence of a God whose perfect universe man had destroyed. In a poem begun in the 1930s but revised over the next thirty years, she conceded that man's "Rotten fruit / Of Knowledge" had led God to drive humanity from Eden, but in the aftermath, man and woman found their own alternatives in the love that binds them together. Humanity and God struggled constantly for control, but neither seemed to win. It was at best a compromise. Humanity is

> . . . the thrust of some most lonely God
> Into a humble earth;
> And through our lips, immune and without touch,
> He tastes this world,
> That is, and is not, His:
> Giving in mystic, equal sacrament
> Drink in return for bread.[35]

Susan Clay Sawitzky was most comfortable with the concept of the Deity as she saw it in her husband. She wrote in her journal that Vassili was her expression of God.[36] In an untitled poem she wrote,

We are only windows [openings] to Infinity;
You look through me at God,
And I through you.[37]

Her definition for God is less important than her search for it. She was unsatisfied with the answers provided her. Southern women were taught to study religion as the keepers of moral tradition, not as theology, but she did not accept completely the traditional role or its answers. As Anne Firor Scott notes in *The Southern Lady*, southern women, unable to express themselves openly, often sought acceptable alternatives to the confinement of cultural expectations. Susan Clay Sawitzky's poetry was that alternative.

More important, in studying seven southern writers, Anne Goodwyn Jones explains the importance of women having a voice. To have a voice politically is to have some power over human affairs and directions, but for a writer to have a voice is to have control over oneself.[38] Susan struggled throughout her life for some measure of control. In the early 1930s her poetic voice may well have been her means of survival.

꒦

CHAPTER NINE

The Comfort of Familiar Things

Forced from Eden:
Deprived of happy singleness of being
By knowledge unsound.
            —"The Shifting Void," SCS Papers

IN HIS LONG LETTER TO Colonel Clay on May 14, 1927, William Sawitzky
had explained his failure to ask for Susan's hand as concern for her
well-being. He described her as a poet and an artist and then, because
the colonel was a soldier, he defined the special qualities of the creative mind.

> I think that poets and artists are the milestones on the road of human
> culture. They are in their emotions, ever so much deeper and more
> sensitive than other people, they suffer immeasurably from the ugliness
> and brutality of life, they are so easily misunderstood and more easily
> hurt. In other words, they have to pay a heavy price for their divine gift,
> which is to express what so many of us feel but are unable to say.[1]

Given the reasons for the letter, one might be inclined to think
Sawitzky's comments somewhat self-serving, but in the aftermath of
the miscarriage his actions indicate that he spoke with conviction.[2]
William Sawitzky proved to be as protective a husband as Colonel
Charles Clay was a protective father. One suspects that he wanted to
shield his wife from "the ugliness and brutality of life" for more traditional reasons than her "artistic" mentality, but he was no less concerned. He knew it would take time and understanding to help Susan

cope with the loss of their child. In 1928, he served as the strong shoulder upon which his wife could lean.

Susan wanted and needed that support, but Sawitzky's tendency to patronize also bothered her. Her frustration led to a poem that might be considered a major contribution to the women's movement. The major concern of the women's movement has been the removal of the restrictions upon women, but a secondary argument is that the freeing of women would also free men from the masculine role. William Sawitzky was playing that role. He sought to meet his wife's needs but did not realize her need to see that he shared her grief. She remembered her father's manly composure at the time of Charley's death, and she knew there was more inside her husband. She wrote "Petition to Jehovah II."

> Bring me a storm, O God of Thunder!
> That I may see into the being of one I love.
> Break thou him
> With a leaping and golden bolt of anger,
> As the night breaks into a geode of jagged crystals
> When thy flying hammer cracks its stillness.
> I can find no flaw in the placid surface of his calm,
> And would see him for one moment
> Sublimely shattered before me.[3]

There are two comparisons within the poem that speak to the strong male image and her realization that beneath the silent, steady, "placid surface of his calm" lay the beauty of sensitivity. Vassili was the night—cool, detached, his thoughts obscured in blackness. Yet stars penetrate the darkness as small hints of the reality behind the facade. Her poetry is replete with images of stars as freedom and understanding. More graphically, she compared Vassili, man, to a geode, a rock hurled from heaven and seared by its entry into earth's atmosphere. From all outward appearances, a geode is a dull, metallic gray or brown rock, but if broken open, its "jagged crystals" are stunningly beautiful. In her poem it takes the storm of a God of Thunder, a bolt of anger, or a flying hammer to break the hard exterior and release the beauty within. She wants him "sublimely shattered" for a moment. Vassili, man, has the potential for sensitivity, tenderness, and beauty if only he will express it. She would later list "Petition to Jehovah II" as one of her "love poems."[4]

Susan's frustration with her husband was short-lived. That part of her which had dreamed of a protective knight not only succumbed to his care but depended on it. The human being who grieved also needed his support. The private Susan could write such lines, but the public Susan found comfort in her husband's concern for her. At that moment she could not or chose not to distinguish between traditional male protectiveness and human sensitivity.

Susan acquiesced to other "traditional" values in her grief. From 1928 to 1935, the public Susan retreated from her early pose as a "modern" woman and began to apologize to her family for the shortcomings of her youth. Vassili first noticed a longing for quiet, peaceful surroundings. They took long rides in the country, stopping in small towns and out-of-the-way places. She sat in fields and beside millponds reflecting on the serenity around her. The New England countryside was not enough, however. Susan wrote to her parents, "The other day while driving in the country I saw a young colt running and snorting in his lot, kicking the damp grass with his little hooves, and homesickness swept over me unbearably."[5] Vassili encouraged Susan to visit Kentucky shortly after the miscarriage, and he continued to arrange yearly visits of at least three to four weeks through 1933. Business trips into the South allowed him to take Susan to Lexington and then pick her up after the completion of his work in New Orleans, Mobile, or Columbia, South Carolina.[6]

The couple traveled slowly on such trips. Susan's letters and postcards to her parents noted that their old car, which they had nicknamed Domie, needed frequent rest stops. Those stops just happened, of course, to coincide with Susan's needs. Domie rested on the beaches, in quiet mountain retreats, or at a secluded inland lake. On such stops Vassili and Susan enjoyed the scenery peculiar to the spot or shared time with their favorites among nature's creatures—the birds and smaller animals. After a business trip in the spring of 1929, Vassili remained in Lexington for a visit of several months. He rented an apartment on South Broadway near the center of Lexington, and they visited frequently with Susan's parents and her uncles, who now lived in the Lafayette Hotel.[7] Susan saw her old friends, and she walked with Vassili in the fields and wooded areas she loved. Even the colonel noted the deep love Vassili and Susan had for each other. Vassili's protective role and Susan's adoration and respect for him conformed to Charles and Ria Clay's concept of what marriage was supposed to be. They noted, in particular, the serenity of Susan's personality and credited the change to Vassili's influence. A year later, the colonel wrote to Vassili thanking him for sending Susan on another visit. In that letter, he also let Vassili know, gentleman to gentleman, that he knew the source of Susan's growing peace and contentment.[8] Charles Clay thus admitted in his way that he had spoken too quickly three years earlier.

Vassili also planned frequent vacations to scenic spots. Susan's Uncle Tom and Uncle George suggested they vacation at a secluded retreat near Ganonoque, Ontario, called the Cragmere Inn.[9] Susan enjoyed it immensely, so once each year, in fall or spring, they spent a month there.[10] The area around Ganonoque was called the "land of a thousand lakes," and the inn occupied a bluff overlooking two large lakes filled with small islands. It was the natural surroundings that appealed to Susan and Vassili. They canoed in the safer inlets, stopping to examine flowers, various types of moss, and rock formations along the banks. They did not venture into the lakes because neither could swim, but they walked the trails leading to points where they could look out over beautiful expanses of blue water. Susan wrote long, rambling letters describing in vivid detail all that she saw and implying the healing effect she was experiencing.

Vassili also arranged a second trip to Europe for the summer of 1930. Susan had enjoyed the first trip so much one can only suspect that Vassili thought it might help her forget their loss. This trip took them into northern Europe. They stopped in Berlin, and Susan's love of history surfaced again. Her letters home did not contain the youthful enthusiasm seen in the letters of her first trip to Europe, but they did indicate that her attention was diverted at least sporadically from the deeper thoughts and questions that occupied her mind.[11] They also visited Vassili's home in Riga, and Susan was delighted to see the places he had known as a child. She met his sisters, Jane and Olga, who lived in Riga, and was delighted by their praise of Vassili and their acceptance of her. By the end of the trip, she was again feeling the pangs of homesickness, and Vassili arranged a trip to Kentucky less than a month after their return from Europe.

Susan's homesickness and the subjects of her letters reflect a greater need for family and the surroundings of her youth. She wrote more frequently to her parents and again asked her mother to write about everyday occurrences at home. How were the family pets? Had the season changed? Were the leaves as vibrant as they had been in earlier years when she had looked from the window of her room? She even referred to specific trees and bushes seen from parlor or dining room. She asked her mother to mention where she was sitting when she wrote and to describe the contents of the room. Her interest was not in changes. No new trees had been added to the Clay lawn, and the same old heirlooms and furnishings occupied virtually the same places in the Clay home as when Susan lived there. Susan craved the security of familiar things.

She also expressed greater concern about her parents' well-being. Colonel Clay was over seventy years old by 1928. A bout with sciatica forced him to limit his activities and worried Susan to the point of hysteria.[12] She gently chastised her family for not telling her when things were wrong at home. She also complained that when they failed to write she began to expect the worse. In sentences Ria Clay could have written thirty years earlier, Susan pleaded, "Please do not keep it from me if there is [something wrong], for long drawn out suspense and apprehension is much worse and creates a worse condition of thought than a single statement of fact. Please someone write and tell me how everyone is . . . to dispel my uneasiness."[13] Susan worried about the uneasiness of her parents too. She feared her poems about death would distress them so she cautioned Metzie to show them "only a select group of poems." "I wouldn't run any risk of worrying Papa and Marm for the world."[14]

A large part of Susan's worry resulted from the state of the Clay farm. Colonel Clay and his farmhands had grown old together, and they could not care for the farm as in an earlier day. Actually, Charles Clay had begun to curtail his farming operation shortly after returning from World War I, but Susan, occupied with her own problems, had not noticed. Now she noticed and decided to take charge. Bob, graduated from West Point and stationed in Oklahoma, could be of no help to his father. Metzie was at home, but Susan never entertained any expectations that she could provide meaningful help. She revealed her adherence to the value system she had sought to reject when she suggested in a letter to Vassili that Metzie, as a woman, could not be expected to handle financial matters.[15]

Susan decided that her parents should sell their farm and move into Lexington. Once she had an idea, everything was supposed to move quickly to its realization so she took the absence of any response to mean the colonel agreed. She and her mother searched Lexington for a suitable apartment. Plans were made to store household goods, and she and Metzie began to rummage through old boxes and trunks stored in forgotten nooks and crannies of the house. Her letters to Vassili indicate her satisfaction that the decision had been made and her excitement over the discoveries in the family attic. She wrote, for example, that they had found numerous letters, Revolutionary War land grants, and other documents and papers with "signatures of Jefferson, Madison, Monroe, Clay and of more local interest, Samuel McDowell, Wilson Cary Nicholas, etc. We had an exciting time opening these brittle brown-spotted pages, so long unhandled that they almost peeled apart. We swore Father and Mother to secrecy, for if Uncle George knows of their existence he is more than apt to sell them."[16]

All the work and preparation was to no avail. Susan returned to New York, and as the weeks and months passed, she finally realized her parents had no intention of moving. She chastised them gently in her letters, continued to worry about them, and frequently gave advice, although it was never requested and rarely followed.

Susan's new concern did not mean an end to family fussing. Her yearly trips to Lexington were still marred by the "electric nervousness" that characterized the Clays. On one occasion her visit "seemed to overstimulate the family at first, and there was the inevitable superfluous discussion and argument."[17] Susan claimed, correctly, "It is such a pity as we are all devoted to each other."[18] Letters after her return to New York, however, were inevitably filled with apologies and protestations of love. "In spite of all our electric nerves, and that I seem to make my family and myself more nervous by blundering remarks, I did

have a lovely happy visit to you all. You are the sweetest, kindest parents and sister in the world, and I love you with all my heart. No place
on earth seems sweeter than home."[19]

Susan not only spoke of home as sweet and her parents as kind, but
increasingly after 1928 she expressed her greater need for home and
family and accepted personal responsibility for past disagreements.
She frequently apologized for her stubbornness and rebelliousness in
the period before her marriage. The most poignant but certainly not
the only such statement was made in a letter to her father in June 1935:
"Looking back over my very blameworthy life I can find no fault with
you or Marm, and wonder how you were able to see through my ill
temper, complexes and exhibitions of dissatisfied ego, to the being that
I really was, loving you devotedly always, and often breaking my heart
over the stupid role in which I had cast myself."[20] She went on to say
that there had never been any real unhappiness in her life but a sort of
haziness that had cleared away. The "cloudy period" before her marriage, she now claimed, had been of her own making and not that of
her parents.

The same apology and a growing feeling of love for her past are
evident in a series of letters Susan wrote to her uncles. Tom and George
Clay were older now and in poor health. When their sister Teetee died
in 1924, they sold Balgowan and moved to the Lafayette Hotel in Lexington. Susan used her descriptive abilities to recall for her uncles
earlier and perhaps happier days. They enjoyed her reminiscences and
her beautiful descriptions of Balgowan, the seasons, and the events of
their lives, now so far in the past. Susan wrote to cheer the two men in
their old age, but the letters leave little doubt that she was feeling the
warm glow of nostalgia as well. She wrote, for example, to her Uncle
Tom on January 31, 1935: "I with my nervous turbulent nature, being
often at odds with the world, used to feel a sort of healing in the very
earth of Balgowan. I walked alone in the fields sometimes, in a sort of
ecstasy, as though with the secrets of things unfolding around me."[21]
Stories about her immediate family also recalled the pleasant times.

Charley and I used to cake walk sometimes at night, going around and
around inside the circle of grown people, Papa or Marm singing and pat-
ting the tune for us. Whenever we passed Grandma's chair we made a

On one of her trips home, Susan posed with her father, mother, and a family pet in the yard beside their home.

deep bow. I was, I am afraid, a little touchy about the performance, being exceedingly timid and sensitive to bursts of grown up laughter, but Charley, who would almost invariably loose [*sic*] his balance and topple over when he made his bow, would get up and continue his dance in my wake as though nothing had happened, holding out his little apron, throwing himself back, and picking up his clumsy little feet as best he could.[22]

She recalled Charley often in those letters. He remained much on her mind. Tied by memory to her past, Susan was mending the fences that surrounded those memories. She wrote to Uncle George Clay in 1933: "I think as one grows older he learns the meaning of kinship, and sees himself against his own background . . . youth wants to rebel and break away, but maturity finds comfort and peace in traditional and familiar things."[23]

Certainly by writing so warmly of the past Susan was attempting to
bring happiness to her parents and her uncles in their old age, but it is
also obvious that tradition no longer "mummified" her as it had in
1921. She now welcomed the support of the traditional family, the Clays
of Kentucky, and recognized the importance of the past in her own
life.[24] She wrote in an untitled and unpublished fragment:

> What can I do
> Who have become
> So much the past
> I who am now
> So gathered
> Behind myself
> Pent up behind the present,—amassed.[25]

Some of her poems also caught the mood of childhood experiences
on Bluegrass farms. "Winter Dusk" is the most purely nature-oriented
of her poems. Written in the early 1930s, the poem is autobiographical,
and it is nostalgic.

> The young colts stamp and shift,
> And small hooves thud
> Against confining wall-boards,
> The darkness smells of straw
> And of fresh manure steaming on the straw-bedded floor.
> Soft noses and lips, loosely moving,
> Sprinkled with delicately perceiving hairs,
> Feel for hidden oats pushed into trough cracks,
> And jerk upward startled
> At a damp release of breath.
>
> Now stooping through a fence
> I feel the jolt
> Of warped, black cypress boards between my knees;
> And my gloves catch the roughness
> Of rain bitten grooves.

The cold is imperceptibly still:
It holds its breath and does not stir,
But ground water swells and hardens
In clods beneath my feet.

I lift my face to feel the hurrying feet of snow.
They touch my cheek timidly
Like small, cold paws:
A great host of them
Come down from the deep Arctic of the skies,
Down from the jammed, cloudy ice floes,—
Little furry, strange things
Padding through the dusk.

And stars that opened quaking petals
At the thin edges of cloud drifts,
Are deeply buried now
Under light-lying heaps of crystal.

No moon or stars
Make this faint illumination
Remote as candle light
Over worn, hoof beaten fields.
Now shallow, circled areas grow bright
Next widths of darkness,
Marking each dent and swelling
Of the ground.

An old road lies here sunken in the field
Worn in by toil of wheels,—
Wheels bound with a hard-shrunken rind of iron,
That dented the damp earth over and over
Under root-toughened grass,
Until the aching mire came through.
They sought as sensitively as a new formed gully
Through untracked stems

To find the essential way from gate to gate;
And now this road is their experience
So deep and certain
That it guides the wheels.

I walk beside it on the brittle sod
Avoiding hard cords of mud
Squeezed up at the wheels' edge,
And dull-eyed puddles
That have closed white lids in sleep.

The dragging gate
Holds stiffly in the road
And grates like rust
In its half circle groove.
I lift it against my hip
And hook its limp-linked chain
Over a nail.

Now up a hill and a thin path
To where the light of windows reaches out
Through crossing boughs.
I look through endless myriads that fall
With slow, weightless sinking.
Did I say furry paws?
It may be all the cloud-cocoons of heaven
Have opened at this hour
And these are wings of ice that thicken the dark.
They seek the grass like tired moths
And cling unsteadily to dried weed stalks,
It may be that the yellow light attracts them:
I hear them pelting softly on the pane.

No one has marred the pure snow on the steps
But I drop foot-prints
Like a fall of leaves across them.
I stamp the fine crust off my boots

And enter in a room of rosy fire-light
Where windows against dusk
Are blue as eyes set in a ruddy face,
And a table covered white beneath a lamp
Has shadows blue across pale gold
Like snow.[26]

Susan Clay Sawitzky walked the farm roads of her youth, felt the rough cypress boards between her knees as she crossed fences, and smelled the special smells of a horse barn on cold winter mornings. Such senses could not be triggered in New York. The poet sought her roots in this poem and carries her readers back with her to special memories of a rural past.

The most striking change in attitude was that which Susan expressed toward her father. She had always loved, indeed, revered him. Yet there was a wall between them. In later life, she said in a letter to her sister that her father and her brother Bob, whom Elizabeth was visiting at the time, were of a military mind—"matter of fact, dictatorial, and physically active"; she, Elizabeth, and Charley had the sensitivity of the intellectual.[27] Nonetheless, she longed to bridge the gap between them. In the early 1930s she began to address her correspondence to both parents again, and it was conciliatory. The relationship with her father also occupied that quiet place reserved for the most troubling questions, her study. A poem entitled "Child and Father," much like "Petition to Jehovah II," seems at first glance to be angry, harsh:

Storm calls to ocean:
"You know me to be black and miserable,
I see it in your grey glance,
I will strike you, I am filled with rage,
I will cry out, jolt you to anger,
I will stripe your face with sorrow:
But I am you,—I will return."

Fatherhood, however, is scatheless,
Though its forehead wrinkles, it knows no deeper hurt,
It has so many times been storm cloud.[28]

Yet the last line of the first stanza and the second stanza explain a different side of the relationship. Child is a product of father as storm cloud is of ocean. Father, like ocean, is too old, too calm, too experienced to let youthful rebellion scathe him. Father was once child, ocean has been storm cloud. Each is patient and uneffacing in its wisdom. The rebellious offspring will in time return.

The theme of the prodigal child presented itself in "Child and Father," but it was more direct in a poem Susan Clay Sawitzky wrote in late 1932 which she titled "Prodigal."

> Man must forsake his source,
> In mystic, periodic wrath,
> Like the great hurl of earth
> Away from light,
> Recanting painful vows of blessedness.
> And so through wastes of bones and age-blind stars
> Flung down by floods of time,
> He wanders sadly, with old thoughts of bliss
> Charring his heart,
> Until he stands on utmost rim of balance
> And a far-faint kiss
> Is spring against his face.
>
> Then sick for parent love he turns,
> And hastens backward
> Toward the moveless sun
> Whose light alone pursues and overtakes;
> The patient father whose effacing brightness
> Has never known recession or return,
> Yet grants eternal charters of new freedom
> That man may go exploring at his will,—
> Grooving his own ellipses
> On tranquil planes of mind.[29]

Susan Clay was declaring herself the prodigal. She had forsaken her source and felt a great deal of wrath. The poem announces her return. Susan wrote to her parents that the poem had a double meaning. She was expressing her concept of the relationship of God and man, but the poem also referred to parent and child. "When I wrote it I thought of you both and me."[30]

Susan's relationship with her father was always marred, however, by the noble, patriarchal figure painted by her mother in her youth and lived by her father after his return from military service. He, too, was the geode of "Petition to Jehovah II." After his death she wrote: "Remembrance of him is dear and deep,—yet I always stood aside, unable to approach him closely. . . . Yet somehow yearning to be near him. I have gone back there many times . . . and tried at this place and that time to tell him, but my voice never carried. It was as though a high wind blew between us. He smiled at times seeing my gestures and my lips moving, yet he never heard what I said."[31] Such was the price of images—to father as well as daughter. A cult of true manhood exacted its costs as well.

The poem "Prodigal" had additional meaning. It was confessional. Her emotions required that she make peace with her past. It was the traditional Susan Clay Sawitzky who wrote sometime between 1928 and 1932 a poem she titled "The Cowed."

> There is that desire in me
> Of the small, creeping ones
> Who would feel about them comforting pressure and stillness
> Of interstice and low set ceiling of stone.
> There is too great and lonely space to move in:
> I need a crack and night,
> With hard and certain ponderousness about me.[32]

In the early 1920s, she had written that walls made "the sensitive places of spirit / Ache like the angles of a close-confined body."[33] Ten years later, tradition, family, community, southern gentility, and values provided "comforting pressure." Susan Clay Sawitzky was never really "cowed," as the title of the poem might suggest, but she had completed another circle. She might "reserve the right to wonder" or "go exploring at [her] will," but the pain of experience harkened her back to the comfort and peace of "traditional and familiar things."

CHAPTER TEN

❦

Depression

Poverty you are kind:
You hasten through the dreary work of time.
You are the burning of leaves
That will not perish of themselves
Though dead
                                    —"Poverty," SCS Papers

THE GREAT DEPRESSION, the hardships of which restored the faith of many Americans in traditional values, enhanced Susan Clay Sawitzky's inclination to embrace her past. William Sawitzky had been a self-employed art dealer since before he married Susan. He combined a knowledge of art and the aristocratic manner required for success in that profession. Wealthy patrons employed his services not only as an agent but as an authority with an excellent record of verifying the authenticity of expensive art pieces.

In the 1920s Sawitzky had made a very comfortable living with an income often in excess of ten thousand dollars per year. When Mrs. Clay became too direct in her concern for Susan's well-being in 1929, Sawitzky wrote that two transactions between October 1 and December 31, 1928, had brought him seven thousand dollars. He continued to earn well above the average national income until 1931. His business was, however, highly competitive, and his attempts to comfort Susan after the miscarriage meant he spent less time at it. His reduced effort in the midst of the Depression quickly affected his income.

Sawitzky tried to combine business with his obligations to his wife. In 1929 and 1930 he left Susan in Lexington during his business trips to

New Orleans and Mobile, Alabama. The trip to Europe in 1930 was also a mixture of business and vacation. By 1930, however, his career began to take a more scholarly direction. The Depression left him few options because the number of clients dwindled, but the process began as a conscious decision, not one of necessity. Initially, Sawitzky saw the more academic tasks of evaluation as a means to involve Susan in productive activity. Shortly after they met, he had encouraged her to pursue her interest in poetry rather than art. At the time, perhaps, he believed more opportunity existed for a woman as a poet. After the miscarriage, her interest in art gave him a good pretext to keep her with him as he worked so as to keep her mind off the loss of their child. Moreover, her artistic ability and her literary skills proved increasingly useful to him. By 1930, Susan had begun to copy his notes in her fine hand, and she developed a filing system so that those notes could be recovered easily. He also increasingly depended on her to help him with English, particularly the American variety.

Sawitzky encouraged her to be his "helpmate" and assistant. He took her with him to evaluate paintings, and he taught her to recognize the way particular artists used a brush, the subtleties of color, and other techniques by which artists could be identified. Increasingly, he asked for her opinions. She proudly wrote to her family that the ideas and opinions of one complemented those of the other. She was obviously delighted to feel useful.[1]

In May 1932, an article entitled "Another Miniature by Gilbert Stuart" appeared in *Antiques* under the authorship of Susan Clay Sawitzky.[2] Susan noted in a letter to her sister that she had been involved in "some art criticism and analysis with Vassili and on my own account under his guidance."[3] Since Sawitzky was the authority on Stuart—he had edited a four-volume study of Gilbert Stuart by Lawrence Park between the time he met Susan and their marriage— there seems little doubt that he was consciously seeking to involve his wife in his efforts. Susan, proud of her article and of her role as her husband's helpmate, lost no opportunity to praise to her parents his "genius" and his pride in her efforts. Vassili's work became their work; their time and energy were spent in research and writing in his field, art history. Though she continued to write poetry, his work became the more important.

Although Sawitzky's work was enhanced by Susan's efforts, her involvement meant that she stopped seeking to publish her poems. She wanted to publish but would not submit her work. The very personal nature of her poetry explains some of the reluctance, but the issue went deeper. Each time she published throughout her life, some person or group had exerted pressure, generally in the form of persistent encouragement, to do so. In 1921, it was Sawitzky who suggested that she submit poems to *Town and Country Magazine*. In 1924, Granville Terrell urged her to seek a publisher. The tone of his note seems to indicate a knowledge of her reluctance. Her poetry, he wrote, made him

> feel like urging you to a broader field of poetic realm . . . I know it is hard to muster courage to place your efforts in critic's hands but talent will always assert itself and overcome any barrier that discouragement may present.
>
> I hope ere long to see some of [*sic*] beautiful gems flashed before the public eye in one of the real journals of today where the lovers of talent are eager to read such verses as you write.[4]

In the period after 1928, the hesitancy implicit in Terrell's letter was apparent again. No one encouraged her; she was, at best, working in isolation, at worst, struggling against subtle discouragement. She frequently sent her poems to Mrs. Clinkenbeard and to her sister, Elizabeth, for their thoughts. Metzie became Susan's most frequent reader from 1928 to 1932. Susan appreciated her sister's "great creative ability" and her "clear analytical sense." She wrote to her parents, "She [Metzie] and I are in such spiritual and mental accord that she can explain exactly my meaning and intentions as well, if not better than I could." Metzie could "deflect me from what is wrong or trite and bring out what is good in them [poems]."[5]

Elizabeth may have understood Susan's poems, and she might criticize them discreetly, but in the 1930s she did not like the direction of Susan's thought. Dark thoughts of pain and death disturbed her religious sensibilities so she eventually refused to read Susan's work. Her sister's alienation seems to have had an effect on Susan. In early 1933, she wrote to the Clays that she had been writing some very cheerful poems "lately" and would send them for the family to read.[6] Yet she could not bring herself to submit them for publication. She wrote to Elizabeth, who eventually relented and resumed reading her sister's poems: "I am always completely at sea as to what to do with my work, but it seems to me that it would be wiser not to try to publish anything for the present. I am trying to reshape all of my poems a little; they have awkward hitches, and have never satisfied me."[7] There is no indication that Elizabeth tried to convince her otherwise.

Susan also wrote in 1935 that she intended to work out the question of where to seek publication through Christian Science. She requested help from one practitioner in overcoming "timidity" and lack of self-confidence in regard to her poetry.[8] An undated note from approximately that time asked another Science practitioner, "Help us find the right place and reception for poems today and know honesty and protection as they are not copyrighted."[9] So much of her is apparent in the note. She wanted to publish yet was hesitant to attempt it. She leaned on faith in Christian Science yet instructed the practitioner on the practical matter of copyright. Susan Clay Sawitzky shared a hesitancy experienced by many women writers.[10]

In the early 1930s, Susan forsook her dream of publishing her poetry, satisfied herself in her husband's work, and did what many capable Clay women had done before her—supported the career of the man of the family. Another change reflected her efforts, conscious or otherwise, to renew her past. By late 1932, she began to express frustration with life in New York and the desire to move to the suburbs of the city. Her comments stand in stark contradiction to those she had written as a "small town poetess" about the freedom of New York and the intellectual stimulation of its people. She now wrote to her sister, "I have nothing to say to these 'smart, wise-cracking' New Yorkers, and have to lapse into a silence embarrassing to me and boring to them. Outside of Vassili I have not a single friend or companion." She went on to insist that because she had Vassili she needed no one else, but obviously her ecstasy over life in the city had waned since 1921.[11] Later, Susan wrote even more pointedly in a letter to her mother:

> Unless you had gone through an experience for nearly five years of New York City life, you could not realize what it means to us to be out of it. For the first time we find peace, clarity of mind and relaxation. Of course

I know that New York affects us in a way that is incomprehensible to
city enthusiasts. To them its ceaseless hurry is stimulating, but to me it
has never seemed anything but a treadmill of resultless effort. So many
people love the atmosphere of night clubs, restaurants, theaters, etc.,
which has never meant anything to us at all. Most people whom I know
do not think at all—they repeat, and their conversation is an adolescent
effort to scandalize and appear "clever." Sometimes I think a human
being reaches, in seclusion, a very advanced sort of sophistication which
could be called enlightened innocence. It makes one look at life with
level eyes, and gives an ability to evaluate which makes one impatient
with the pretense which the average person calls "life." We have very
few friends as most people bore us and we bore them, approaching the
world in a different way with different interests.[12]

She wrote as if completely oblivious to earlier statements referring
contemptuously to small towns and dull people or to her rather "clever"
articles in the *Louisville Herald*.

It seems doubtful that "seclusion" had led to any "advanced sort of
sophistication." Rather, her attitude fits a pattern of changes in her
life. The miscarriage confronted Susan with the pain of the real world.
She wanted less of that world than she had thought. The peace and
security of the cocoon in which she had grown up, the comfort of
traditional and familiar things, the protection and quietude grew more
appealing. William Sawitzky, aware of his dwindling savings, was willing to perpetuate that existence for her by urging a move from the city
to more peaceful, and cheaper, lodgings in the suburbs.

In September 1932, Susan and Vassili rented rooms in the home of a
southern-born woman, a Mrs. Caskey, in White Plains, New York. It
was the first of a series of moves from one set of rooms to another until
1935, when they rented a small house. For Susan it provided the opportunity to experience again the rural surroundings she had known in
her youth. Vassili and Susan worked in the mornings, but after lunch
they often drove or walked to fields or millponds where they observed
birds and insects. Susan's thick notebooks, describing what she had
seen, also revealed the contentment such outings brought.

Vassili enjoyed the more leisurely pace as well. They could be closer
to the fields and ponds, he argued, but return to the city for research

or to evaluate paintings. Coincidentally, he could keep from Susan for a little longer the frightening reality of their financial circumstances. Susan undertook their move with characteristic excitement. She cleaned their rooms thoroughly, then decorated them with items indicating Vassili's heritage and her own. On her trip to Kentucky in 1933 she even attempted to learn to cook by spending a day in the kitchen with Millie Lawson.[13]

If Susan's optimism and training initially blinded her to the financial realities of the Depression, realization was no less stressful when it came. She became nervous, complaining frequently of a skin problem, the symptoms of which seem similar to those of nerve-related disorders. She also became increasingly intolerant of the actions of others. In September 1932, Susan described their new landlord, Mrs. Caskey, as "a well born, pleasant, gracious woman" from North Carolina and Virginia. By December, however, she was an "inveterate telephoner" whose "soft, drawling voice penetrates even closed upstairs doors." She also complained about Joe, the houseman, who went "from room to room with a roaring vacuum cleaner while he whistles like a canary."[14]

The noise, and perhaps the arrears in rent, led them to leave Mrs. Caskey's house at the end of the year. It was not, however, the last time they would complain about noisy apartments or insist upon "quietude" before agreeing to rent. At their first apartment in Stamford, Connecticut, another small town in a rural setting within easy driving distance of New York City, the source of the problem was the young niece of the owner, who "thumps at intervals on the piano all day." "She is an amusing, but much indulged child, and her aunt regards this persistency as a symptom of musical genius, suggestive of the infant Mozart."[15]

Their other major complaint about rented rooms was the lack of cleanliness. They often had to share bathroom facilities with the family from whom they rented. Understandably, Susan was never happy with the arrangement and generally found fault with the habits of others. Eating with others was no less traumatic for her. At the Leckies', their meals were included with the rent. She explained the reasons for her annoyance in a letter to her mother.

The dishes are washed usually without soap with a filthy brush and wiped on towels that look as though the floor had been wiped with them. They have a poor sweet old cat who is blind, but who is allowed so many privileges that it is impossible to stand it. He is handed each dish as it is finished to lick clean before our eyes, and these dishes are then washed with the rest indiscriminately. His hairs permeate the house and float into cream, butter etc.[16]

Susan and Vassili quickly resumed their practice of eating in restaurants. Even in the worst days of the Depression, when they were four to five months behind in rent, they spent $1.67 a day to take their meals in a local restaurant.[17]

Susan's greatest impatience was with the humiliations Vassili suffered at the hands of others. Slow to sense the toll the Depression was taking on her husband, she made up for it with the depths of feeling so characteristic of her overly sensitive nature. To her, he was the noblest of men. When Sawitzky's efforts to find work in his field failed, Susan was angry. People had money, she said, but they refused to buy artwork for fear of adverse publicity and criticism. A month later she wrote dejectedly:

It is like some sort of terrible spell. Vassili has tried everything on earth— to get a position in some line for which he is trained or a subsidy from some organization that is supposed to exist for the purpose, but has met with chilling apathy and stupidity. He has borrowed until there is no one whom we can approach anymore, and the discouragement and humiliation is telling on him. It almost kills me to see the frustration and despair on his dear face sometimes.[18]

Susan lashed out at those who caused his despair. The wealthy bought cars, foods, and furs and went to the theater, but they talked poor, a "sort of hypocritical pose with many wealthy people."[19] She wrote to her Uncle Tom in a similar vein: "It is astonishing to hear so much talk of poverty, and then see nearly every third woman on 5th avenue wearing a mink coat, and to read of the crowded theaters and places of amusement."[20]

Susan reached her lowest point in 1935. Vassili's poor health accentuated her awareness of their financial plight. He was fifty-five years of age and suffered from emphysema aggravated by persistent colds and attacks of influenza. In 1933, he developed a painful eye problem. Although not a Christian Scientist himself, Vassili gave Susan permission to contact her practitioner because there was no money for expensive doctors.[21] Susan spoke of her concern for Vassili in her letters to her parents but not of her deeper fears. Those fears, however, were apparent in less direct ways. Her notebooks of 1933–35 contained numerous fragments of poems interrupted by lists of expenditures or possible sources of income. She could not keep her mind from wandering back to practical issues of survival. She also complained of her own petty illnesses—nervous neuralgia, headaches, and the ever-present skin disorder.[22]

Hardship notwithstanding, like many who experienced the Depression, Susan Sawitzky would look back later and remember the good times. Difficulties of arrears in rent, noisy apartments, and "difficult" or "surly" landlords paled with time; Susan and Vassili were drawn closer by the Depression and its confinement. She explained their practice of taking their meals in restaurants as the opportunity to meet pleasant, unassuming people and to experience the joy of riding through the Connecticut countryside. She wrote of fresh, neatly scrubbed children waiting beside the road in the mornings, of horses and other animals in the fields, and of the changing seasons. She and Vassili enjoyed classical music and, seated arm in arm on the comfortable but aged sofa in their "parlor," spent Saturday afternoons listening to Tchaikovsky on the radio.

They attended an occasional movie. In 1933 Susan urged her parents to watch for the arrival in Lexington of any film by a "delightful young actress named Katherine Hepburn." They had also seen Mae West but warned that she was "a consistent low-brow."[23] They found an out-of-the-way theater and attended performances of more classic plays for a cheaper price. Vassili, of course, worked at preparing articles for journals or on a series of books about early American painters for which he was beginning the research. Susan helped him or retired to her own writing and reading in her study area of the apartment. This was a part of their happy life as well. They were intellectually inclined, and the Depression years enhanced that side of their personalities.[24]

Pressed by economic difficulties, Susan sought security in religious faith. Just as with the death of her child, financial hardships caused her thoughts to turn to Christian Science. She spoke frequently of the law of supply and believed that if her faith was right God would provide their financial needs. She read the *Christian Science Journal* and the *Sentinel* thanks to subscriptions given to her by her mother.[25] She also used Science practitioners, but here also there were two Susan Sawitzkys. She used practitioners in Stamford and New Haven to discuss financial matters. Personal matters, however, were reserved for her Kentucky practitioners. In a sign of her growing awareness of her origins and their hold over her, she wrote that the New England practitioners "would never be able to understand Metzie's and my Kentucky background and our cast of mind." Sickness and financial problems are impersonal, but "a Southern woman's idiosyncrasies and vagaries she [a New England practitioner] would not sympathize with. Mrs. Sandifer, on the other hand, has had infinite patience with us both, knowing the same social structure, locality, etc."[26] Such views certainly did not conform to the best principles of Christian Science, but they comforted Susan. She was convinced that through Science "some unexpected way is always opened to replenish us."[27]

Vassili, again sensing Susan's need, did not object to her use of much-needed money to secure the aid of practitioners. Susan would send fifty cents asking for help with her recurring skin disorder, in locating the proper apartment, or for the means to meet their current and past due financial obligations. She wrote her parents: "If it were not for Science I would feel at my rope's end, but somehow I know that this will sooner or later adjust things, and in the meantime care for us from day to day, as it has done, in spite of the anxiety which I cannot overcome."[28] Susan later affirmed to her sister and her mother that Science was responsible for all the good things in her life.

The Depression also strengthened her ties to her Kentucky family in a very practical way. In 1933, the Clays began to send Susan and Vassili money each month to meet some of their expenses. The farm cushioned the Clays from the worst of the economic problems. There was little money coming in, and, unbeknown to Susan, the colonel was also borrowing money. But the land produced food for the family and their servants. The wages of the Clay servants were cut by half early in the Depression, but their needs were not forgotten. Food and used clothing, firewood from the farm, and virtually anything else of use was given to the people who had served them faithfully for years. Millie Lawson carried supper home from the Clay house most evenings.[29]

The Clays worried most about their eldest daughter. There was nothing new about that concern, but Colonel Clay was more aware of economic conditions than his daughter and perhaps William Sawitzky as well. On May 22, 1932, he wrote directly to Sawitzky inviting him to spend the summer with them in Kentucky. It is a most interesting letter both for its suggestion and for the mood in which it was written.

My dear Mr. Sawitzky:

Let me join Mrs. Clay in a most cordial and insistent invitation to both you and Susan to spend the summer with us. I know full well the terrible conditions all over the country. If you will come to us it will add nothing to our expense and will give us more happiness and peace of mind than you can conceive.

I believe we can make you comfortable and happy. You have little or no work during the summer and I can see no reason why you should be subjected to any expense or anxiety.

Now do not let me receive no for an answer for we really want you. You can drive through in your machine and the trip will cost you very little. You will then have your mind at ease and have time to mature your plans for the future. We three are alone this summer and we really need you. Give my dearest love to Susan.[30]

The colonel's suggestion was a practical one. His remark that the family needed them was probably closer to the truth than either he or Sawitzky realized. Vassili and Susan would have been no great burden financially or otherwise, and Vassili, with his significant horticultural background, might have carried the Clays forward one more generation as Bluegrass landowners, albeit with a name strange to the region.

The letter, however, came too early and recalled too many memories. Vassili was not ready to give up on his career. In May 1932, their financial situation was still acceptable, and there was reason to hope for improvement. Sawitzky had also made an important discovery in his field in 1931. The February 1931 issue of *International Studio* contained a picture of a portrait attributed for over one hundred years to Sir Joshua Reynolds. Sawitzky recognized it as a portrait of Caleb Whitefoord, a friend of Benjamin Franklin, painted by Gilbert Stuart around 1784. Whitefoord had sat for Reynolds, but this portrait, Sawitzky maintained, was in the style characteristic of Stuart. The *New York Times* announced his discovery on March 14, 1931, and *International Studio* published his justifications in its April 1931 issue.[31] Other articles on early American portrait painters were being accepted for publication, and Sawitzky's reputation as an honest and accurate evaluator of art pieces was growing. Just as Susan had reason to believe her career showed promise in 1921, Sawitzky believed his efforts would open doors to paying positions. For Sawitzky, there was also the matter of pride. Colonel Clay's letter seemed formal, almost patronizing. In fact, the letter suggests a very real effort by Clay to set Sawitzky's mind at ease. The colonel would never have penned such phrases as "you will give us more happiness and peace of mind than you can conceive" or "we really need you" unless he meant them. Sawitzky, however, was not ready to admit to his father-in-law or himself his failure at the manly task of providing for his wife.

Sawitzky was wise enough not to say much to Susan. In August 1932, they went back to Ganonoque for a vacation, and Susan wrote the following note to her parents.

> You are sweet and lovely to offer us a home with you and I confess it gives me a grateful feeling of reassurance and refuge to think that if things prove impossible for us, that my Father's and Mother's home is open to us. But naturally Vassili doesn't want to give up unless he has to do so. All his work is here, and he feels that to leave it . . . would be a mistake at this time. He feels he can't let go, and even the most pessimistic businessmen say conditions are steadily improving.[32]

Conditions were not improving, however. By Christmas of 1932 Susan realized the seriousness of their financial plight. Torn between her own fears and a hesitancy to cause her parents distress, her letters were characterized by inconsistencies. On December 21, 1932, she wrote that she would not be able to send Christmas gifts. After that pro-nouncement, however, she continued, "Remember we are perfectly comfortable, warm, well-fed and happy in spite of the present lack of ready money, and expect to spend a pleasant Christmas. I believe things are breaking for us and that relief is on the far horizon."[33] Shortly after Christmas, Colonel and Mrs. Clay sent money to their daughter.[34]

Susan received her parents' gift with dismay. Unaware of her own role in creating their concern, she wrote to her father admonishing him against sending money: "Papa, you must not try to send me money. You are everlastingly sweet and generous, but it is not necessary, so I am returning the five you sent me. I love you and Marm with all my heart and so does Vassili, but we can't let you do this."[35] But the same pattern appeared again. After attempting to set their minds at ease, Susan would make an off-the-cuff statement that rekindled their con-cern. In one instance she proclaimed that Christian Science had helped them by finding a source from which Vassili could borrow money. Four days later, she asked her mother to call Mrs. Clinkenbeard, the practi-tioner, about treating Vassili's eye problem. They "had no money for expensive doctors."[36]

The Clays began to send five or ten dollars every three weeks or so as they could spare it. Susan occasionally complained but more fre-quently thanked them profusely for being so loving and kind. Vassili, she said on one occasion, was particularly struck by the generosity of the Clays compared with the other family with which he had been associated, one of the few references to his earlier marriage.

In 1934, the Sawitzkys also began to receive aid from Susan's Uncle Tom Clay. George Clay died that year, and when the estate was settled Uncle Tom began to send Susan twenty-five dollars a month. She pro-tested bitterly to her parents, thinking that they had encouraged him to send her money.

> Please, *never* under any conditions, ask Uncle Tom to send me money, or infer that I am in need of it. He has been perfectly wonderful to me, and has sent me substantial gifts repeatedly, having done so again the other day, but I have a perfect horror of becoming a burden and would rather die than ask for money or have anyone do it for me. So never mention our financial ups and downs to him.[37]

Susan kept her parents on a roller coaster of emotions. She shared the slightest financial success but could not contain the depths to which she sank.

It is little wonder that Colonel and Mrs. Clay became thoroughly frustrated with Susan. With unprecedented frankness for a male so wedded to nineteenth-century values, Charles Clay wrote to discuss financial matters with his daughter. He said he wanted to help Susan financially, but to do so he needed answers to specific questions. How much did the rent cost? Was coal used for fuel? How much did it cost per ton? Was there a refrigerator in the house? How much did milk and other necessities cost? Finally, he demanded immediate and straightforward answers. Beneath the gruffness, Colonel Clay was a loving father, deeply concerned about her and demanding to know what was needed to assure her well-being.[38] Two months later, Ria Clay wrote an equally revealing letter to her daughter. She insisted that Susan mail her laundry home to Kentucky. Millie would be more than happy to do it for Susan, she said, and it was too difficult a task for a lady. Equally frank with her daughter, she wrote, "Use every care to keep well and happy. Trust God, be practical, *cut out the super sensitiveness* and both you and we will be much happier."[39]

Again, however, Susan's happiness, and that of her mother, was confronted by sudden tragedy. On November 29, 1935, Colonel Charles Clay died suddenly. Susan told Vassili in a letter written after she had rushed to her mother's side that he seemed to realize only as the blow struck him. He cried, "O God," then fell to the floor, dead of heart failure at the age of seventy-eight.[40]

Just as at Charley's death, Susan consoled her mother. For the first time, she handled grief with the stoic grace of her grandmothers Clay and Pepper. Only the brief lines expressing her love and her inability to feel close to him marked his passing. The image she held of her father, more prominent in death, had always been more comforting than the reality.

CHAPTER ELEVEN

Recovery

And all in lap of God are fed,
And all beneath His brow are warm.
                    —"Beloved Beast-children," SCS Papers

IN SEPTEMBER 1935, Susan and Vassili made their last change of residence. It was intended to be another cost-saving effort but in fact coincided with improvements in both their financial situation and their general peace of mind.

The couple rented a small cottage just outside Stamford, Connecticut, from Augusta Williams, who quickly became a close friend as well as a landlord. They loved the little house from the start. It had only four rooms, but to them, cramped in tiny apartments or rented rooms for all their married life, it was a mansion equal to Ashland itself. Each now had work space sufficiently private to avoid disturbing the other's "quietude." Vassili used one of the larger rooms so he could spread his work out, while Susan used a smaller, closet like room as a study.

They used one room as a parlor. It was there on Saturday afternoons that they sat together to listen to the radio broadcasts of classical music. In the winter, Vassili made a fire in the large stone fireplace, a reminder of Susan's home in Kentucky. Susan's print of Ashland adorned one wall of the parlor. Other prints, paintings, and portraits, along with trays, pieces of china, and crystal objects acquired by inheritance as her parents' generation died, gave the parlor a distinctly Kentucky and Clay flavor. The house also contained a small kitchen, the least-used room. Susan prepared Vassili's poached egg for breakfast, a cold plate for lunch, and, having discovered the *Bluegrass Cook*

Book containing traditional recipes, including one by her cousin Nanny McDowell and others by the "Paris Clays,"[1] she occasionally experimented with their evening meal. It was only a matter of weeks, however, before her letters indicated that they were eating in restaurants again.

The house was surrounded by two acres of land, dotted with clumps of trees and bushes. Susan could view the workings of nature from inside or walk the lawns when she tired of her study. She made friends with the squirrels and the birds that came to feeders Vassili built. Her home was the closest thing to Kentucky she had experienced since leaving her father's house. Scarred by the "brutalities" of a broader world, Susan Clay Sawitzky found comfort in the same things that had brought security in her youth.

An additional advantage of the cottage was its cost. Because Stamford was more rural than urban in the 1930s, they paid less rent as well as lower utility bills. Their finances improved for other reasons too. Susan learned, although reluctantly, to accept support from her family. Ria Clay sent money periodically, but Uncle Tom provided the greatest aid. In 1936, he began to send Susan fifty dollars per month. At first she protested, but Marm argued that it would all go to Susan, Metzie, and Bob someday anyway, and Susan saw the logic of her explanation.

Throughout the late 1930s, legacies from other relations helped pay outstanding debts and allowed them to renew their vacations at the Cragmere Inn in Ganonoque. In 1938, an inheritance from her Aunt Lena, Ria Clay's half-sister, enabled Susan to bring her mother and Metzie to Connecticut for a visit. Ria Clay stayed the summer while Metzie used her share of the inheritance to travel in Europe.

Uncle Tom also prepared a will at this time, leaving each of his nieces and nephew approximately twenty-thousand dollars upon his death. In a fashion perfectly in keeping with family and southern gender values, Bob, the only nephew, received his share in fee simple and was made executor of trusts established for Susan and Metzie. The interest provided an income for both nieces; the principal remained to provide lifelong security.[2] It proved to be Tom Clay's characteristically practical way of protecting his nieces.

Their financial situation also improved as a result of Vassili's successful endeavors. In 1935, Yale University asked him to write the foreword and prepare a catalog for a Ralph Earl exhibition, and he also

Named assistant curator at the New-York Historical Society in 1940, William Sawitzky already suffered from emphysema and low blood pressure.

began to examine and evaluate the collection of the Historical Society of Pennsylvania. For a short time in late 1935, the New-York Historical Society paid him seventy-five dollars per month to evaluate its collection. In 1936, an anonymous patron began to pay Vassili a monthly stipend to evaluate paintings for purchase. His work involved a good deal of travel throughout the Atlantic states so the patron provided the funds that allowed them to replace Domie with a new "machine."[3]

Throughout the 1930s Vassili's reputation as an authority on American art grew. In 1940, their dreams and Susan's predictions to her parents were realized when the Carnegie Foundation awarded a grant funding a position as assistant curator of the New-York Historical Society. Vassili also taught part-time at New York University, lecturing on early American art, and the foundation funded his research for a series of studies on early American artists.

The natural surroundings at their little cottage provided the third element upon which their happiness was based. The love and enjoyment of nature had sustained them in the years of greatest hardship, drawing them even closer as they experienced its unfolding, season by season, together. They seemed to gain strength from the cycles of creation, each leading to new birth. Field, stream, and millpond were their theaters. Bees and butterflies, frogs, opossums, and even skunks were joyfully observed in a natural setting. Even as Vassili's work increased, an afternoon, and sometimes two, each week found them out in the countryside. Susan wrote letters to her mother best described as prose poems, describing the hues of leaf and sky, noting differences between New England and Kentucky, and asking questions concerning the stage of the season at home.[4]

Susan's attitude toward nature was an interesting mixture of art and poetry and owed much to her Clay upbringing. Looking at nature with the eyes of an artist and poet, she filled her letters with vivid descriptions that shared her delight in what she saw. Fall in New England was "thickets of dogwoods with rosy leaves and sumac with brilliant curious hues. Now many of the trees are bare, but the wine shades of the oak keep the woods rich."[5] In describing cattle at a fair, she wrote that they were "sweet as cream, their horns and hooves polished, their bodies faultlessly groomed." The Brown Swiss cows were not brown but "mouse gray, with ivory noses and ears lined with peach colored velvet." Susan could also give more somber word pictures. Bulls of a particular breed had "flanks like dark mountains, their small eyes filled with primeval rage, their nostrils snorting hot volcanic breath at the close peering crowd, that found a thrill in coming so physically near these Babylonian gods."[6]

The Sawitzkys had much more patience with animals, fierce or gentle, than with people. They kept birds as pets and frequently cared for injured animals of all species. In 1933, Susan found an injured pigeon outside the Metropolitan Museum. She wrote her mother that the poor bird rode on her lap as quietly as a kitten the forty-five miles home. Several pages of description followed, filled with language of tenderness and care which she rarely used to describe humans.[7] An injured lizard was cared for until restored to health, then taken to Kentucky by Susan and released in less populated surroundings. Vassili asked in his first letter if the lizard liked its new home. A kitten found abandoned in a post office, "unnoticed and hungry in the midst of a throng of people," was brought home and revived. In their worst days financially, they bought ground-up raw meat, "or hamburger as it is called," and condensed milk to feed the cat. Susan could become angry over lack of cleanliness, but she jokingly remarked that she was forever getting the cat down from tables, mantle pieces, and other household furnishings.[8] She also placed food behind the books on the shelves so that field mice that came in for the winter would have a meal.[9] Letters and papers, gnawed at the edges, indicate that the mice were not content with Susan's rations.

The couple became emotionally attached to their animal friends. They spent hours caring for some animals and observing others. Susan would brave drifted snow and strong winds to provide food for the birds and squirrels. Several of her letters to her parents describing her encounters could have been shaped and molded into short stories or prose poems for publication.[10] Indeed, Susan may have missed a calling that could have led to the contribution to society and even the prominence she expected of herself. Her vivid descriptions and warm, sensitive stories might easily have been turned into children's books. For example, the death of a little dog prompted a long letter to her mother in May 1935, describing their friendship and her sorrow at its death.

The little dog, named Pal, belonged to a young boy who lived across the street. Pal was not popular with everyone in the neighborhood for reasons she explained in the letter. But first she described the physical features of the little dog so her mother could see as she read.

Pal was a cocker spaniel of a red gold color, with long, limp ears that hung down like golden locks at the sides of his little snub face. He had the large moist, dim-looking eyes of his breed that seem so full of world sadness, and a short muzzle that filled the bones of his face loosely like a velvet bag. Looked at face to face, that is when Pal was on the terrace and we on the driveway below, his lip lifted a little on the right side showing his teeth, and his ferocity, as Vassili said. He had a compact sturdy little body, silky "feather feet," and a stump of a tail that betrayed him many a time behind his back when he was trying to look like a dangerous dog in front of it.

Then she described Pal's personality. The little dog had an inferiority complex "owing to his small size," which probably accounted for his frequent and loud barking. Many of the neighbors disliked him because of the noise. Mrs. Delanoy disliked him because he "watered her stoop." But Pal had likes and dislikes, too. For example, he thought the local newspaper unfit to read; therefore, the boy who delivered it was denied admission to his yard. Nor did he like boys on bicycles, the junkman, or the postman who befriended his rival, a German shepherd named Duke. Beneath the harsh exterior, however, there was a gentle soul apparent to those who cared enough to look. Susan described for her mother how she and Vassili had discovered the real Pal.

> We were crazy about him from the moment we saw him, and at once entered into negotiation with him for his good will. These transactions were carried out very cautiously on his part, for he was strangely timid and unbelieving. When we called him he would come across the road, into the edge of our yard, then wait for us to stoop down to his level and beg him to come nearer. This fulfilled, he would prostrate himself in turn, lying with his back legs spread out frog-fashion. Vassili always called this disarming, or the laying down of all imaginary weapons on both sides,—a symbolic ceremony of good faith. Now he would slowly drag himself along on his front paws, while we coaxed and reassured him, until he arrived at last at our feet. Here he allowed himself to be patted and stroked along his ears and back and over his forehead where the soft, loose skin would slip back from his eye-balls. Finally he would roll over on his back to be scratched underneath and let us hold his soft thick little paws. In time he became so confident that he would come silently, without being called, when we went out of the front door, but

we always observed the latter part of the surrendering of weapons pantomime."

Susan expressed her sorrow that Pal would not come again to greet
them. He had jumped from his owner's car and been killed. Susan and
Vassili were so distraught they had accomplished nothing for days.
Susan had written nearly twenty handwritten pages about Pal but noted
that the Clay family felt about animals as she and Vassili did so they
would understand.

Indeed, Mrs. Clay could understand. Such a letter was not the least
bit surprising, nor was it the only lengthy letter written about the things
she loved. Susan had a lifelong fascination with butterflies, and many
letters were written on the subject. Some of those letters were as moving as the one concerning her friend Pal. Others were more "scientific."
In 1934, for example, she wrote a twenty-page letter that dealt exclu-
sively with the life cycle of a milkweed butterfly. Others described the
mating dances of pheasants and bluebirds building nests, which she
had spent hours observing from the window. All were characterized by
excellent descriptions, childlike curiosity, and sensitivity. Among her
papers, there are nearly a thousand photographs of birds and trees, lakes,
and other natural scenes taken with their old Brownie camera. There
are also hundreds of cards containing descriptions of birds in Vassili's
handwriting and notebooks filled with Susan's research on butterflies.

They were not "systematic naturalists," as they quickly noted, but
rarely have two people enjoyed their efforts more. Indeed, they seemed
to prefer the company of animals and protected them against the "wan-
ton cruelty and thoughtlessness of the average person who looks upon
them from a selfish, limited and utilitarian view."[12] Unless animals served
the "human beast," they were considered a nuisance. Vassili and Susan were both hurt and angered by what they believed was most people's
approach to nature, the tendency to tease or to kill. Susan complained
that Mrs. Delanoy taught Georgette, the infant Mozart, "to fear and
dislike dogs, because they bite children, soil their dresses, and give
them distemper, to avoid red ants because they crawl into the ears of
children, to run from bees or wasps as they sting them, etc."[13] She
expressed their philosophy of nature in a letter to her parents in the
summer of 1934.

People sometimes look on Vassili and me as childish and almost stupid in our interest in those things but it is our greatest joy and recreation. Nature is as fresh as if it were the Garden of Eden, and we the only human beings in the world at the moment of our experience. Occasionally we borrow something from her, but we always return it intact, losing more and more the desire to take and possess. We are not systematic naturalists, but in these intermittent contacts are perfect experiences that we never lose.[14]

The Sawitzkys found more pleasure in nature during these difficult times than they did in people. To some degree, such a choice resulted from the embarrassment of borrowing but not being able to repay close friends. It also resulted from the sense of peace and security Susan craved. In a draft letter to her mother she wrote that her love of nature and its creatures helped "wipe away all the grime of human experiences." Crossing through the phrase, she replaced it with "soothe all the soreness of human contact." In a final version she referred in the same context to the "pain" of the human experience.[15] Despite a quick temper and her own ability to be very critical in judging people, she craved a simple and innocent world. Increasingly, she searched for beauty and order just as her youthful education, at home and in school, had taught her to do.

The Sawitzkys did maintain contact with a few human friends. Oscar Cesare and his wife, Ann, and poet Hortense Flexner King and her husband, Wyncie, a cartoonist and book illustrator, were their most frequent guests. The Kings met frequently with Susan and Vassili for dinner, or the couples visited each others' homes.[16] Susan found their company and conversation especially stimulating. She began to draw again, testing each of her visual character studies against Wyncie King's sharp senses. The same relationship applied to their conversations. She was herself again, excited, animated, quick to leap into the verbal fray. King required her to stay close to reason, and she thrived on the challenge of their repartee.

Hortense King became a critic of a different sort. The two women read and discussed each other's poetry. Just as the Clays helped with financial recovery, Hortense King nurtured Susan Clay Sawitzky's poetic recovery. She sensed Susan's sensitivity. Unlike her husband's, Mrs.

King's critiques were cautious. Susan accepted criticism of her draw-ings or her conversation; her poetry, however, was at the center of her sense of self. Hortense King praised first. She thought Susan's imag-ery truly brilliant. She applauded the blending of philosophy and po-etry and only in guise of afterthought suggested a revision, more thought on the wording of a given line, or the danger of losing the reader in abstraction. All comments ended positively, and increasingly she urged Susan to submit her work to publishers.

Susan had written many poems during the 1930s. Indeed, most of her nature poems had their origins in the decade between the death of her child and the close association with Hortense King. Yet she had labored for her husband's success, helping him to publish rather than seeking publication herself. She wrote for her own pleasure or, as she said, therapy.

In the late 1930s, as in 1921 with the New York trip and Professor Terrell and the Scribbler's Club in 1924, an outside impetus, in this case Hortense King, led Susan to seek publication. In 1938, she began a cautious effort to publish. Her notebooks contained addresses of journals and practice letters to editors. She also began to divide her poems by topic. She compiled collections, reworked some of her po-ems, typed manuscripts, and, finally, summoned the courage to sub-mit them for publication. She mentioned submitting poems to Viking Press and to a poetry contest. In February, she wrote to her mother that she was trying to find the right place to publish her poems. She remained tentative, telling her mother to tell no one lest the poems be rejected but declaring her intent to dedicate them to Mrs. Clay and Vassili if they were accepted.[17]

It seemed a hopeless task. On June 14 she wrote to her mother:

I have tried so hard in Science lately, and have been singularly unsuc-cessful. My book of poems which means so much to me has been re-peatedly refuted, with the most meaningless and conflicting comments, after weeks of tense waiting in each instance for a decision. I feel utterly perplexed and discouraged, restless, sterile minded with almost com-plete loss of mental appetite. I seem to be going through some murky personal experience.[18]

Those remarks show why Susan, and, indeed, perhaps many poets, hesitate to submit their work. She never seemed to fear rejection when writing articles on art history, but they were not so personal. More important, she and her husband had better connections with publishers of works on art history. The ties to the world of poetry Susan had developed in the early 1920s were given up after she married. Susan's poetry was written in isolation.[19] Nevertheless, rejection of her poetry left her "sterile minded," drained, "with almost complete loss of mental appetite."

There seems little doubt that Susan would have given up had Hortense King not encouraged her. King sensed Susan's fears and hesitancy to set herself up, time after time, for rejection. She encouraged Susan, suggested changes in the poems, and submitting them to publishers of single poems as well as book-length collections. Finally, there was some success. Susan's poem "Mariner" appeared in the highly regarded *Poetry: A Magazine of Verse* in the February 1941 issue.[20]

"Mariner" is without question one of her better poems. It also expressed her personal struggle. Susan Clay Sawitzky was the voyager, the dreamer, the prospector of freedom. Like her mariners, she wandered over narrow boards—her pedestal. She beheld freedom and was intrigued by it, but she was withheld from it by external and internal forces. She was woman, not enslaved but not free.

CHAPTER TWELVE

Poetry

The confident grip of earth set feet
Is not for you,
You who can never lose
The reeling sense of vast velocity.
                    —"Mariner," *The Circling Thread*

"MARINER" WAS THE FINAL POEM that Susan Sawitzky published, but it
was not the last that she wrote, nor did it stand as the high point of the
thought process upon which the body of her work was based. Financial recovery and the encouragement of Hortense King gave her new
confidence. Her poems of the late 1930s, begun before "Mariner" was
published, exhibited a new dimension, which she called cosmic imagery, and its scope required significant confidence. She still sought answers, however, to the old questions, and many of her poems spoke of
balance, both human and heavenly.

Susan spent much of her time after the publication of "Mariner"
creating a collection of poems in the hope of publishing them in book
form. Each collection emphasized the circling thread of life from birth
through the complexities and limitations of earthly existence to death,
the freedom and understanding that death brought, and the repeti-
tion of the process again and again as she saw it in the world of nature. She dealt continuously with the issues that gave her difficulty.
Despite the complexity of theme and her own constant searching for
understanding of the pain and sorrow she had experienced, her treatment of every issue was in language that evoked beauty. She chose

words carefully for their beauty as her teachers had taught her years
earlier, but increasingly, she used fewer and more precise words, and
though she rarely used rhyme, she employed phrases that trigger the
senses. Susan sought in her ideas the same ordered, beautiful world in
which she had grown up. Like many poets, particularly those she preferred, Tennyson, Blake, and Whitman, she searched increasingly in
mystical realms for that perfect understanding.[1]

From 1928 to 1941, Susan Sawitzky wrote approximately one hundred poems and many fragments which she left incomplete in notebooks or on scraps of paper. Most of those poems fit the same general
theme. Woodridge Spears used her title "The Circling Thread" for his
collection of Susan's poems published by the *Kentucky Poetry Review*
in 1984. By doing so, he was remaining faithful to her own interpretations of her work. She saw her poetry as the completion of a circle.
From the earliest examples of her poems, short, rhymed verse controlled somewhat by the values of her teachers, to her last effort, a six-
page freewheeling romp through the heavens called "Strange Universe,"
her work can best be described as a circling thread. In fact, there were
several circles, ever enlarging circles of a Ptolemaic bent, encompassing central Kentucky, earth, the universe, the struggles of a young southern woman, of women generally, and then of humanity as a whole. Her
own circles came together to create new ones. The influence of her
reading in Indian religions combined with her poetic neo-Platonism
and her Christian Science faith provided a base for her view of souls
among the stars, returning time and time again to be "shod with flesh."
Life was a circling thread, she wrote, through two holes, birth and
death, and thus lost innocence was recoverable.

Her own life had been a circle; the two holes were confinement and
freedom, lost innocence and the search for it, a world filled with romance—King Arthur and rainbows—and too much reality. Her earthly
life was a circle of confinement by family and community values. Susan was the real version of Carol Milford Kennicott, the major character in *Main Street*. She rebelled and sought escape through marriage
and flight to a large city. She had a "working brain," but she could not
escape the "village virus."[2] Unlike Kennicott, Susan did not return to
her own Gopher Prairie. Confrontation with death and economic depression brought her back to intellectual confinement—entrapment

by the same values—but this time largely self-imposed. Freedom for women of that generation was not easily won.

Susan shared the themes of lost innocence, self-doubt, and mysticism with scores of other poets and novelists who craved a world serene and peaceful, simple and complete. Her search, however, may have been more complicated because she sought to travel two paths simultaneously in her quest. Her efforts to rediscover lost innocence were obstructed and eventually thwarted by the innocence she never lost. The values of the southern gentry, particularly those transmitted to women, proved difficult to escape. Susan Clay Sawitzky remained the genteel proper lady, a descendant of the plantation gentleman and statesman of Kentucky, Henry Clay.

Then there was the second path. Try as she might, as guilty as she sometimes felt, that special world of her mind would not be contained. Susan created a poetic world, a small space where the rules did not apply, and in that space she pondered, searched, and wrote about the issues that confronted her. In the late 1930s and early 1940s, she refined in a more tranquil state of mind the powerful feelings that had arisen with the loss of her child. She liked to say that the poems came to her as a burst of inspiration. That was one reason, she argued, why she could not revise them. Although there is an element of truth in her account of their origin, that explanation is also misleading.

Five lines from a poem written in the 1930s explain the development of her poetry better than any of her pronouncements related specifically to the subject. She first titled the poem "The Mighty" and later "Coordinate Miracle."

> One idea cleaves itself and becomes two,
> New ideas thrust themselves between the old,
> Like life that swells and breaks
> In the shut womb,
> Sliced and divided into oneness.[3]

These lines not only explain the development of her poetry but are another example of a circle. Ideas are created as life itself develops, slicing, dividing, swelling, breaking into more ideas and a unity of explanation at the same time.

Ideas did come to her at times in a burst of inspiration, but it was not unusual for her to revise a poem over many years. As Susan sat beside ponds and fields, she wrote descriptions in verse, a kind of free poetic form. Those notes do not constitute poems, but neither are they notes as most people would take them. They have a rhythm that implies the poetic. At some later time a line or portion of the line might appear in a poem either as an idea, an image, or a nearly word-for-word section. Then, writing in pencil, she worked at preciseness of language. Only a few poems made it to a typed stage. Even then, numerous penciled changes would occur before the poem might be considered finished. She changed lines, deleted some, added others, and she labored over an exact word or phrase, sometimes carrying an option in parenthesis through several copies. "The Shifting Void" is an excellent example. Elements of the poem appear in her notebooks before her marriage, but a dated copy with the changes in Susan's hand is included in a collection of poems she worked on in the 1960s, more than thirty years later.[4]

Like many southern writers, Susan wrote in a world unto herself.[5] After her marriage, she lost the contacts made in the early 1920s, and only Hortense King offered suggestions for revisions. Her isolation from other poets explains at least in part her failure to publish and the "hitches" in her poems. She never settled into any particular school. In 1924, Anna Blanche McGill placed her among the Imagists when she reviewed Susan's first book of poems. Although her poetry has similarities to that of the Imagists, other influences were at work as well. Like many American poets of the period, she was particularly fond of the French Symbolists, and their influence on her poetry is apparent. She also read Emily Dickinson but initially was not overly impressed, preferring Tennyson, Blake, and other poets she had read since youth, especially Walt Whitman.[6] Her "Walt Whitman's Poems" praised him as a symbol for all poets.

> The earth uprisen
> In a sun-drawn, yellow tide;
> A thrusting upward of arms in harvest gladness,
> These are your great unscythed, ungarnered poems:
> Like ripe wheat

Stretched between field and sun,
Where the slow rhythm of breathing
Swims like hot wind.

And you, O hoary child
Lashed by the shining
Of golden, monotonous lines,
Their flood against your breast,
Call out to us who tread the dusty road:

"Come, there is plenty,—plenty for each and all!
Thresh them, these bending stalks, the grain is yours.
Carry it into your barns
In the pinched, blue days of Winter to warm you,
To bring strength to your sagging arms.
Sow it again and again as the years turn,—
With every planting more yours, less mine,
A thinner crop, yet with my nourishment in it.
Abundance now, plenty for all,
Take, eat,—my body and soul."[7]

His "great unscythed, ungarnered poems" were "Like ripe wheat" which Whitman offered those tired and hungry poets who traveled the difficult road. He was, she proclaimed, the only mystic she ever understood.[8]

By the early 1940s Susan's newer poems ran the danger of being too abstract because of her efforts to limit the number of words. Hortense King gently warned her against the dangers of losing her reader.[9] Although Susan experimented with language, seeking to present the most precise meanings possible, the most important characteristic of her poetry was her imagery. Much of that imagery came from her Kentucky background. She saw in Kentucky few "boats and their down turned images" lying "like open shell valves." The surface theme of "Mariner" was purely New England. But she had been in New England for some years when she wrote of "soft noses and lips, loosely moving, / Sprinkled with delicately perceiving hairs," of old roads sunken in fields, and gates in half-circle grooves. Those were her Kentucky experiences.

She called specifically on her Kentucky experience in a most perceptive passage from "Winter Morning." The poet stands before a fresh snow contemplating new beginnings.

> And while I hesitate
> A negro farm hand
> Trudges through the trees,
> With every layer of warmth he has about him
> Pinned and patched,
> Looking like battered husks
> About old ears of corn,
> His chapped face like a brown leaf
> Silvered with frost:
> And all his foot-steps follow him across the hill.
>
> So he records himself in beauty,
> And so the simple-hearted track themselves
> Across God's breast,
> While others, conscious and fearful,
> Stand aside.[10]

Even in this poem heavy with nostalgia, the theme of her collected work is present. She searches after God and understanding yet is uncertain over the path to take. The simple one accepts on faith and tracks "Across God's breast," while the other Susan, the thinker, stands aside in contemplation.

Susan divided her poetry by subject, yet all her poems contain similar or interrelated themes. A chart in one of her notebooks listed some of her poems under four major and several lesser categories. The major categories were Spirit, Death, Nature, and Love. The most important of the lesser categories were those dealing with her lost child. The others, listed as Time, Inspiration, Analysis, and Sensitiveness, could easily be considered as subcategories of Spirit. The lists of poems under each of these categories do not include many of the fragments or unfinished and untitled poems in her manuscript collections or her papers. A very obvious topic of her poetry which she failed to list was a lifelong effort to define the nature of God. As with "Winter Morning," which is listed under Nature, however, the "two great mysteries of Life" appear in many of her poems, if not as the principal subject then as imagery or simile.

All the poems listed under Spirit raise questions relative to the human's role or the ability to survive in this world. The early poems portray humanity as weak and ill-equipped to understand life's vagaries. In "Ego," the author is unperceiving.

> I see as water sees,
> Eyes filled but unperceiving,
> Strewn lightly with the long dreams of the world.
> I keep a shut and secret brightness
> Fast ceilinged with its own unearthly image.
> Do not ask that I behold you,
> Ask only that you find yourself in me.[11]

In "Gift," humans are shallow.

> Must the bleached ankles of rushes
> Or the span of a lily stem
> Measure my shallowness,
> When the sky itself comes into me
> And hollows me out to its own immensity?
>
> I feel the clutch of roots
> In dull grey mist of mud,
> But miles within me
> Lies the ooze of cloud,
> And in the night the sharp-edged, time crushed stars
> Sink to their height in me,
> Settling like sand across a floorless deep.[12]

Despite the shallowness, however, she sees potential in mankind. Clouds for Susan were symbols of freedom; the ooze of cloud is then the potential for freedom.

"The Shifting Void" is not merely the story of some universal void or cosmic phenomena, but where one finds him- or herself if only temporarily. Human beings seek fullness and understanding, but as soon as enlightenment occurs, new areas of darkness appear. There is here a kind of poetic Hegelian dialectic. At first, Susan Sawitzky seems to view the creation of antithesis negatively, but in its very creation she seems to be trying to create true synthesis, combining opposites.[13] Freedom and confinement, emotion and reason, romance and reality—all struggle in her poetry and in her life. One is reminded of the dialectic that existed in Kentucky, the border state: North and South meeting, attempting to coexist in a region that was neither. Susan grew to maturity in an environment that perpetually sought balance.

Enlightenment was possible, but did it result from compete submission to the Deity or through human intellectual ability? "Winter Morning" implied the simple view as the best answer. A fragment reveals her efforts to hold on.

> He who can believe in something
> Is fed, clothed and free.
> Moving in ordered universe
> The doubter is the bound one
> Faltering with ball and chain
> In treadmill . . .[14]

In "Mariner," it is God who "grants eternal charters of new freedom" so that humans can search for answers. Yet the search appears futile in the poem. The contradiction is never really resolved. Only in the making of the poem is there solution. Within her being is contradiction. Her intellect seeks expansion; her training pulls her back. Prophetically, or as afterthought, she wrote:

> I found amid much darkness
> This grave, celestial truth:
> That suns involved in wisdom
> Burn back again to youth.[15]

In "The Mighty" the reliance on "traditional" wisdom appears again:

> He knows man as an out-thrust, growing bough
> That in old youth

Hides the wise child maturity;
And that the cold, and crumpled inner leaves
Of evolution
Slowly unbind
About a small, tight knot
Of final flower,
Which any eager hand may break apart
But no thing loosen
Except its own awareness.[16]

Susan Sawitzky still struggled with the concept of confinement and freedom. She merely traded earthly father for a heavenly one, southern woman for all of humanity. Freedom and the freedom to think become things to shut out. Her poem "The Cowed" pointed that out. Two fragments speak to the same issue.

Over this small house which is my life
A wind moves, wild and dark
Scented by fields of cloud,
Sweet with the dark ripeness of
    snow cloud.
It shakes the weak walls of my (self) body
It cries for entrance with rising importunate cries
With its lips to my shut lips.

Why do you come to me
Rough child of heavenly freedom?
I have barred the doors of my
    life against you.
To feel you within me is madness
To give birth to you is such
    liberating death.
Yet within my soul already
Your chill unearthly breath
The white flakes of your presence
Sift like snow across the threshold
    of my spirit.[17]

The second fragment is less polished, but her nagging concern over the presence of thought is apparent.

> Your prison guard asleep
> And you out in the moonlight staggering
> Too weak to run away
> But making swashbuckling passes with
>   your thoughts.
> Like the foolish gestures of a bough
> Philosophying with the wind.
> The sudden gusts of laughter
>   lift themselves and wailed for you
> But you knew you could never escape
> The glare of tomorrow's soberness.[18]

The two remaining categories into which she divided the poetry of the 1930s were much smaller. She included under Nature eight poems—"Spring Song," "March Water," "The Least," "Skylarks," "Briars" (Homecoming), "Winter Dusk," "Winter Morning," and "Skunk Cabbage." Although the theme of each is taken directly from nature, Susan's probing questions regarding humankind are apparent throughout these poems as well. In "Skunk Cabbage," the poet drew from the discoveries that she and her husband made as they walked in the fields. The plant's aroma reminded her of decay and death. The poem, however, turned death to positive use, in a tribute to spring.

> Too soon arisen
> You who lightly sleep,
> Dark cerements twisted
> Rank with burial scent:
>
> The first then, furtive life of Spring
> Shall find
> Your parted shroud,
> And quicken on the fetid taste of death.[19]

Out of last year's decay and death the tender shoots of a new spring grow.

These poems express more than an appreciation of nature. They are also autobiographical. Susan Clay Sawitzky walked the farm roads of her youth, recalled winter snows and spring thaws, smelled the skunk cabbage and the horse barn. She sought her own past in those poems. They carried Susan back mentally to a time of security, a time before her rebellion, when the world had seemed to be full of promise instead of dread, "perfect and joyous" rather than insecure. They also provided a degree of security in the present as she learned to live with, though not accept, the losses she had endured.

The final category into which Susan divided her poetry was Love. She wrote short, pleasant pieces on the subject, yet they are not what one might expect. Her papers contain fragments that appear to be attempts at traditional love poems. She usually gave up, slashing through them in obvious frustration or leaving them in rough form. She did, however, write a few poems which she considered love poems, messages to Vassili. The earliest, "Secret," is warm, colorful, and full of imagery.

> Who could know
> that my love for you
> Is colored with ruby and emerald?
>
> For it goes with humming-bird wariness
> Beating its wings into grey mist.[20]

"Message" was similar in tone:

> As a dove folds its cry in its throat
>   I called you
> As a gentian speaks with shut lips
>   I whispered your name:
>
> And through the thin walls of my heart
>   Beloved, you heard.[21]

Throughout the 1930s, Susan thought more about the cyclical nature of life, and her poems to and about Vassili changed as well. She was constantly amazed that they, such like-minded people, had found each other over so great a distance. In the poem "Triangle," she noted the difference in their origins.

> You and I looked upward at one star
> Though the shoulder of the world was thick between us
> And at this apex our eyes met.[22]

Their finding each other by looking upward at one star was not a chance occurrence. It tied her love for Vassili to the other events of her life. Her child still soared among the stars. Moreover, she had decided that only destiny could have brought her and Vassili together. She completes the circle in a short, untitled note: "Even in your childhood when I was not yet born I was with you."[23]

Susan included "Petition to Jehovah II" in her list of poems about love. She wanted to shatter the outer, earth-imposed crust and see the natural beauty she knew existed within her husband. A very rough fragment carried something of the same theme but without the anger.

> Is love the yearning to encompass
> To ingest
> To exchange (to interchange) substance
> To draw down (in) the opening of space
> To a small nest.[24]

"Jehovah II" and this fragment are hardly love poems in the traditional sense.

Among the last of the works Susan wrote in the decade of the 1930s were three poems she called "Some Poems on Extension." They were entitled "Of Space," "Of Magnitude," and "Of Ending." Collectively they form a proper conclusion to her work of the 1930s and early 1940s. In notebooks dating from the late 1930s Susan collected quotations from newspaper articles, books, and magazines which dealt with astronomy. Her thoughts on the human struggle for survival on earth led her beyond its boundaries.

In "Of Space" she found man capable of controlling both God and his world.

No being nor brain too small
For my democracy,
No being too great
For this most ample world.

For space is measure of the creature scope,
And from an ego
Calipers of mind
Mark out its bounds.[25]

Worlds, she wrote, could sit together in a room; a skull, a mind, contained years of heaven's sweep. Though physically bound to earth, man is nevertheless free to comprehend cosmic thoughts. The second poem, "Of Magnitude," treated the restriction of dimensions.

Height, breadth, depth
These three
Box us to place.
A fourth takes down our walls,—
For omnipresence
Is extent of each.

Dimension of idea
That knows no where
Yet finds ubiquitous center.[26]

Susan again sought freedom through ideas. She applied a mathematical truth to man—that there is no number greater than one, no number less than one. Since matter continues, death, or ending, as she calls it in the third poem of the series, means nothing. The end will come, not once but over and over again. She concludes that the universe is the unity of all matter. She is one, or will be one, with her child, her brother, Papa, and all who have experienced death. Susan Clay Sawitzky is far removed from her Kentucky roots in one sense. In another, they are there; there is consistency. Her poetry was escape; it was understanding. It provided answers, if only temporary ones, to questions she was not supposed to ask. It also linked her to a past.

᭦

CHAPTER THIRTEEN

Fear of Forever

Each line of life is so essential
The loosening of one small stitch
Would cause the whole of Spirit to unravel.
> —untitled fragment, SCS Papers

THE TEN YEARS FROM 1938 to 1947 were the happiest and most reward-
ing of Susan's and Vassili's marriage. They had survived the difficult
Depression years together and had labored as a team to conduct research and to publish a series of articles so that Vassili's reputation
could be established and he could obtain a paying position. Sawitzky's
work was favorably received. He was respected for his objectivity and
his integrity. A careful researcher, he presented evidence in a meticu-
lous, some would say pedantic, manner. His advice on the subject of
eighteenth-century America painters was eagerly sought, and virtually
no verdict was secure until he had evaluated the painting in question.
His commissions and invitations to give guest lectures had increased
after 1935. Finally, in 1940, the coveted grant he had sought for so long
crowned his career.

No one could have been happier than Susan. In her mind and heart
she had believed for years in Vassili's "genius," which was finally being
recognized and rewarded. It was coincidental, of course, that success
justified his refusal in 1932 and again in 1935 to forsake his career and
wait out the Depression on the Clay farm.

Vassili's success was also Susan's though she did not share equally
in the credit. She worked by his side throughout the years and became

well-versed in the field of art history. In 1942, in the foreword to his *Paintings and Miniatures in the Historical Society of Pennsylvania,* Sawitzky acknowledged Susan's role in the publication and her personal knowledge of the field. He almost credited her with joint authorship though he left no doubt of his ultimate authority. Susan would not have expected otherwise. She was fulfilling her prescribed role as helpmate in the development of her husband's career.

The success, albeit belated, gave Susan and Vassili some peace of mind. They renewed their fall and spring visits to Canada and the little inn among the thousand lakes. The surroundings had been altered somewhat by the construction of a highway which cut through the pathways they had enjoyed in earlier days. Susan referred contemptuously to the effects of "progress." But Susan and Vassili had changed, too. Their activities were more slowly paced. Vassili had aged rapidly, and emphysema prevented him from walking more than short distances. They enjoyed the same things as before—the beautiful landscape of trees and rocks descending to the water's edge and their little friends, the wild creatures, that played about the rustic surroundings of the inn. The difference was that they now observed from the chairs and swings. Susan frequently read to Vassili, pausing to discuss the birds or butterflies. They talked of art and music, sharing a peaceful and relatively carefree time together.

Susan doted on Vassili more than ever. Though much younger than he, she seemed to want to grow old with him. If Vassili could not walk the paths, Susan would enjoy the swings and settees. She slowed her pace to match his and even seemed to prefer the clothing of an older woman.

The fact that her parents' generation was now almost gone also seemed to draw her closer to Vassili. Her mother died suddenly in 1939 followed by her Uncle Tom a few months later. Susan accepted the deaths, particularly that of her mother, with surprising resolve. She went to Kentucky to be at her mother's bedside. After her death she returned to Vassili, but little was said or written directly about her mother's death. Ria Clay had exercised significant influence of both a positive and negative nature on her daughter. Elizabeth Clay spoke of the bond between them, created, she believed, when Susan was a baby and Ria worried frantically about her husband's safety.[1] Ria Clay was as responsible as the colonel for suffocating her adolescent daughter, but Susan mostly blamed her father. She wrote letters to her mother throughout her life. They shared the same idealistic view of the world as well as a romantic definition of marriage. Susan had written to her mother in 1938 that she respected Vassili so much it was easy to obey him, just as Marm had told her would happen in a good marriage.[2] And now she turned to her husband just as her mother would have done.

The deaths of so many relatives in the last years of the 1930s caused Susan to give greater thought or at least more reverent thought to family matters. No Clay could escape the name. Susan did not try; Clay was always a part of her signature. Now, however, the heirlooms divided with Bob and Elizabeth, the last survivors of their branch of the family, provided more physical reminders of the Clay heritage in the small cottage where she lived. Her mother's death also brought Susan and her sister closer. Metzie, the last of the members of the James B. Clay branch to reside in the Bluegrass country, moved to New York. The two sisters saw each other more frequently, meeting occasionally for lunch in New York City or talking on the telephone for hours at a time. In 1942, the three great-grandchildren of Henry Clay, Susan, Elizabeth, and Bob, met briefly in New York for lunch and shared memories. Bob was on his way overseas, another Clay serving in another American war. His sisters saw him off, then shared his letters throughout the war years. On Sunday afternoons, Elizabeth often joined Vassili and Susan for a light lunch at one of the restaurants they frequented. Vassili was very charming, as he always was, and Elizabeth developed a strong and enduring attachment to him.

The youngest of the four children, Elizabeth had suffered most from the suffocating control of her parents. Like Susan, she found that no man passed the tests imposed by Colonel and Mrs. Clay.[3] Elizabeth involved herself in theater and in writing groups at the University of Kentucky, but the requirements incumbent on a nineteenth-century lady severely restricted her activities. Like several generations of Clays, Elizabeth believed the community scoffed at her family. She wanted to leave yet could not take the forceful action her sister had. Even when her Aunt Lizzie and a Christian Science practitioner interceded, arguing with Ria that she was ruining Elizabeth's life, the strangle hold of culture and tradition could not be broken. Only death freed her from the most obvious limitations.

Despite her own experiences, Susan at first assumed a parenting role with Elizabeth, guiding and protecting her as their mother had done, even insisting on the standards of conduct she had earlier rebelled against.[4] Initially, Elizabeth was not happy in New York. Like Susan as a young woman in Washington, D.C., she did not have the skills to match her goals for employment. She dreamed of holding positions of authority; she took a job as a clerk at the Metropolitan Museum of Art. Her unhappiness enhanced Susan's efforts to mother her. Vassili finally intervened. While providing security for both Clay women in his own way, he gently suggested for the benefit of both that Elizabeth was capable of caring for herself. Old enough to be Elizabeth's father, Vassili served as big brother instead.

Once such matters were resolved, Susan and Metzie talked of the family and began to share an interest in genealogy. They read each other's poetry again and Susan introduced her sister to Oscar Cesare and others she thought could help Elizabeth with her literary efforts. Elizabeth had written a play based on Millie Lawson's stories, which she hoped to sell. Susan offered suggestions and tried to serve as literary agent for her younger sister, a role someone needed to play for her. Circumstances threw the two sisters together, and for six years they enjoyed each other's company as they had never done before. That closeness helped both women endure in the years to follow.

Elizabeth's sustaining influence was needed for reasons more crushing than Susan could have contemplated. On February 2, 1947, Vassili died. His death was neither sudden nor unexpected, yet for Susan, sensitive and dependent as she was, it was both. This death she could not accept stoically. William Sawitzky had sensed for nearly ten years that he would not recover from the illnesses that plagued him. The physical problems he suffered in the Depression years had not been properly treated for lack of money. His more serious physical disabilities were emphysema and low blood pressure. Originally more a nuisance than anything else, the emphysema grew worse each year until he could hardly move from his chair to the lectern without stopping to catch his breath.[5] As early as September 14, 1940, Vassili, addressing Susan almost as a parent would a child, explained his concerns for the future. She admitted that she had refused to contemplate thoughts of his death. Vassili told her that there was no choice and reluctantly, hesitantly, she acknowledged that truth.

Vassili and Susan went to bed after their conversation, but Susan could not sleep. At dawn on the morning of September 15, 1940, Susan sat alone. She might acquiesce to Vassili's logic as a loving and dutiful wife should, but her mind was filled with alien thoughts. As was her manner, she wrote:

> This morning I made up my mind to go with him, Vassili my darling, when he dies. I would go with him anywhere here, why should I hesitate at death? It would be easier than many changes and decisions we make here, because there are so few arrangements to make. Just step, and ask him to hold to me. I have no ties in the human world but him,—no one would grieve deeply, my sister and brother would be shocked, but they would quickly and wisely turn their backs on it, and would realize too that it was best for me. I would miss the world, the dear world of nature, but it is more bound with association than we know. Without him it might lose its value, be a sort of currency without backing. When he is at my side, sharing it with me I see deeply into the very veins and juices and essences, without him I am lost and blind.

She was relieved by her decision. It was as if a burden had been lifted from her shoulders. She resolved to make the most of nature while they could share it together. She stopped to look at two squirrels, long-time friends, playing outside her study window, and wrote about their antics. She then returned to her theme.

> O beloved, there can be no separation from you. We are inseparable as water bound in the stream. . . . Why is there this superstitious non-sense about suicide, a certain degree of civilization is the blindest thing—to become more civilized is to see clearly, calmly like an Indian. You cannot take life. What would death be? It would be a change, a momentary discontinuance, a non-conformity, a new disposition of belief. . . . God speaks through him to me.[6]

Given her love and respect for Vassili, her explanation almost appears rational. There was no life, she thought, without him. Her study of Hindu philosophy, Christian Science, and the evolution of her own thought were evident in the poem, too. Mary Baker Eddy had called death an illusion. Life was merely a thread circling through birth and death.

Some time after September 15, 1940, Susan expressed her thoughts in a poem. It was called "The Revelation." It referred to the things she learned and felt that night.

Must rifts of sorrow
Open in the soul,
Loss and the fear of loss,
Sky draughts of terror,—
To send out love
To upward streaming brightness?
To light familiar faces
To this gauntness
Of new perceiving?

O when I look at you
Standing alone
—Immaculate—
As one who hides farewell,
Touching me
With the late, long reaching glance
Of tired eyes,
And holding God's sealed message to Himself
Vised in your hand,
The past so far,
The future swerving near,—
Then crags of chaos
Light with rearing love:
And I
To deaf, uncarrying space cry out
To close
This cleft of seeing.

> This angel
> Darting suddenly through heaven
> His wings on fire with death—
> Creating outraged,
> Inadmissible vacuum,
> —Lesion in breast of God
> Spurting arterial light
> Of pitying love;—
> With cry of God
> Clapped helpless at his heels.[7]

Once again, the reality of death was invading her pristine world, and she cried out against it. Her poem is the cry of widow or widower. Life alone was frightening in a deeper sense than merely facing the world. The chaos of which she spoke was intellectual and emotional. Vassili's death created an "inadmissible vacuum." The soul, perfect world of man, again confronted by reality, rifts of sorrow, produced terror, her fear of forever.

But Susan Sawitzky would not commit suicide. That prospect was quashed when she shared it with Vassili. He apparently spoke strongly against it. She obeyed him, but the "gauntness of new perceiving" left her again longing for the release death would bring. The haunting aphorisms written after the death of her child reappeared in her notebooks. The ugliness and brutality of life once again left her "sterile minded" and helpless.

Vassili requested cremation, and in the spring of 1947, Susan, with Elizabeth waiting nearby, silently spread his ashes near a favorite pond where they had watched blue herons wade. Elizabeth stayed with her sister for several months. Family loyalty required it.

Susan Sawitzky was still a young woman, not yet fifty years old, when Vassili died, but she lived for only one reason after his death. She had promised she would. Once again, William Sawitzky anticipated his wife's needs and sought to protect her as best he could. He left her with little financial support, but he was more concerned with her will to live. As in 1930, his work, "their work," provided him the means of giving her the will to continue. As early as 1939, he had proposed to the Carnegie Corporation a series of monographs on the major eighteenth-century American painters. The project included works on Matthew Pratt, Thomas McIlworth, Lawrence Kilburn, William Johnston and his associates Joseph Blackburn and J. S. Copley, Ralph Earl, and Reuben Moulthrop. A secondary plan called for volumes on John Watson, Abraham Delanoy, John Durand, Ralph G. W. Earl, and a revision of his edition of Lawrence Park's four-volume work on Gilbert Stuart. The project was approved in 1940, and the first volume, *Matthew Pratt: 1734–1805*, appeared in 1942. It was also the last monograph published. Thereafter, he and Susan collected information, photographed paintings, and made preliminary evaluations relating to all the subjects of the proposed volumes. At the time of Vassili's death, research was nearly completed on all the projected studies in the first set and on John Watson, Abraham Delanoy, and the Stuart volume in the second set.

It seems doubtful that William Sawitzky intended to finish the volumes. Instead, he collected the research, involved his wife in the work, emphasized the importance of the studies, and, finally, exacted from her a promise to complete it after his death. Sawitzky's motivation was not egotistic but based on an evaluation of his wife's temperament. Susan Sawitzky would live if for no other reason than to complete the work of her beloved husband, which he called "their work." She certainly contributed, but her main purpose was to complete the work as a memorial to him. She would endure pain, but she would not commit suicide.

People rallied to support Susan in the aftermath of Vassili's death. She was too stunned to make decisions, and her sister and friends essentially took over. Elizabeth and a distant relative who practiced law in the area handled the legal affairs. Elizabeth urged Susan to leave the little cottage in Stamford that held so many memories. When Susan balked, Augusta Williams, her landlord, insisted. She told Susan she planned to sell the house. Elizabeth Blanford claimed that Williams's decision was not a financial one but an act of concern for Susan. Susan moved to New Haven, Connecticut. She and Vassili had worked regularly at the Yale University library and she could continue to work on "their" projects there. Conveniently, a friend in New Haven planned to visit Europe and needed someone to occupy her apartment. There were also other friends in the area who would watch after her.

One friend in particular stood by Susan through those difficult years. At the end of the summer, Emily Whitney, a gentlewoman nearly eighty years of age, invited Susan to live in her home. Whitney was typical of Susan's friends after Vassili's death. From a distinguished New England family that counted among its members the inventor of the cotton gin, she exhibited that gentility and refinement typical of elderly women in Susan's mother's and grandmother's circles years earlier. Whitney spoke knowledgeably on a variety of subjects within Susan's areas of interest. They were kindred souls with different strengths. Susan was bright, spontaneous, a gifted conversationalist. Whitney too had those attributes but was a practical woman who furnished the day-to-day support Susan required. She took Susan into her home, encouraging her and subtly providing a guiding hand. She introduced Susan to a circle of elderly ladies who quickly became her closest friends. They frequently dined in New Haven's better restaurants or planned dinner parties to be enjoyed at Whitney's home. The women, all older than Susan, enjoyed her spirited conversation and perhaps also the feeling that Susan needed them in a time of grief most of them had already experienced.

Emily Whitney looked after Susan almost as Vassili had. They searched for an apartment so Susan would have her own place although she remained in Whitney's home most of the time. Whitney would go out of town for brief visits, then longer ones. When she returned, however, she invited Susan to stay with her. She fussed about Susan's eating habits or insisted on picking out a new dress or a hat for her and paying for it. That circle of women provided a source of support central to the experiences of many women yet one Susan had not enjoyed since her school days.

Her time with Emily Whitney and their friends was generally reserved for evenings. Weekdays were spent fulfilling her promise to Vassili. She worked constantly on his research, sometimes from dawn to dusk, becoming, in her own words, "almost a recluse." Frequently, only Whitney's insistence pulled her away. The work became in her mind a monument to Vassili's genius that she must complete. It was her purpose in life to finish it; when the promise was fulfilled, she would be free, she implied, to join him in death.[8]

As she studied Vassili's notes, the doubts that had plagued her own work arose again. She questioned her ability to remain true to his goals, to be "the instrument for carrying out his ideas, opinions and directions."[9] Consequently, she went back to the paintings to evaluate them again, rechecked probate records, and even searched New England cemeteries for gravestones, becoming as hesitant as she was about her poetry. It was a slow, tedious business, but she would do it no other way.[10]

The New-York Historical Society, convinced of the importance of Sawitzky's research, agreed to continue paying Susan a monthly salary while she completed the project. Charles E. Baker served as liaison for the society. Like the circle of women, Baker provided much needed support for Susan. He assured her that she could do the work, prodding her toward its completion. In a steady stream of letters he told her that she was the only one who could maintain the integrity of Vassili's opinions. He helped her find new material and scheduled appointments for her to see paintings held privately. His letters had a paternalistic tone. He asked about her health, her research, even her relatives. Susan's state of mind was fragile, and her relations with landlords and neighbors suffered. Baker tried to be supportive. Occasionally, he joked with her in a light vein, as Vassili might have done. On February 15, 1950, he wrote, "How is Reuben [Moulthrop] behaving himself these days? I think his mama has been spoiling him." A year later he wrote, "I hope all goes well with you and that both Watson and Earl are being well mannered untroublesome guests in your home."[11]

Aware of Susan's loneliness and deep despondency, Baker tried to encourage her in any way possible. But he could not protect her from the inevitable. As expenses mounted and little evidence of production was presented, the society felt it necessary to act. R. W. G. Vail, the director of the society, wrote letters questioning one of Vassili's conclusions, undoubtedly the quickest means to gain Susan's animosity.[12] He also queried her regarding her expenses. The society stopped paying her salary in 1949 but continued to pay for her travel and her supplies. Still, by 1954, a single article was all that Susan had published. Moreover, throughout the early 1950s she refused to meet any deadlines established by the society.

In February 1955, Susan made a lengthy proposal to the society, requesting to be placed on its payroll again. Susan first explained the difficulties under which she had been working. She had tried to do too much too soon, compounding the grief she suffered. She had also labored under extreme financial hardship and itemized her income to prove the point. She recounted the litany of problems in finding suitable apartments and the difficulties and disagreements with landlords and neighbors. Despite the problems, she now felt "new life" in her work.

Susan must have realized the society would not accept her proposal without a strong argument. She asked to be paid a salary of $100 per month for six years. In return, she provided a schedule for completing the work on five subjects. If the subjects were completed early, she would add additional projects to finish the six-year agreement. Additionally, she proposed that the society buy from her some of the remaining Clay heritage. In an appendix she listed two oil paintings, a miniature, and an inscribed silver tray, their estimated value of $3,800 and her asking price from the society of $2,000. The money would be spent on Vassili's project, and in return she would will to the society the research notes accumulated by Vassili and herself.[13]

Apparently, the value of the materials Susan promised was sufficient to convince R. W. G. Vail to overlook the difficulties he had experienced with Susan: the society agreed to place her on salary again. The decision was certainly not based on her productivity, although that did increase after the arrangements were made. In 1955, the society published "Portraits by Reuben Moulthrop: A Checklist of William Sawitzky."[14] A year later, Susan published another piece on Moulthrop, "New Light on the Early Work of Reuben Moulthrop," in *Art in America*.[15] In 1957, she published again in the *New-York Historical Society Quarterly* on Abraham Delanoy.[16]

The increased productivity did not end her troubles with the society, however. She still moved too slowly and sought too frequently to use the *Quarterly*'s pages to eulogize her husband. The society constantly negotiated with her through Charles Baker to remove personal references.[17] The old questions about expenses and slowness also arose again. The society eventually realized that Susan was incapable of completing the project; a decade's work had resulted in five articles.

Susan, too, was disappointed and upset over her scholarly production. Her letters to her sister show that her sense of obligation was all that kept her going. In July 1948, she wrote, "It is only when fatigue finally brings me to myself that loneliness hits me like a blow across the face. . . . It is my zero hour." In the same letter she said, "If it were not for my beloved Vassili and the work he asked me to do I don't think I could go on, but I will see it through for his sake."[18] She complained repeatedly about the interruptions and the petty illnesses that plagued her. She wrote to Elizabeth:

> I feel so ashamed that I haven't written to you . . . but my powers of accomplishment seem so low that if I can creep ahead with a few pages a day on Moulthrop I am thankful. Nothing seems to cure the low vitality, discouragement and despondence that I have gone through for three years, and the realization that I get nowhere fills me with anguish and shame that I have let Vassili down this way.[19]

Susan stopped her work completely in 1949 to visit Elizabeth, avoiding "a severe nervous breakdown . . . until I could gain sufficient mastery over my shaken condition."[20] Things were no better when she returned. Her "anguish and shame" made her defensive and suspicious. Disagreements with landlords and other tenants interrupted her work repeatedly. She also suspected that other scholars were trying to steal Vassili's work. By 1957, the society, again through Baker, encouraged her to cooperate with other scholars. Baker reminded her that the society could not block the efforts of others to publish material on "Vassili's" topics. When a young scholar, L. B. Goodrich, contacted the society about his research on Ralph Earl and a projected trip to England, Baker saw it as an excellent opportunity to help Susan.[21] She saw the matter quite differently: "Mr. Baker of the New-York Historical Society sent me your letter requesting the information gathered by my husband on Ralph Earl's paintings in England. I think, if you will give the matter consideration, you will realize that no one interested in the publication of William Sawitzky's work could possibly be willing to give his material to someone else."[22] Such cryptic remarks and strained relationships were the rule rather than the exception after Vassili's death. She fought the deep sense of loss and meaninglessness that plagued her and could not control the sharp responses her discomfort caused. Emily Whitney and Charles E. Baker fought the symptoms rather than the cause. The problem was not landlords, unfeeling neighbors, or greedy young scholars. Rather, the undisciplined Susan Clay, shrill, frightened, and depressed, returned after the death of Vassili. She lashed out at everyone from a grief that she disguised but could not conquer.

Unfortunately, her last trip to Kentucky occurred in this difficult time in her life. In the summer of 1951 she needed money to use for her research and focused on the family heirlooms as a source of funds. She first attempted to sell them to the Ashland collection, but the Clay Foundation did not have the money to buy them. She interpreted its refusal as the old "hostility of Lexington" against her family. Old friends, she noted, went out of their way to be nice to her, but she implied that there were sinister designs behind the scenes to hurt the Clays once again. Nothing had changed, she complained; Lexington's citizenry still found petty things to criticize and gossiped maliciously: "They were all charming and gracious, but there was the old incessant, damaging gossip, and a sort of thoughtless cruel criticism that made me feel I would never, under any circumstances, return there to live."[23] Though her charges had some justification, Susan carried the defensiveness of several generations in her mind.

Back in the East, she had disagreements with a group of "young professional women" in an apartment where she lived. She shared with them a common bath, and their untidiness made life miserable for her. In turn, they mocked her southern, aristocratic manner. She moved to another apartment, but her life without Vassili remained tension-filled. When a group of workmen began tarring the roof of a neighboring building, she became angry, fearing the pigeons she had befriended would become stuck in the tar. She chastised the workmen in language uncharacteristic of the stereotypical southern lady. In her anger she even called a Christian Science practitioner in Louisville to complain and ask for support. The animals, the birds, nature was all she had left to love.[24]

Even Elizabeth was not immune from attack. Metzie Clay married William Blanford, a fellow Kentuckian, in 1948. Tall and massively built, a gifted pianist with large hands and a winning smile, he was an excellent conversationalist, inquisitive by nature, and well-read. Susan liked Bill Blanford; she was pleased that her sister had found a man of her own choosing instead of the military types she had been thrown with by the family. Nevertheless, Susan bristled at differences from her opinion or even at questions meant to allow her to enlarge upon her opinions, a particular strength of Blanford. In 1953, the Blanfords moved to New England after two and a half years in California. Susan went to visit them, and disagreements followed. After returning home, her first letter to her "dear sister Metzie" opened with the type of apology formerly associated with family visits.

> I did have a lovely time with you and Bill and am sorry that Bill's and my faulty dispositions and immature lack of self-control should have put blots on our being together. I suggest that Bill and I form an organization called "nerve addicts anonymous," and each try to keep his or her shirt on until September when we will meet again, changed and charming individuals.[25]

The letter has both a frustrating and a sad quality. Susan Sawitzky had a "faulty disposition" and an "immature lack of self-control." On numerous occasions she became angry with her brother-in-law if she called to talk to her sister and Metzie had gone out.[26] On another occasion, Susan became angry at Elizabeth for not trying a diet she had recommended and saw her sister's refusal as a test of her love: "You claim to be fond of me, so prove it by doing this one thing that means so much to me."[27] Yet she deeply loved her sister and brother-in-law and was instrumental in helping establish contacts for Blanford with the Beauport Museum in Gloucester, Massachusetts. Employed as curator in 1956, he would remain there until he retired in 1979. She also sent money when they needed help, just as they would send it to her.[28]

There were other signs of erratic and unusual behavior. In 1949, in defiance of the principles of Christian Science, Susan began attempting to reach Vassili literally "beyond the walls of death." A perfect target for frauds and con artists, she spent a large sum of money seeking help from spiritualists and might have spent considerably more had not one medium made the mistake of bringing William Sawitzky back as a Polish-speaking spirit. Susan immediately broke off the sessions.[29]

Still, she continued to believe that Vassili could be contacted, and she fervently studied spiritualism. She communicated regularly with Arthur Ford, a much published author on spiritualism, and talked at length with friends on the subject.[30] Given the philosophy of life and death evident in her poetry, her quest is not surprising. She had written when struggling with the finality of her husband's illness:

> I will find you
> Because there is no road
> Too intricate in distance
> In this world,
> And simple so to grasp your dear loved hand
> Through the thin folds of death.

and

> As in rushing foam locks into foam
> Like white fingers joined beneath water,
> So shall I reach and find you
> In the hollow behind death.[31]

Death was, after all, merely a transition. Consequently, for nearly ten years, Susan sought to contact Vassili through an ouija board. Historians tend to dismiss such action as the product of a deranged mind. To do so, however, at least in this case, is to disregard significant information. Susan copied in a hurried, frequently illegible hand her questions and Sawitzky's alleged responses in approximately two hundred pages of notes.[32] Those notes reveal Susan's extremely fragile mental state in the aftermath of her husband's death, but they also contain a record of the issues that dominated her thinking in that period of her worst grief.

The accounts inevitably began, were frequently interrupted by, and ended with almost mournful statements of love and longing for Vassili. She also expressed her desire for death by her own hand and her rejection of it because of his opposition. She asked how long she would have to wait before she joined him. The "Answers" told her it was not her time to die with her work yet unfinished. Indicative of Susan's psychological needs, in these "conversations" Vassili urged her to seek

solace through Christian Science. She wrote that he pointed out specific passages from *Science and Health*. For example, in September
1951, she was deeply despondent and threatening suicide. Her notes
indicate that Vassili encouraged her to read a section defining life in
Science and Health: "Life is divine Principle, Mind, Soul, Spirit. Life
is without beginning and without end. Eternity, not time, express the
thought of Life, and time is no part of eternity."[33] But Sawitzky had
never studied Christian Science.

Though the ouija board may be a strange medium, it is not uncommon for elderly people who have spent many years with a spouse to
feel the need to talk with him or her. Susan discussed personal problems with her husband, told him about the seasons, recalled shared
experiences, and mentioned her animal friends. Another important issue began to appear. Susan believed Vassili suggested as early as 1951
that their papers should eventually be left to the New-York Historical
Society. Certainly Charles Baker was not aware of it, but the ouija
board eased his task of acquiring the papers. Finally, Susan told Vassili
that she did not think that she could complete his work and should let
others share in his research. Her notes indicate his agreement.[34]

It would be easy to dismiss Susan's ouija board notes as the work of
a tortured mind, but that is exactly why they are valuable. Susan Clay
Sawitzky was a lonely, tortured woman in those years. The topics she
broached were of deep concern to her.[35] And over time, the evolution
of those "conversations" is a statement about the strength of the human will. Somewhere in her mind, through reason or without it, Susan Clay Sawitzky realized that she had to stop working on her husband's
projects. Her upbringing—the training to play the role of the dutiful
wife—and her love, by her definition as lasting and as beautiful as its
literary counterparts, required her to believe Vassili wanted her to stop
working in his field and begin again on her own work. She seemed
incapable of making a decision without his approval. Vassili was dead,
but she was still a prisoner in a man's house. She had accepted his
protection so completely that she lost the freedom to make her own
decisions.

CHAPTER FOURTEEN

❦

Circle Complete

> Height, breadth, depth
> These three
> Box us to place . . . .
> Dimension of idea
> That knows no where
> —"Of Magnitude," *The Circling Thread*

FOR FIFTEEN YEARS AFTER Vassili's death, Susan suppressed her own creativity to complete his work. Little of her was evident in those projects. Her letters indicate a slavish loyalty to his thoughts and interpretations. In 1962, that changed. There was no slow evolution, no long periods of meek acceptance as had characterized her in adolescence.

Susan mentioned her poetry in a casual conversation with Ann Cesare. The two women, both widows, renewed their friendship in the fall of 1961. While visiting in Stamford, Susan asked Ann to lunch, and the two women began to correspond, talk on the telephone, and visit occasionally. Ann Cesare asked to read some of Susan's poems. Her enthusiasm was, Susan wrote to Hortense King, the "only spark I needed for a conflagration, for since showing it to her I have been seized with a desire to write more."[1]

King's response indicates both the hold of traditional values and the need for self-expression. It is also apparent from the letter that the problem was not Susan's alone.

I certainly bless Mrs. Ann Cesare for persuading you to take out your poetry, to read it again, and to lose yourself in writing (and re-writing) those two beautiful, condensed and marvelously original poems—I was never more delighted than to read how this—your own personal preoccupation re-asserted itself—and I will confide in you that I do not think it was only Mrs. Cesare, but William, somehow, somewhere who persuaded you to return to your own gift—It does not mean you will give up his work—but maybe you will feel more alert and able to do the tasks you have been occupied with for 15 years, if you give time to what can only be called inspiration of your own. I think the feeling of creating fires the whole mind, "flushes new blood through capillaries long deceased"—(a new one by H. F.) and that this will result in renewed mental life that will be reflected in your work and his too.—

So, do not reproach yourself—there has never been anybody so faithful and careful as you. But make full use of this spurt of joyous excitement, and don't think it is "the thing you greatly feared come upon you"—feed it, keep on working at his and your tasks together.[2]

In 1962 the men in Susan's life were dead, yet their memory confined her. For fifteen years, she had struggled to complete her husband's work, fighting the desire to turn to her own inspiration, her poetry, and trying to convince herself that his work had become hers. When it went slowly, she felt guilt and shame, often to such a degree that she became ill. King was also a widow. She voiced a woman's traditional sense of responsibility to her husband's work but also the human need to pursue one's own gift.

The new excitement was not without the ever-present sense of guilt. Susan admitted that she had not looked at her poetry "for fear it would interrupt the very difficult work I have long been struggling to do for Vassili." King's letters sought to allay such fears, but her concern was unnecessary. Susan wrote that she was neglecting work she ought to be doing, but "I vow each day I will not look at my poems, then I spend the day writing them." She declared with characteristic enthusiasm that she was experiencing "one of the happiest times in my whole life."[3]

Susan's life was, at least temporarily, reborn. She did not stop working on Vassili's projects. In fact, as King suggested, her own "inspiration" seemed to stimulate her efforts. She began to pull together the Ralph Earl manuscript and made sufficient progress that in 1963 she was awarded a grant from the Ford Foundation.[4] For a time she was able to work as much as six hours a day on Vassili's material. But she also read again and wrote on topics of her own choosing. It was her third and final period of creative expression.

Hortense King quickly assumed as important a role in Susan's life as Ann Cesare. Susan and King began to read the same works and then write to each other about them. Ironically, those letters and a few that critique King's collection of poems, *Half a Star,* contain Susan Sawitzky's most direct statements about the nature of poetry. She was most concerned with subject and accuracy of treatment. Occasionally, accuracy meant agreement with her own ideas, and unlike Hortense King, Susan expressed her criticisms bluntly. For example, she expressed displeasure when King compared the scrapings of a particular summer insect with machinery. Susan said she loved the little insects but hated machinery so that the comparison hurt her deeply. Another poem, she said, was charming but not large in thought. She revealed her own definition of poetry when she declared, "There is always in your work the longer, deeper meaning beautifully revealed in immediate subject." Susan paid particular attention to wording and the rhythm of language. She praised one poem for the choice of words and for the beautiful pictures it created. "They [the poems] take hold of life and its mysteries in a very original, tragic and beautiful way and your use of words and images is unusual and arresting."[5]

Susan raised some critical questions about her own poems. Her old work, she complained, depended too much on imagery and lacked a larger meaning. Her new work seemed little different except that the emphasis was on cosmic imagery rather than earthly metaphor. She also stressed composition. She chastised King for having weak endings to several poems. Then Susan attempted to soften the criticism by saying poor endings were perhaps her greatest fault as well.[6]

The letters between King and Susan also show her preferences in literature and her evaluation of it. Susan, probably at the insistence of Ann Cesare, rediscovered reading in the 1960s. In the evenings, fortified by a martini, she read for several hours before retiring. It was an exhilarating experience for her. "What a delight it is, and one you can have all alone, to wander through the certainties of literature, one road or pathway leading to another, and curiosity endlessly aroused."[7]

But she did not have to read alone. Her two friends read with her, and then they shared their ideas in long letters or over the telephone.

Only Susan's letters to Hortense King have been preserved. Susan wrote letters as she had years earlier to her mother, ten to twenty pages of free discussion. Her assessment of poetry, drama, and essay reveals a mind still active and alert despite eccentricities that increasingly characterized most of her relationships. She gained a new appreciation of Dickinson and read Shakespeare and English history again. When she read a translation of Ovid's *Metamorphoses* she itemized characteristics that Shakespeare could "have noticed and absorbed"— close observation of nature and character, the unusual choice of words, vivid narration, beauty, humor, and a sort of homeliness. She was not the first to see such influences, but she very well may have found them independently.[8]

She read Ben Jonson again. His works, she thought, were "metrical exercises in Elizabethan 'wit,'—not poetry." Jonson was too flattering of the king and his patrons, insulting to those who disliked or disagreed with him, and too egotistical. She did find merit in his descriptions; though "disgusting," they were interesting. She read Boris Pasternak, but his descriptions brought back painful memories of Vassili, and Yevgeny Yevtushenko's *A Precious Autobiography*, which did not impress her. His was a bandwagon role, she said. It was not his views as much as the prostitution of the genre to which she objected. She admitted that he was in tune with the world, "with its self-celebration of ideologies," but she did not believe he was a poet.[9] Ironically, Susan now read more critically than at any other time in her life. The romantic self-delusion of her formal education had lost some of its hold on her.

At King's suggestion, Susan read Mary Chesnut's diary of life in the South. She had expressed many of the same criticisms for years. She thought the region's people were guilty of hypocrisy. She agreed with Chesnut's charge that the South put too much emphasis on personal or physical beauty. She recalled it as a "cruel point of view," and unpleasant memories of her youth caused her pain.[10] Reading Mary Chesnut perhaps produced pain for other reasons as well. Chesnut wrote movingly about her inability to have a child and the shame others placed on her because of it. Susan had known the pain; she certainly could understand compromises Mary Chesnut made because they were not unlike her own despite the century that separated them.[11]

Susan listed her favorite poets as Shakespeare, Chaucer, Villon, Dickinson, Whitman, Hopkins, Blake, Rimbaud, and Rilke. Above all, she wrote, she preferred the "poets of the Bible as the King James version translates them."[12] Again, the circle is complete. Tradition pulled her back. With the exception of Dickinson and Hopkins, she had read the same poets in her youth. Her best poems near the end of her life are replete with biblical themes. The madness of modern man is seen as "seed of Eden's fruit," but there is also a new political bent because concern over possible nuclear holocaust led her to new considerations of freedom and knowledge.[13] Susan Sawitzky wrote and revised. She put together a kaleidoscopic survey of her work, which included the short love poems "Secret" and "Message." "Lullaby," "The Least," and "The Flight" recalled the loss of her child, "To Charley," that of a brother and friend, and "Revelation," her beloved Vassili. Poems such as "Fear of Forever," "Threshold," "Spring Melting," "Gift," and "Winter Dusk" symbolized her evolution from grief over the death of her child to balance and survival. "The Shifting Void" and "Equivocal Answer," twenty years in the making, were included in their final form. New poems completed the poetic journey as well as the circle. "Strange Universe" was a new poem encompassing man's history from the Garden of Eden to eternity. It was a circle in itself from the destruction of man as ideal, the expulsion from the garden, to "New joke / Of ancient fiend," man's destruction in a nuclear Armageddon. Its scope and length reflect the optimism and joy she experienced in the early 1960s.

In this late burst of energy and optimism, Susan seemed very close to achieving, intellectually at least, the freedom she had craved so long. Heaven's realm was not only that of "the poets of the Bible" but of stars, planets, and everything else that had symbolized freedom for her in earlier days. Her poems were longer now. "Equivocal Answer" was four stanzas, "The Shifting Void" nearly four pages, and "Strange Universe" six pages. The lines were short, every word layered in meaning. Hortense King warned her that she occasionally lost her reader but encouraged her to write more and to seek publication of her new and "best" poems.

The themes never changed. A new poem, "Nebulae," written in 1962, was "Leonids" again but more sophisticated and its author more active, less a helpless victim of fate. Instead of watching as her baby passed in flight with other children, she could now write:

> I lose not
> In your flight centrifugal
> Through heights of death;
> But trap you fast
> In circling love,
> Fleeter than light
> And placid rush of stars.[14]

She wrote of love again in "Visions," taking a cool, analytical approach that stressed that the knowledge of love brought intimacy, both physical and intellectual.[15] The universe and the relationship of God and man in it were constant topics of her new poems. "Lucifer" treats the fallen angel which, like humankind, is guilty of rebellion against God. Humans are twisted, contorted, but God, dealing with humans, is also less than omnipotent. He is "debased / In effigy of man" and after centuries "no wiser" to the inconsistencies of those he created.[16]

In a new poem titled "Escape," Susan treated a familiar theme but with a new maturity of thought, and the circling thread completes its path and begins again.

> This sentient, wincing, yearning
> Bit of dust
> Pinched up from death—
> Organized, bound
> Identified,
> Legged, winged or strung,
> Given a membrane
> To adjust the wind;
> Set going a moment,
> Crawling, stepping forth,
> Obliquely whirling
> To grass:

This knot of self
Hoarding its meek
Arrangement of illusion
Fleeing disbandment,
Hiding its small cache
Of immortality
In slit of leaf or mud
Or risen flesh,
Or in the pocket
Of the walking wind;
Stitching identity
To further loop:
Is small
Belittling greater
By a sameness.

Strange God
Who nails corruption to eternity
With mystic feel of quickening
In decay,
Reversing Crucifixion:
Know in compassion
Dream concerns itself,
Seeking defense
Against unbearable spirit;
Pity your thoughts belied
In blameless evil
Running to death
For cover,
Wrapping in decency
Or dissolution
—Diaper of leaves or womb—
The crumbling me
Against exposure of infinity.[17]

Susan's quest for both confinement and freedom is apparent in "Escape." Or perhaps one should say both Susans are here. The poem's

title contradicts its contents in part. Man's position is defensive. He is crawling, then stepping forth. He whirls not to an implied escape but to grass, back to the confinement of "poppy stems" and "the tall knees of the mountains" she wrote about as a young woman. He hoards illusion, hides his cache. In an interesting combination of ideas, human immortality and human freedom must be secreted away in some close, confined place.

A second circle is apparent in "Escape." Man is again locked in contest with forces of life—God, earth, death. Man, however, seems far smaller and less significant than the "brute divine" of "The Shifting Void." Man hoards even his illusions of importance and clings to his "small cache / Of immortality." Creation, search for identity, lost innocence, escape through death to begin again—there forms the philosophical circle, birth to death and life a mere thread circling between the two. In "Escape" Susan contemplates a "Strange God." The last stanza confronts her own mortality and, because Susan finds life in death, God reverses Crucifixion.

In "The Shifting Void" most of the characteristics of her later poetry are readily apparent (see appendix). "The Shifting Void" describes creation, expulsion from the Garden of Eden, and human response to God's punishment. The mood of the poem and the rhythm of language, even when dealing with secular themes, bring to mind her "poets of the Bible as the King James version translates them." Yet one cannot assume blind submission to traditional Christianity. It is a modern theme of the earth's creation that she describes. "Some think that earth was made / From spurting of the sun's side, / Wrenched by the passing / Of a mightier star." In her description of the world thus made, she suggests an evolutionary process. Hills erupt from the molten core, cool, grow old, and crumble to fill the valleys. The moisture of oceans becomes heaven and then ocean again. "Life seethes, expands." In anticipation of a later poem, she suggests that all is continuum; nothing is lost, merely changed. More important perhaps, she describes earth in feminine terms. The sun was earth's womb, creation a "giant birth." Indeed, creation itself is an incident in maternity, and the child, earth, is described as an organism with "molten blood / [that] Wells up in breast of stone: / Slow heaving, / Shifting weight of self / On rigid heart."

In the third stanza, she turns to man and his disgrace in the Garden of Eden. Adam was disgraced because he had been lured by the "rotting fruit of knowledge." The perfect universe, "Patterned on plane of heaven," was left in shambles by man and his penchant for thought. There is, however, a surprise at the poem's end. God, it seems, could get the upper hand with Susan Sawitzky, but he could not keep it for long. Expelled from Paradise, Adam and Eve, the latter mentioned for the first time, found some solace in the "pure, exclusive love" they discovered. Moreover, there was balance in the power of man and God. Just as earth evolves out of man-shattered, God-created Paradise, man and woman found a new world, less than Paradise but more than they, and maybe God, expected.[18]

While one part of Susan Sawitzky struggled to understand God, the universe, and the totality of existence and to place humanity in the context of it all, the other side of her found instant gratification in the relationship of simple animals to that same God. The creatures of earth, sky, and sea become angels under God's special protection. In "Beloved Beast-Children," a joyous God created, loved, and fed "the simple ones." They were contented in the lap of God, and the implication is again that happiness results from unquestioning acceptance, from the innocence of the simple field hand, the unthinking one, or Susan in her youth.[19] In another poem of the 1960s, "Decadent," she wrote of "a tired brain's combative anguish."[20] Susan was torn by the two images she had of herself. The daughter of the nineteenth century was tired of questioning, tired of a world where those she cared most about were no more, tired of a world that seemed to be a shattered Paradise. A more modern woman used modern ideas to answer ageless questions.

It is ironic perhaps that Susan Clay, the poet, the "alien-seed" in the family of politicians, made a political statement in two of the last poems she wrote. In "Decadent" she could be talking about her own family, the Clays; she most certainly is talking about the human family.

> You, carrying in your veins
> A family death,
> —Race death—
> Taxed with some earlier over-potency,
> Look, as through shadow, at our confident glow,

Aware of thronged and dusky margins
That ring mortality.

Matter to you
No stuff to take between the hands,
But to scan sharply
Doubt and deny;
A world persistent, thin,
With tensile toughness
Giving before a tired brain's combative anguish.

In you there are caverns
That suck the flesh,
There are dark and restful vacuums
That kiss the flesh,—
Like a field where graves are.

You are grey, brown, black,
Accordant,—
There is no hard-packed health in you
Who need and nurture sorrow:
Who, poking in the wastage of the world,
May lift the corners of annihilation
To find new-naked, primal patch of life.[21]

Susan's relationship with her family was similar to those of many women of her era. She had been trained from youth to respect the family and to exhibit loyalty to it; the name and the family were always a part of her. She began late in life to trace her family's history. Several boxes of genealogical materials relating to both the Clays and the Peppers are included in her papers. She could not resist, however, a certain excitement at the hint of weakness or scandal even if it was a fleeting notion. For example, in 1968, she remarked in a letter to her sister that Bob Clay had always planned to write a book about family members revealing "all their idiosyncrasies." She looked forward to it "even though I will be one of the victims."[22] A more revealing incident arose from her genealogical research. She traced the Peppers back to the Culpeppers of Virginia, a family that claimed prominent members. But she was more delighted by an illegitimacy that she erroneously believed linked the family to the Indian woman Pocahontas. Even when she discovered that the link was in an associated line rather than her own, she wrote to tell her sister how delighted she would be to discover such an occurrence in the family.

Susan made several references to impurities in the family during this period of her life. She was intrigued by them. The Clays knew southern history too well not to have some questions about their own ancestors. Yet she remained uncomfortable with her thoughts. The words "You, carrying in your veins / A family death, / —Race death—" may have resulted from her fears. The death of her nephew Robert Clay Jr. may be a more important link between the poem and her family. He died while scuba diving in 1973. He was the last hope that the Clay name would be carried on by those directly descended from Henry Clay. There were many descendants of the great statesman, but with the exception of her brother, no males remained. Susan might scoff at her family at times, but she was a Clay; the end of the family line was a serious matter.

The poem refers to the family of man as well. She was concerned about nuclear weapons and their impact, and the "corners of annihilation" and the "wastage of a world" were probably her first statements on that subject.

The last of her poems was entitled "Strange Universe." Covering six typed pages, it was her most ambitious poem and perhaps her best.

> Shuffle the centuries,
> Blink the eyes,
> In glance from birth to death;

"Glance from birth to death" it does, and one dares not blink on this tremendous ride from Joshua before Jericho to new prophets, astronauts, riding giant arrows in pursuit of the moon. Television, pollution, and nuclear destruction are merely a few of the themes she treats in terse, pregnant terminology. Yet as with death, horror is handled in striking language and images. The mushroom cloud is replaced as a symbol of atomic explosion with images of a huge and hideous tree spreading out over the world. The tree grew "From ultimate seed / of Eden fruit." Later, she referred to the concept of nuclear weapons as "New joke / Of ancient fiend." Both statements imply a connection between nuclear destruction and man's sinful search for knowledge. Both events lead to pain and destruction. Near the end of the stanza, she compares the two events again. Adam and Eve's sin in the Garden resulted in punishment of their children and all later generations of children. Nuclear explosion, in a similar manner, released "Invisible pollen, / Gened with monstrous birth, / In blight of man unborn." Unborn generations are equally affected by man's rash use of faulty knowledge.

There is a hint of conclusion in "Strange Universe." Susan Clay Sawitzky incorporates into it most of the grand themes apparent in her poetry. Though human thought is less than perfect, she does not respect "horde driven" minds either. Like many of her later poems, this one includes the realization of the need for balance in all things. Earth still confines and the skies liberate; birth and death are connected. Her beloved beast children are included, "Pinned out in stars / On zodiac path." Even in universal themes, Susan charts her own earthly orbit. She returns to the land of her origins and in a pleasant way domesticates the universe in images of a Kentucky horse farm. Short, poignant lines follow one upon the other, full of contrast, powerful in their brevity, with not a wasted word anywhere, merely novelty in condensations. All is continuum; all curves back upon itself.[23] It is fitting that "Strange Universe" was the last of her writings. At least in an intellectual sense, she had finally escaped the men's houses in which she had lived. She roamed the universe free and unfettered.

CHAPTER FIFTEEN

❦

Give Me Death

One must be very quiet to waken into death;
So quiet that the heart stops still to listen,
And no stirred leaf of thought makes the spirit tremble.
—"Threshhold," SCS Papers

"STRANGE UNIVERSE" WAS THE product of Susan's last burst of energy. In it she achieved a measure of the intellectual freedom she had sought for so many years. Even as she wrote, however, the real world and her own fears were encroaching on that special world she had created. She again collected poems, prepared manuscripts, and typed copies of individual poems to be sent to publishers. None, however, was published. According to Elizabeth Clay Blanford, editors were willing to publish if certain revisions were made. What those revisions were is no longer known. Apparently, Susan threw the letters away in disgust.[1]

Susan Clay Sawitzky was always particular about her poems. She wrote to Hortense King on May 17, 1962, "I don't know what to do about my stuff. I have suffered so from the 'art world,' my heart sinks at the thought of trying the 'world of poetry.'" Fearful that King might secretly submit poems sent only to be criticized, she wrote, "Please never, under any conditions, lend or send away anything of mine." The very thought led her to look back through her own poems and destroy "much of the old work." She promised to submit her work but "not just yet, as I am continually rewriting."[2]

The problem continued to occupy her mind. In 1964, again to Hortense King, she expressed the duplicity of her feelings—fearing publication yet wanting to publish. In March she threatened never to publish. In August she expressed the opposite view.

> I feel I must do something about mine [poems] before long, if anything is ever to be done, for I can't leave them to my family who are indifferent to them or even hostile—my sister positively dislikes them, and my brother and nieces are busy with their own concerns. I have only two friends in the world, you and Ann [Cesare], and I would never burden either of you with them. They have to be launched by me or die with me, and the world would lose nothing in either case. However, there is something about wanting your child to live, undistinguished as it may be.[3]

The poet was, despite the freedom of "Strange Universe," still a prisoner in her own house, not a man's house per se, but she could not accept the strain of rejection or criticism implicit in the process required for publication. Criticism was another attempt to imprison her. Suggestion of change was not an avenue of escape but a further effort at controlling or manipulating her thoughts as well as her actions.

By the mid-1960s, her confinement resulted also from a changing world. The nation was caught up in the civil rights movement. Her neighborhood in New Haven underwent a transformation common to older sections in many communities. Its population quickly became urban working class and then an ethnic mixture as African Americans and Hispanics moved into its apartments and homes.

Susan supported the civil rights movement in principle. Her memories of the faithful family servants in Kentucky made her sympathetic to the cause of African Americans. She was also inclined to be sympathetic because of the sense of noblesse oblige passed to her as it had been to each generation of Clays. Male members of the southern gentry had frequently been the "protectors" of the African American community. Her father had interceded many times on behalf of the faithful servants when their children had difficulties with the law or lower-class whites. She attributed those same characteristics to President John F. Kennedy.

> I lamented the death of Kennedy, because, though caught in all this tumult, he seemed to have some touch of the spiritual brotherhood of

man, a willingness to put himself in the place of less fortunate human beings, to see their needs *from their standpoint,* not his own, and to try to relieve them in spite of the inconvenience to the rich, and even to himself. He could see the 'terrible trampling of guinea pigs' in the lives of the helpless and poor.[4]

To live from 1897 through the 1960s and 1970s, however, required considerable flexibility. To adapt to the changes occurring in her community was more difficult. A series of robberies in her apartment building were, the police told her, the crimes of a group of young black men. Then, in November 1969, she came home just as a young man broke through her door with a crowbar. The police graphically described what could have happened to Susan. Several days later, a second attempt was made to enter her apartment. Her father and Vassili were gone. Emily Whitney and Charles Baker had tried to assume the protective role, but neither was in a position to care for her as her father and husband had done. Consequently, Susan began to retreat within herself and her apartment. Fears that had a strong basis in fact became a constant state of terror.[5] Susan considered moving from New Haven. She talked with Hortense King about moving to England and to Louisville. She asked Elizabeth to find her an apartment in Gloucester and spoke occasionally of moving to Mississippi, where her brother Bob lived.[6]

But she did not move. If such thoughts were any more than whims of a moment, Susan's eccentricities confined her options. In her New Haven apartment she hired a carpenter at her own expense to nail celotex panels to the walls to shut out the noise, to place bars on the windows, and to install a second door over the original with multiple locking systems. She demanded similar alterations when she talked to property owners about apartments.[7]

For a brief time, Elizabeth contemplated moving Susan into her home. She and her husband occupied a small cottage on the grounds of the Beauport Museum, but Elizabeth was moved by a strong sense of duty to her sister. Again, Susan's eccentricities proved insurmountable. Susan was often difficult to get along with, but in old age she had grown worse. She seemed particularly quick to quarrel with William Blanford. It was decided that Susan would stay in New Haven. Imprisoned for so long, she became a perpetrator of her own incarceration. Susan Clay Sawitzky spent the last years of her life behind locked doors and soundproofed walls. She read, busied herself with Vassili's papers, and talked on the telephone.[8] The deaths of Ann Cesare in 1966 and Hortense King in 1973 created even greater isolation. Throughout the 1960s, she repeatedly wrote that they were her only friends. Emily Whitney and her circle had all died.[9] Consequently, Susan slipped further into the "close confining angles" of her tiny apartment. She refused to meet relatives who lived or visited in the area and did not want them to come to her apartment. Elizabeth begged to come to New Haven, but Susan refused, insisting it was too dangerous. When Elizabeth threatened to come anyway Susan said she would not answer the door.[10]

Susan hired a young couple to handle business matters and to bring her food. They took her checks to the bank, mailed her letters, and brought books she requested. She left the apartment only when they escorted her to a doctor or dentist.[11] In her last years Susan Sawitzky was literally a prisoner in her own house and in her own mind. On July 11, 1981, she wakened softly into death, as one of her poems suggested, free at last from the confinement of earth and flesh.

Elizabeth rushed to New Haven to handle the arrangements. In the apartment, she found hundreds of books and the collection of papers, notes, letters, and photographs that tell the story of Susan's life. She also found boxes of poems organized into collections as if Susan meant to send them to publishers. Most were bound with small pink ribbons.

At first glance, those materials seem to contain the elements of a romantic novel. The origins of stereotypes become readily apparent, but there is also a clear picture of a woman who faced the twentieth century and its mixed signals to women. She wanted the opportunities it promised. Her Clay heritage cried out for achievement. That heritage also called her back. As a Clay she probably had greater opportunities than most women to overcome the obstacles. She did not.

Those neatly bound volumes of poetry are also misleading. A fabric woven from words and phrases she chose for their beauty masks a struggle experienced by southern women, American women, indeed, in some instances by humanity regardless of gender. How good is that poetry? Because of her limited publication, it has had little attention from literary critics. But she clearly had ability. "Lullaby," "Mariner," and "Winter Dusk" certainly stand on their own merit. "The Shifting Void," "Strange Universe," and "Equivocal Answer" have powerful lines and stanzas. A judgment of her work as poetry, however, must await evaluation by critics.

Her poetry is certainly valuable from a historical perspective. She thought of herself as a poet, and she had some success being published. Whatever the assessment of her work, it reflects the issues she confronted as a woman. The predominant theme, evident in poems written over a period of sixty years, is the tension prevalent in women's lives. Given the episodes of her public life, it is surprising that she could or would state so clearly and analytically her personal struggle and continue to develop that theme over so long a period. That consistency speaks to her will. She never stopped seeking answers. By writing, she continued to search for definition of self. It also speaks to her perceived potential. Though she should have sought publication more consistently, she did seek it as early as 1913 and as late as 1964.

The evolution of her poems contains the dynamic of a woman's struggle. Her early poems spoke of confinement in romantic images. The concept of freedom had not yet entered her consciousness. She saw with the eye of artist and poet and combined the somewhat contrived language of her traditional training with her modern theme. Pretty language and romantic expression were characteristic of her writing throughout her life. As in the work of many southern women writers, romance and reality blend inseparably in her work.[12] Her thought became more analytical as she matured, however. Soft, lighted fireflies spoke romantically to her theme, but family portraits, sternly posed, denoted purpose, morality, tradition, responsibility, and unforgiveness of transgression in forceful terms. One of her most powerful statements as a young woman was her indictment of the image society required of its females. Forced to think, dress, and act alike, southern women accepted a fleeting and shallow definition of beauty. Mary Chesnut had expressed the criticism a century earlier, but southern values changed very slowly. Susan cried out for the right of women to pursue their potential. Later poetry addressed issues forbidden to women who reached maturity in the years when Victorianism was a major influence. The sense of helplessness as a woman is apparent throughout her poetry, yet she questioned the strong, emotionless, omnipotent male image. She asked poetically if she was responsible for her miscarriage, and she refused to take personal blame. She defiantly expressed her joy in and the purity of the sexual act that had created her child. Moreover, her poetry consistently contained definitions and descriptions crafted in terms derived from her female experiences and outlook.

Her later poems emphasized the unity of humanity. Though the origins of her poetry are found in her personal struggle against the artificial restrictions placed on women, her thought carried it to obstacles confronted by humanity. Certainly, high on her pedestal, the southern lady was "withheld from freedom and beholding it," but her mariners and all who had felt the "tick of reason in a skull" knew both the freedom and confinement of thought as well as the limits of nature, earth, human frailty, and subservience to a Deity. The struggle between human confidence and the need for a superior being is not limited by gender. In searching for her own freedom, she sought to define the limitations that affect all humanity.[13]

Susan Clay Sawitzky was no philosopher, but she raised the philosophical questions of those who live, work, and survive, the issues that confront every person, stronger or weaker than she, throughout a lifetime. Like many of those human beings, she sought answers from within herself. Much of her poetry relates directly to thoughts born of crises, but as resolution came to her, she searched for the perfect world promised in youth. She sought through the power of mind to achieve freedom from confusion and a lack of control over her own affairs. She used the tools that presented themselves, borrowing liberally from Christian Science, Hinduism, and the romantic literature she had read in her youth. Her search led her to the dilemma of human experience. Thought frees man from the confines of body but confronts him with other limitations. Virtues carried to extremes are no longer virtuous. Human knowledge creates answers and more questions; it pursues truth, but it can be destructive as well. Birth assures death, and out of death comes new life. Each path seemed to circle back upon itself. Susan Clay Sawitzky captured the unwritten philosophy of survivors.

Humanity craves freedom and security but actually wants balance. In "The Shifting Void," she wrote about an "everlasting, restless search for balance" and a "craving" for the "substance of the filled," for peace, comfort, contentment. In her last poem, "Strange Universe," she recognized the dilemma with which she had struggled for nearly sixty years. She described human existence as

> Continuum curved
> To content
> Of Enigma.

The poet, the private Susan Clay Sawitzky, left a record of her will to be free, but it was not a published record. That, too, is explained at least in part by her upbringing and the problems of the woman poet. She wrote in isolation, sacrificing her poetic contacts for marriage and the traditional belief that a woman's responsibility was to help her husband in his career. She, however, did not receive the support from him that would have allowed her to seek publication aggressively. That support came only when Hortense King began to read her poetry. Publishers expressed interest in some of her poems, but Susan was not inclined to revise them. That part of her personality had been molded in her formative years by the adults around her. Her refusal to revise also stemmed in part from the personal nature of her poetry. There was too much of herself in her poems to accept change.

The directions of her own affairs also limited her ability to publish. Foolishly, she abandoned her contacts with publishers when she married, and after the miscarriage she was too busy seeking sanity, her attention drawn inward by the pain she experienced. In the 1930s and again in the 1940s, Sawitzky, apparently for the best of reasons, sought to involve her in his work, and the success implied by the Carnegie grant inspired her again to abandon efforts to publish her work in support of her husband. She deserves significant credit for "their" contribution in art history, but it has never been given to her. Her "best" years were spent like those of many women, aiding her husband's pursuit of success rather than her own.

Sawitzky was certainly dedicated to his own career, but his definition of "poetess" and "artist" also dictated his actions regarding his wife. In the 1930s, he sought to lift her spirits by creating something important for her. After 1947, his work would give her a reason to live as well as an income. He could have been more supportive at other times during their marriage. He had encouraged her to publish before their marriage, and she would have revised her work if he had suggested it. He never objected to her poetic efforts, but to publish would involve criticism, and that would have been detrimental to his efforts to protect the "beloved one." Susan's husband was as protective and paternalistic as her father; he merely had a different, perhaps even more disarming, approach. If the men in her life had been less protective, Susan certainly could have been more independent. Protectiveness begets the need for protection, gender notwithstanding.

Sixty years of writing, then, led to little published work. Susan must bear the responsibility to a large degree, but other factors make her weakness more understandable. Susan's "gift" was little more than a hobby to those around her and in some ways to her as well. It can also be seen as an escape—not to freedom, but from reality. In her study she fussed and fumed, then returned to her real world as lady and dutiful wife. Finally, she did not have the nonpoetic skills necessary to pursue publication relentlessly. The pursuit of a theme over sixty years indicates her internal strength, but it also suggests the powerful forces of her background and training. Those forces inclined her to rationalize, forsaking what was important to her.

If the private Susan Clay Sawitzky left a record of her will to be free, the public Susan Clay Sawitzky, the southern lady, left a record of confinement and compromise. Her life invites the criticisms born of stereotypes. Raised in relative luxury, the heir to a great heritage, pretty and talented, she could have moved easily from adolescence to the comfort and security of adulthood within the Bluegrass gentry. Perhaps she set her expectations too high, both in regard to her own potential and in defining the man she could marry. She was spoiled and pampered, wanted the best of both worlds, and exhibited characteristics that guaranteed failure in professional employment. She can be accused of choosing to remain on the pedestal in her husband's house rather than perform the mundane tasks that would have eased their financial burdens. She can be charged with not really wanting freedom, preferring to be the protected, refined lady of leisure. She wrote about freedom while accepting money from her parents and uncle.

She never took a realistic view of crisis, responding in a highly emotional, overly sensitive manner. She refused to come off the pedestal,
making feeble, timid efforts that had little chance of success.

Like the stereotypes of women, each statement is based in truth,
but a second Susan Clay Sawitzky can be posited. Margaret Ripley
Wolfe echoes many scholars when she notes that women were haunted
by the specter of the southern woman. Anne Goodwyn Jones makes
the theme more personal. At least some women, incapable of open
rebellion, created a public persona akin to the image of the southern
lady while maintaining an inner self. The dual persona, however, can
create serious difficulties for an individual. Typically, Jones argues,
southern women neither freed the beast within nor killed it in its cage.[14]
Such an interpretation seems appropriate to Susan Clay Sawitzky. Her
poetry is evidence of the "beast" within, but she continued to be haunted
by the southern lady.

The record of her life reveals the tenacity and the complexity of the
myths that limited women, the subtleties by which they were instilled,
and the cumulative effect they had even as Susan, like many women,
struggled against them. Susan Clay Sawitzky lived in the twentieth
century but had an education more fitting to the mid-nineteenth century or, more accurately perhaps, to fictional accounts of that era. That
education occurred at the hands of family members as much as in a
formal setting. Indeed, her life indicates the immense power of the
family to instill values and styles. The Clays were certainly not an average family. Their stories were grander and there were special reasons
why the family sought so forcefully to instill their values, but other
families teach loyalty, duty, an interpretation of history, and a distinct
set of values. Elizabeth Stone argues in *Black Sheep and Kissing Cousins: How Our Family Stories Shape Us* that, regardless of class, family
stories delineate the rules and define the family for its members.[15] Many
women of the early twentieth century, and perhaps later, learned their
places within the family as they grew up in it. Susan Clay Sawitzky was
certainly not the only helpmate to husband or loyal daughter. She was
not the only one to feel the pull of traditional values when she tried to
open new doors. Values instilled by example as well as overt lesson in
an age that moved far more slowly than the present lay dormant for
years until recalled by a situation or a crisis.

The Clays also provide an example of how the roles of the sexes in the family actually functioned, a critical factor in understanding the family.[16] A great-great-great-grandson of Henry Clay recently recalled to me seeing a photograph of old Grandmother Clay, sitting in her large wheeled chair, surrounded by family members. He noted that she looked quite "matriarchal." In subtle ways he learned, though generations removed, the power exercised by the matriarchal figure. A dignified but loving uncle, a family jokester, nurturing aunts, and queenly grandmothers provided the stereotypes in Susan's life, or the myths by which families define themselves.

Protective males abounded in the Clay family. The great patriarch, Henry, or Grandfather as he was known in the family, looked down on them all, regardless of gender. Uncle Tom, the gallant Charley, and Bob played manly roles. The most significant male figure for Susan, of course, was Colonel Charles Clay. His attempts to fulfill the requirements of a cult of true manhood had a painful effect on the male and female members of his family. Charles D. Clay was "old-fashioned" and demanding. He very likely would have shot William Sawitzky in 1927, but during the Depression he sent money to be shared by his daughter and her husband. Susan saw her father for what he was: the geode. He was no Mr. Barrett and certainly not a Cassius Marcellus Clay. Susan resented his unbending attitude, but she found it impossible to question his love for her.

Susan was continually plagued by the image of her brave, soldierly, gentlemanly father. Her marriage to a man seventeen years older than she, with a brave, scholarly, gentlemanly image, is not surprising. If either man had been a bona fide ogre, Susan might have broken the hold of dependency. She grew impatient at times, but she also craved the love and support of her father and husband. In emotionally traumatic times, there is a very thin line between sensitivity and a patronizing attitude. Most humans, male and female, want the former, objecting only when the line is crossed. Susan's poem "Petition to Jehovah II" shows how complex the issue can be. Susan Sawitzky, like most women, frequently grew frustrated with the males in her life, but she saw a positive side too, acquiesced to male protectiveness, and consequently lost the ability to exercise independence. The issue developed over a lifetime, but it began in the bosom of the family.

Susan's dependency throughout her life is obvious, but it is clearest in the years after Vassili's death. Many women born near the turn of the century experienced the death of a husband and found themselves poorly equipped to survive on their own. It was certainly not a matter of intelligence but an absence of work skills required in the marketplace, a definition of self as incomplete without a husband, and a learned sense of inferiority. Susan labored to complete her husband's work, felt inferior to the task in light of his "genius," and felt guilty for finding personal fulfillment in her poetry. She was so dependent she could not make a decision without talking to her dead husband to get his approval. She longed for her own death so she could be with him.

Though the values that confined women seemed to work to the advantage of men, it is simplistic and counterproductive to place all responsibilities on males. Women played a large role in perpetrating those confining values. Margaret Ripley Wolfe notes that if a male plot existed to subjugate women, then "many southern women have been all-too-willing accomplices."[17] Susan's Grandmothers Clay and Pepper, Aunt Teetee, and mother instilled the values and insisted that family members follow them. Why did women perpetuate the very myths that limited their potential? Certainly they had little choice. Ria Clay's actions between 1897 and 1908 indicate the lack of alternatives. It also seems, however, that they perpetuated the system because to a degree they believed it too. Susan named the "enemy" early in her writing. In the poem "Portrait," she stated that the Clays were "mummified by tradition." The weight of tradition has been a significant burden to many women.

Susan's formal education was equally indoctrinating. Studies of women's education at the turn of the century have emphasized its failures for all classes of women. Miss Ella Williams' School did not attempt to create a critical-thinking, aggressive, or ambitious woman. It taught traditional social skills and "Sir Walter's disease." As Vassili said of Susan's letters from Europe, her education was "too filled with King Arthur and rainbows." Such a description evokes a southern image. Bordwick and Douvan suggest that young women of the middle class in a more modern era had a similar experience. Susan's education and upbringing resemble that which Susan Juhasz describes for another woman poet, Sylvia Plath. Juhasz suggests that Plath "swallowed whole the myth of the All-Round Student." Pretty, popular, smart, and an overachiever in high school and college, this middle-class New England poet later found it impossible to resolve the conflict between woman and poet, or one might add, between two images of self. She found the solution in suicide.[18] Susan swallowed not quite whole a similar myth. She thought about suicide, but she survived.[19]

Susan refused to quit. Many young women of her era, and others, acquiesced to the master plan. They made "good" marriages and took their places in their proper social classes. How many of them harbored a resentment as Susan did? Susan Clay refused to accept less of herself or a potential husband than she desired. She fought back, slowly, narrowly, attempting to remain within the socially acceptable parameters. She attempted to break free of family and community in 1919 and in 1921. Each time traditional values pulled her back. Her brother's death and her mother's grief triggered traditional values—human values of sensitivity and family loyalty.

The most courageous act the public Susan Clay ever took was to elope with William Sawitzky. She risked the derision of her community. A half-century later, Lexington's octogenarians still talked disapprovingly of the "strange" Russian who stole her away, and the embarrassment of the Clays at the time is frequently related with cautious delight. She also risked permanent separation from her family. Such actions do not constitute weak acquiescence or timidity.

Susan Clay Sawitzky is subject, perhaps, to greater criticism than Susan Clay. Susan Clay escaped the small town and protective family. Susan Clay Sawitzky lived in a major metropolitan area where she must have seen a more modern attitude toward women and the right to self-expression. Yet her marriage did not bring the freedom she envisioned. Sawitzky's views were only slightly less traditional than those of Colonel Clay. Equally important, Susan carried with her a traditional view of marriage. Vassili was, in her mind, the epic character of literature and the gallant gentleman her mother had married and described to her as a child. The "King Arthur and rainbows" view of life was so deeply ingrained that she made "fetishes" out of her husband's faults if she saw them at all.

Perhaps the examples of metropolitan New York would have had more effect had it not been for crises that drained her sense of confidence.

The miscarriage drew her toward husband and family for support. The economic need and fear created by the Depression also strengthened family ties. Knowledge of her husband's impending death tied her to the completion of his work rather than pursuit of her own. Yet Susan Clay Sawitzky survived thirty-four years as a widow. The modern feminist movement complains about the apathy of the majority of women. The life of Susan Clay Sawitzky suggests that the problem may be bewilderment, guilt, and fatigue, but certainly not apathy.

Just as there were two Susan Clay Sawitzkys, there are two interpretations of her life. Was she weak and timid, responsible for her own fate? Or was she slowly worn down by the weight of the obstacles arrayed against her? Perhaps there is no single answer. Perhaps she was both. To choose one interpretation may say more about the present than about the past, oversimplify the issues, and distort the complexity of her choices.

It certainly seems clear that she would have had a better chance of realizing her dreams if she had had more support. Successful modern women have the advantage of networking with one another. Susan Clay Sawitzky was most productive when she had individuals or groups encouraging her. The social clubs of the 1920s provoked strong action. The Scribbler's Club and Hortense King encouraged her to publish her poems, and Charles Baker helped develop the confidence she needed to publish five articles based on the research she had done with her husband. Unfortunately, there were too few such individuals or groups to help offset those who protected traditional values. Many women of the early twentieth century were forced to do battle in isolation.

The two sides of Susan Clay Sawitzky may be the two sides of women. She was first and foremost an upper-class southern woman, but her life and poetry denote the experience of American women. Many women, at least in the middle and upper classes, have experienced not only similar incidents of discrimination but similar sequencings of limitations that culminate in fatigue and compromise. Class, region, and poetic inclination blur description, but the fabric of discrimination is much the same.

Susan Clay Sawitzky's life suggests why there were so few "superwomen." In a broad sense, she epitomizes the American "every woman."

Never really free, she was never tamed either. There was always that irresistible longing that would not be confined by father, tradition, society, husband, or self. She struggled to acquire independence yet remained incapable of obtaining it. She compromised begrudgingly. Death might have been for her the great escape, but she chose to survive. Susan Clay Sawitzky exemplifies the struggle of women—their goals, dreams, strengths, weaknesses, and compromises. In no small sense, she exemplifies the struggle of humanity. All are withheld from freedom yet beholding it.

Appendix

ᵥᵽ

The Shifting Void

What ancient void is this
That matter shifts
Opening new gaps for every wound made whole?

This loss, repairing,
Emptying, pouring in,—
This everlasting, restless search for balance,
This craving
For the substance of the filled.

What estrangements,
What changes, reconciled,
Have sped you here
Rain, snow, and light of sun?

The discontented winds
Seek vacancy:
Spreading in meadows high and buoyant,
Shelving in fields of cold;
In stretched, invisible cordons
Loosely bound,
Levering, floating,
Rushing in the wake
Of other winds;

Blowing new days and seasons,
Mapped in air,
Round bends of plotted globe.

Dark pits of sea drag down
Its swellings from beneath;
Muscles of waves
Slow flexed, released,
Bind and unbind the power of waters.

When young hills, dizzy with desire
For growth,
Heave themselves,
Like cattle, from the earth,
Dark places of the dust move
To compensate creation.

The tired herd
Of hills grown old
Sinks down,
Rounded and quiet,
Their great bones strew the levels,
Their flesh builds up the valleys.

Oceans breathe on the cold sky, forever,
That continents may sweeten
At its dripping.

Some think that earth was made
From spurting of the sun's side,
Wrenched by the passing
Of a mightier star;
Like burst of bulb
Its golden stuff grew high,
Waving in space:

But a sun, more terrible, plucked it
To form a world.

Cold now, and unmolested in its path
It moves;
But molten blood
Wells up in breasts of stone:
Slow heaving,—
Shifting weight of self
On rigid heart.

Like knuckled, hollowed fist
Leveled to sphere
In brim of oceans huge,
It grips sidereal violence within,
Remembering womb of sun, and giant birth,
And kidnapped babe of world:
Abandoned in black fields
To cool,
And weep its bitter seas.

2

Something is lost
That kept us whole and still,—
Life seethes, expands
With leavening bubbles of death.

All is measure on measure
Of pulse and breathing:
The wave beats of blood must continue,
And tide of the breath may not cease.

And one must seek in other,
Kind to kind,

To close the vacuum of loneliness,
And ease its plenitude.

3

Adam disgraced, with beast and worm,
And belly-writhing angel
Forced from Eden:
Deprived of happy singleness of being,
By knowledge unsound,
Banned in strict laws of heaven;
And comradeship
Of those who walk alone,
Yet hand in hand,—
Like mystic love of angels,
And the dead
Who turn from earth;
Male, female,
Creatures paired,
Unmated,
In their pure, exclusive love,
Like stars two-fold,
Pulled taut in mutual bliss,
Must swing about a center of desire
Between themselves set far,—
In touch immaculate.

Two of each sort,
Complete, eternal made,
(Therefore no age, no child,—helpless, beloved—
In sacred garden world.)
Yet holding in themselves
Intrinsic alien seed
Of spurious creation:

Pending woe of choice,
And first desire
To taste inebriate wisdom of untruth.

Secret of earth
Unguessed of God,
Save for deserted nettle-waste of Eden,
And rotting fruit of knowledge
Strewed in grass,—
Whereon He ponders still
In cool of time;
Wrecked universe,
Patterned on plan of heaven,
With man—not mortal then—
But brute divine
At head:
Trial no more essayed.

4
Thus we, unwhole,
Together turn,
And fasten each in each
With anguished kiss
Of naked spirit, flayed of innocence
In virgin flesh:
Its lust of wholeness
Answered by the cries
Of those involved, sucked in,
From waiting limbos of the soul,
Aroused and slain in one.

Caress of holy curse
—this kiss—

Deeper than flesh and bone,—
Absolved in sweet exchange
Of fullness given,
Replenished emptiness:—
Expedient found
In shattered Paradise.

Strange Universe

1

Shuffle the centuries,
Blink the eyes,
In glance from birth to death;
Deal out kaleidoscopic fall
Of symboled days
Marked, yet, with love and labour,
Riches, grief,
And motley, crowned with power.

2

Joshua bidden
Suns stand still,
Babels pile high,
and tongues make strife,
Gritting between the sliding worlds;
Whirl-winds sweep up
In fiery death
New prophets
Lusting God;
And riding
Giant arrows
Feathered white
With drool of cloud,
Great hunters leap
In arc of sky
To chase the fleeing moon.

Horde driven minds
Gather in daze
To seek new peace
In storm and sea;
And wings,
For wasteful wedding flight put on,

Loosen
And sift in grass.

And earth writhes deep
Beneath its heights
Of daring,
Timeless-new,
In bloody molten
Need of balance;
While gazers
At commotion in the stars,
Choke
In their falling dust.

3
And now, behold
The hideous tree,
Split huge
From ultimate seed
Of Eden fruit:
Of mighty trunk
And bulging head,
And roots curled lightly over death;
With mimicked faces
Peering from its mass
Of swelling foliage,—
New joke
Of ancient fiend.

In moment grown,
Butting the sky
And spreading over world;
Knotted and dripped with age
Like candle stump,—
Older than time;

Millenniums spent
In roar of instant growth,
And rage at secret
Bounding from the dark,
In genitals
Too small
For mortal sight,
But not for mortal probing,
Mortal quest
For self destruction.

At last, the tree
Seen in portentous tales:
Blasting beneath
Its rounded, bull-like head,
All life;
And bellowing
On the wind
Invisible pollen,
Gened with monstrous birth,
In blight of man unborn.

4

While old
In mist,
And gathering new
The hosts who wait,
Bemused
In bounds of bliss:
Who find this waiting—end;
Yet lean
Across the tilt of wheeling space,
For feel of earth,—
Its pull
In dregs of soul.

Their plight
Unknown to them, being blind,
Or to those holy beings
Round about,
Free of all time and measure
Vantage point
And rule:
Severed in liberty, serene,
Too full awake
To see.

Restless,
With many plans,
And yet no goal,
Or happy in idyllic lethargy,
Or in some love
Of other time
Regained;
Cynical, now, of heaven
As realm
Miraculous of transport;
But seeking in horizons
Of the mind,
Never achieved,
Answer long given,—
The leached, invisible sky
Touched blue on brow.

Fleshless,
Mandrake formed,
Mortals enchained in immortality:
Dream on untasted birth,
Remembered death,
Orgasm sweet
Of spirit's nakedness.

5

Yet He,
Absorbed, and mortal-deaf
In midst of chittering shift,
(Fainter than stir of blade
On insect limb:)

Bends out eternal walls
For roomier heaven;
Worlds take root
And ravel leafy fire,
And star grain
Germinates the dark
In crops
Of powdery light.

Great beasts
Pinned out in stars
On zodiac path,
Or treading round the poles,
Are fed by Him,
And comets come to nuzzle at His hand,—
Their beam-haired tails
Adrift, behind.

Angels grow tall enough
To lean
With bowering height,
Shading the meek
In glades of wings;
Man, animals,
And creeping things
Confer on laws of love;
And birds' intrinsic songs
Small themes of race,

Precious in egg
And throat,
Claiming their kind;
Tinkled in tiny scope
Of power immense,
Whisper
The secret vastness
Of His Word:—
Tension, unbearable,
Of Love,
Released, in stir minute,
Of manifold.

Embrace of mystic sphere,
Star-rivered,
Plucked with whirl pools
Of His wonder;
Bedded with dark for rest,
And sacred chaos
Of His privacy,
Where still creation moves.
White to all else,
This Presence,
Hushed, involved,
Within Itself;
But here,
—As all is He,
In sanctuary of Absolute—
His light, enwound to whiteness,
Streams beyond,
Bending through mighty prism
Of His Mind,—
Where thoughts,
Unknown to Him,
Detach themselves,
And stand, estranged, yet bound;
Broken to colour

Of created things:
Turning upon themselves
Beholding,—
Plant, rock, man, beast, and star . . .

6

Strange Universe
With flaw of aspect
Closed
In walls of Oneness:
Unknowing
Of all charts
And balances;
Shaped variously
By view
Of creature eyes,
And secret, inner flight
Through space and time,
Like goaded star
Cupped in eternity;
The scape of infinite
Laid out
To match celerity of mote,
Observed from windowed vehicle
Of skull,
And checked by yardstick
Wincing to the speed
Of sky or heart asunder.

Obscure
To sight of those
Who peer from earth
Through maze
Of massed trajectories,—
Scratched, as by skater's blade,
On skim of space.

7

Continuum curved
To content
Of enigma,—
Opening in mystery
Of infinitude;
Its breathing scope
White-flowered
On the chill
Of nothingness:
Too deep for heel of star
Pricking its rowels
In the flying dark,
Or hurtling grave
Plowed round a planet's girth,—
Or veering orbit
Of the myriad brain,
Linked on its burning pebble
Swept in night.

Notes

Introduction

1. Susan Clay Sawitzky, "Mariner," *Poetry: A Magazine of Verse* 57 (1941): 306. The poem was also included in Woodridge Spears, ed., "The Circling Thread: Poems by Susan Clay Sawitzky," *Kentucky Poetry Review*, Jan. 1984, 34.

2. Her husband, William Sawitzky, complained at one point that letters she wrote from England to her parents were "too filled with King Arthur and rainbows." It seems an apt description of her education.

3. Susan Clay, "A Christmas Disappointment," *Lexington Leader*, Dec. 21, 1913.

4. The examples are far too numerous to mention all of them. Regarding southern women one must begin with Anne Firor Scott, *The Southern Lady: From Pedestal to Politics, 1830–1930* (Chicago: University of Chicago Press, 1970). Catherine Clinton's *Plantation Mistress: Women's World in the Old South* (New York: Pantheon Books, 1982) shows an earlier version of strong southern women. See also Virginia Bernhard, Betty Brandon, Elizabeth Fox-Genovese, Theda Perdue, and Elizabeth Hayes Turner, eds., *Hidden Histories of Women in the New South* (Columbia: University of Missouri Press, 1994); Nancy A. Hewitt and Suzanne Lebsock, eds., *Visible Women: New Essays on American Activism* (Urbana: University of Illinois Press, 1993); Sara Alpern, Joyce Antler, Elizabeth Israels Perry, and Ingrid Winther Scobie, eds., *The Challenge of Feminist Biography: Writing the Lives of Modern American Women* (Urbana: University of Illinois Press, 1992); Marjorie Spruill Wheeler, *New Women of the New South: The Leaders of the Woman Suffrage Movement in the Southern States* (New York: Oxford University Press, 1993).

5. Hewitt and Lebsock, eds., *Visible Women*, 6, 9; Margaret Ripley Wolfe, *Daughters of Canaan: A Saga of Southern Women* (Lexington: University Press of Kentucky, 1995), 134; Wolfe, "Fallen Leaves and Missing Pages: Women in Kentucky History," *Register of the Kentucky Historical Society* 90 (1992): 86. Emphasis added.

6. Anne Firor Scott did note the hold of traditional values on southern women and their use of family, class, and manners in their reform efforts in *The Southern Lady*, 169, 180. Caroline Matheny Dillman also argued that maintaining traditions was important to southern women because they defined themselves by their values and gentil-

ity. See Dillman, "Southern Women: In Continuity or Change?" in *Women in the South: An Anthropological Perspective,* ed. Holly F. Mathews (Athens: University of Georgia Press, 1989), 4, 8–17. See also Susan Middleton-Keirn, "Magnolias and Microchips: Regional Subcultural Constructions of Femininity," *Sociological Spectrum* 6 (1986): 83–107. Some of the best examples, however, are of a more personal nature. Sallie Bingham's autobiographical *Passion and Prejudice: A Family Memoir* (New York: Applause Books, 1989), notes her own struggle against traditional values in a Kentucky family somewhat similar to that of Susan Clay Sawitzky. Lillian Smith's *Killers of the Dream* (New York: Norton, 1949) and Shirley Abbott's *Womenfolk: Growing Up Down South* (New York: Ticknor and Fields, 1983) also explain the role of tradition.

7. Joanne V. Hawks and Sheila L. Skemp, eds., *Sex, Race, and the Role of Women in the South* (Jackson: University Press of Mississippi, 1983), xii.

8. Sandra M. Gilbert and Susan Gubar, *The Madwoman in the Attic: The Woman and the Nineteenth-Century Literary Imagination* (New Haven: Yale University Press, 1979), 83. As in every area of her life, Susan Clay Sawitzky's attempt to write and publish her poems reveals the obstacles women faced in a male-dominated world. See Anne Goodwyn Jones, "Southern Literary Women as Chroniclers of Southern Life," in *Sex, Race, and the Role of Women in the South,* ed. Hawks and Skemp, 79–80.

9. Barbara Welter, *Dimity Convictions: The American Woman in the Nineteenth Century* (Athens: Ohio University Press, 1976), 21; Linda K. Kerber, "Separate Spheres, Female Worlds, Woman's Place: The Rhetoric of Women's History," *Journal of American History* 75 (June 1988): 22. See also Bingham, *Passion and Prejudice,* 65–78; Wolfe, *Daughters of Canaan,* 61.

10. Wolfe, *Daughters of Canaan,* 59.

11. See Paul E. Fuller, *Laura Clay and the Woman's Rights Movement* (Lexington: University Press of Kentucky, 1975), and Melba Porter Hay, *Madeline McDowell Breckinridge: Kentucky Suffragist and Progressive Reformer* (Ann Arbor: University Microfilms International, 1980).

12. Anne Firor Scott, "Historians Construct the Southern Woman," in *Sex, Race, and the Role of Women in the South,* ed. Hawks and Skemp, 96; Scott, *Southern Lady,* x. Scott also noted the importance of the Little Colonel books in the formation of her own images of the South.

13. Shirley Abbott captures the tenacity of southern values on women even when they have left much of it behind them in *Womenfolk.*

14. Carolyn G. Heilbrun, *Writing a Woman's Life* (New York: Ballantine Books, 1988), 81.

15. Carl N. Degler, *At Odds: Women and the Family in America from the Revolution to the Present* (Oxford: Oxford University Press, 1980), vi.

16. Clinton, *Plantation Mistress,* xv; Anne Goodwyn Jones, *Tomorrow Is Another Day: The Woman Writer of the South, 1859–1936* (Baton Rouge: Louisiana State University Press, 1981), 25. Jones says style may differ, but women were all "dancing to someone else's music."

17. "The Revelation," unpublished poem, Susan Clay Sawitzky Papers, currently in possession of the author (hereafter SCS Papers).

1. The Setting

1. Elizabeth Clay Blanford, interview with the author. I had telephone conversations with Blanford, the sister of Susan Clay Sawitzky, two and three times a week from 1984 until 1993. Bettie Kerr, the director of the Henry Clay Estate, and I produced oral history tapes in the summer of 1986. Those tapes are at the Margaret I. King Library, University of Kentucky. Other tapes are in my possession. Blanford told the same stories repeatedly with scarcely an adjective or an adverb changing with the tellings. Her accuracy has been tested many times, and her memory of factual detail is astounding. On only one occasion did I find her in error. She believed her sister had graduated from high school in 1915. Susan Clay finished school in June 1914. Of course, her interpretations generally placed family members in the most favorable light, but that was the way she learned the family saga. Her description of life in the Pepper homes is supported by the extensive family photograph collection, a novel by Robert Burns Wilson titled *Until the Day Break* (New York: Charles Scribner's Sons, 1900), which used the Pepper homes as the basis for its fictional residences, and various newspaper stories saved by the family. See also Willard Rouse Jillson, *Romance and Reality* (Frankfort, Ky.: Roberts Printing Co., 1953).

2. Ria, a shortened version of Mariah, was pronounced like the last syllables of her given name, Rya.

3. James C. Klotter, *The Breckinridges of Kentucky* (Lexington: University Press of Kentucky, 1986), 193, 212–13; John D. Wright Jr., *Lexington: Heart of the Bluegrass* (Lexington: Lexington–Fayette County Historical Commission, 1982); Elizabeth Murphey Simpson, *The Enchanted Bluegrass* (Lexington: Transylvania Press, 1938); John Rothenstein, *Summer's Lease: Autobiography, 1901–1938* (London: Hamish Hamilton, 1965). Rothenstein taught for a time at the University of Kentucky and married a Lexington woman. See also Hambleton Tapp and James Klotter, *Kentucky: Decades of Discord, 1865–1900* (Frankfort, Ky.: Kentucky Historical Society, 1977), 95–96. Like many authors, Tapp and Klotter accept the first hint of change with too much optimism. The traditional values remained strong even as progressivism created the first signs of change.

4. Blanford interview with the author.

5. Johnston's initial work was based on the relationship of a little girl and her maternal grandfather who refused to speak to his daughter. The grandfather was a Confederate veteran. His daughter had married a Union veteran. Tapp and Klotter suggest that Civil War animosities were partially responsible and were an excuse for the feuds that characterized the state in the second half of the nineteenth century (*Decades of Discord*, 1–18).

6. Sue Lynn McGuire, "The Little Colonel: A Phenomenon in Popular Literary Culture," *Register of the Kentucky Historical Society* 89 (Spring 1991): 121–46; Anne Firor Scott, *Making the Invisible Woman Visible* (Urbana: University of Illinois Press, 1984), 243. The impact of myths on southern women is noted in Sally G. McMillen, *Southern Women: Black and White in the Old South* (Arlington Heights, Ill.: Harlan Davidson, 1992), 1.

7. Several studies indicate that traditional social values retain their influence far longer than political or economic ones. See Scott, *Southern Lady*, x–xi, 169, 180;

Middleton-Keirn, "Magnolias and Microchips," 83-105; Wheeler, *New Women of the New South*, 5-6. Wheeler notes that the effort to preserve the values of "the Lost Cause" continued well into the twentieth century. The building of monuments and the strength of organizations such as the Daughters of the Confederacy and the United Confederate Veterans peaked between 1890 and 1910, the period of Susan Clay's youth. Both an aunt and an uncle were state officers in such organizations. McMillen noted that southern women remained victims of myth and exaggeration (*Southern Women*, 1).

8. See early numbers of the *Kentucky Gazette*. Frontier society as a whole was quite crude. Pigs rooted in the muddy streets of Lexington, Kentucky, and a higher species fought literally with tooth, nail, knife, and gun to prove their manliness or because they had consumed too much Kentucky whiskey.

9. Victoirée Charlotte Mentelle to M. et Mme Mentelle, Dec. 28, 1803, Clay Papers, Kenner Collection, Special Collections, University of Kentucky. The *Kentucky Gazette,* Lexington's first newspaper, contained letters and articles indicating that others recognized the contradiction. Mentelle, however, succumbed to regional and aristocratic values. She learned to accept the support of the Bluegrass elite and eventually became a slave owner as well.

10. Newcomers to the community noted a strong air of pretentiousness. Mary Austin Holley, who came from Boston when her husband accepted the presidency of Transylvania College, wrote to friends about it. See Rebecca Smith Lee, *Mary Austin Holley: A Biography* (Austin: University of Texas Press, 1962), 120-21. Mary Todd Lincoln, a native, found the city's social airs stifling. See Jean H. Baker, *Mary Todd Lincoln: A Biography* (New York: Norton, 1987), 53-73. For Susan Clay's era see Simpson, *Enchanted Bluegrass*, preface.

11. Wheeler, *New Women in the New South*, 5-6; McMillen, *Southern Women*, 1.

12. Simpson, *Enchanted Bluegrass*, preface.

13. Bertram Wyatt-Brown, *Southern Honor: Ethics and Behavior in the Old South* (New York: Oxford University Press, 1982), 120-23. The newspapers indicate that applicability to central Kentucky both in the antebellum era and in Susan's time. See also Klotter, *The Breckinridges*, xv-xviii. The Clays resorted to nicknames to eliminate their own confusion. James's son Henry was called Harry, and his daughter Lucretia, named of course for the wife of Henry Clay, was called Teetee. There were three Susan Jacob Clays in as many generations. For the sake of clarity, Mrs. James Brown Clay, Susan's grandmother, will be referred to as Susan M. Clay or Grandmother Clay.

14. Family papers in the University of Kentucky Special Collections contain numerous references. See as examples the January Papers. The concerns remained into a later era as well. See Bingham, *Passion and Prejudice*, 76, 84.

15. Wright, *Lexington*, 126-29. George H. Clay, Susan's uncle, had continuing disagreements with his neighbor William Wright, the flour magnate who developed Calumet Farm. Clay took Wright to court over the whitewashing of fences between their properties. Eventually, however, the Clays would sell their land to Wright.

16. Nancy K. Forderhase, "The Clear Call of Thoroughbred Women: The Kentucky Federation of Women's Clubs and the Crusade for Educational Reform, 1903-1909," *Register of the Kentucky Historical Society* 83 (1985): 19; Scott, *Southern Lady,* 180-81.

17. Helen Deiss Irwin, *Women in Kentucky* (Lexington: University Press of Kentucky, 1979), 91. William Chafe argues that the suffrage issue brought few of the changes envisioned by its proponents. The underlying structure of society remained unchanged (*Women and Equality: Changing Patters in American Culture* [New York: Oxford University Press, 1979]). The society columns of local newspapers indicate the same was true of the Bluegrass. The gentry's social functions continued as before, and the names of those involved in the suffrage movement appeared as chaperons.

18. Blanford interview with the author.

19. Wilson, *Until the Day Break*; Jillson, *Romance and Reality*. Mrs. Pepper's efforts to raise her daughters properly though exercising considerable independence herself is very similar to that attributed by Sallie Bingham to her own grandmother and mother (*Passion and Prejudice*, 65–87).

20. In the 1920s the farm was purchased by the Wrights, who incorporated it into their Calumet Farm, one of the best-known horse farms in thoroughbred racing.

21. Susan M. Clay to Charles, Aug. 21, 1889, SCS Papers. Letters from Mrs. Clay and her daughter used the term repeatedly. After Mrs. Clay's death, Lucretia used it only when she was frustrated with some member of the family. References can also be found in the Thomas J. Clay Papers, Library of Congress (hereafter cited as LC).

22. This attitude is not uncommon among the descendants of famous men. See Paul C. Nagel, *Descent from Glory: Four Generations of the John Adams Family* (Oxford: Oxford University Press, 1983), 3; Klotter, *The Breckinridges*, 323–24. Edward Kennedy noted similar feelings in an article published in *Time*, May 31, 1976, 18.

23. Susan M. Clay to Charles Clay, Dec. 24, 1901, SCS Papers. Susan M. Clay was deeply affected by her financial difficulties. She consistently talked about the family's poverty although they were poor only in comparison to earlier wealth. A slip of paper listed her assets around 1865 at approximately two hundred thousand dollars. Admittedly, much of the wealth was in property, but she repeatedly warned her children that they could not tolerate poverty. On October 31, 1882, for example, she wrote to Charles, "If a man has no means of his own, he should marry a women who has, or not at all." She went on to tell him to quit being silly about a young woman. The letter indicated she had given the same advice to her son Tom. Three of Susan M. Clay's children died before reaching the age to marry, but of the remaining seven, only two married. Her influence in such matters was considerable.

24. See SCS Papers. The family saved various army publications indicating the ranking of officers participating in special training schools.

25. Susan M. Clay to Charles D. Clay, Oct. 31, 1882, SCS Papers.

26. From 1888 to 1894 Ria Pepper kept a scrapbook which when completed was nearly twenty inches thick. It contained the information cited in the text. One young man received a strong letter of rebuke for being too forward, and his name did not appear again on her dance cards or as an escort.

27. Though Ria Clay did not like his formality at first, her mother urged her to be patient. Charles's mellowing is evidenced by a series of approximately one hundred letters they exchanged between January and September 1896, when he was stationed at Fort Apache, Arizona. It was also Charles who preserved most of the letters. See SCS Papers.

28. Ria to Charles, Feb. 2, Mar. 5, 11, 1896; Charles to Ria, Aug. 3, 12, 1896; Charles to Lucretia Clay, Aug. 12, 1896, all in SCS Papers.

2. Childhood

1. Ria Clay to Charles Clay, Feb. [n.d], 1899, Feb. 10, 1902; Elizabeth Pepper to Charles Clay, Feb. 6, 1902, SCS Papers.

2. Susan M. Clay to Ria, Jan. 31, 1899, SCS Papers.

3. Ria to Charles, [n.d., during Spanish-American War], SCS Papers.

4. Susan M. Clay to Charles Clay, July 28, 1898; Susan M. Clay to Ria Clay, Mar. 26, 1899; Susan M. Clay to Charles, Apr. 24, 1898, Ria to Charles, June 12, 1898; Teetee to Ria, July 19, 1898; Teetee to Charles, July 11, 1898; Ria to Charles, June 30, 1898; Teetee to Ria, Jan. 31, 1899, all in SCS Papers.

5. George Clay to Ria, Aug. 9, 1897; Teetee to Ria, July 19, 1898, SCS Papers.

6. Charles to Ria, Sept. 11, 1897, Apr. 27, 1898, SCS Papers.

7. As George Clay's letter cited in note 5 would indicate, Ria's task was not difficult. Charles Clay was a part of an army that emphasized a strong masculine image. See Donald J. Morzek, "The Habit of Victory: The American Military and the Cult of Manliness," in *Manliness and Morality: Middle-Class Masculinity in Britain and America, 1800–1940,* ed. J. A. Mangan and James Walvin (New York: St. Martin's Press, 1987), 35–51.

8. Ria to Charles, Jan. 29, Feb. [n.d.] 1899; Charles to Ria, June 15–27, 1898. Charles wrote a long diary letter to his wife while on board the ship carrying him to Cuba.

9. Ria to Charles, [n.d.—Apr.–June 1898]. The letter can be dated by its contents and because it was addressed to Charles in Cuba. George Clay to Ria, Aug. 9, 1897; Ria to Charles, n.d.–Feb. 1898, Feb. 10, 1902, SCS Papers.

10. Ria to Charles, Mar. 1, 1902, Mar. 13, 1899, SCS Papers.

11. Susan M. Clay to Ria, Jan. 31, 1899; Charles to Susan M. Clay and family, Dec. 10, 1901; Ria to Charles, Dec. 16, 1901, all in SCS Papers. Melba Porter Hay notes that training in the concept of noblesse oblige had begun early in the life of Madeline McDowell Breckinridge. In her life it became an impetus for reform (*Madeline McDowell Breckinridge,* vii–viii, 219–20).

12. Newspaper clipping dated July 23, 1902, Box 61, Thomas J. Clay Papers.

13. Ria to Charles, July 22, 1898, Mar. 13, 1899, Aug. 11, 1898, SCS Papers.

14. Wyatt-Brown, *Southern Honor,* 141. The case of Susan Clay raises questions regarding Wyatt-Brown's contention. Though true in the broadest sense, the very presence of a dominant male certainly provided young women with at least a vague understanding of the "natural order." In the absence of her father, Susan became the dominant member of the family. Her father returned in 1908, but Susan's confidence seems to have been too deeply established. She knew how to be submissive and demure, but those characteristics fought a continuous battle with her confidence, spontaneity, and spirit.

15. George Clay to Ria, Aug. 9, 1897, SCS Papers.

16. Ria's letters indicate clearly her concerns for his safety. She wanted to be patriotic and to believe God was on the side of the United States, but faith did not overcome fear, and patriotism waned in the absence of her husband. She wanted her "dear old

man" at home. A long period without a letter, rumors, or a look at the jingoistic news-papers caused near panic. In July 1898, she wrote, for example, "My precious long looked for letter came this morning. You don't know with how much love and home-sickness I read it. I took a real hard cry over it. This is not the only homesick cry I have had" (July 13, 1898). On another occasion she wrote, "God help a poor half demented wife who adores her dear husband" (July 2, 1898). She prayed that he would do his duty but come home soon (June 15–24, 1898). Charles urged his wife not to read the papers and assured her that he was well and happy, except for missing her and baby Susan. Once in battle, he became caught up in the excitement, and, forgetting to be protec-tive, wrote more honestly, but he was back in the United States with Ria before she received those letters.

17. Charles to Ria, Apr. 2, 9, 1899, SCS Papers.

18. Blanford interview with the author. Ria's sister Pinnie accompanied Clay on the trip back to Lexington, then rejoined her husband, who was also stationed in the Phil-ippines with the Seventeenth Infantry. See also newspaper accounts in SCS Papers.

19. Copy of a letter from Captain John C. Gregg to Mrs. John L. Kirk, Mar. 28, 1899. Captain Gregg, a friend of Charles Clay's, was later killed, but he had written to his sister describing Clay's wound and the near certainty of his fellow officers that Clay would die. Mrs. Kirk sent a copy of the letter to Ria Clay. See also Will Aldnach to Charles Clay, Jan. 30, 1900, SCS Papers.

20. Blanford interview with the author.

21. Mrs. Charles Clay to Robert Clay, May 15, 1924, SCS Papers.

22. Margery Fox, "Protest in Piety: Christian Science Revisited," *International Jour-nal of Women's Studies* 1 (July–Aug. 1978): 402, 413–14.

23. Susan recalled such memories in a series of letters to her uncles written in the 1930s. See Susan to Thomas J. Clay, July 10, 1935, SCS Papers.

24. Elizabeth Clay Blanford, "La Petite," an unpublished reminiscence of Balgowan and Aunt Teetee, SCS Papers.

25. Blanford interview with the author.

26. In the 1920s Elizabeth Clay Blanford developed many of the tales into Negro dialect stories popular in that era. Many of those stories are in the SCS Papers.

27. Millie could not write, but she dictated letters to her daughter Susie (Susan Brown, telephone interview with the author, Sept. 5, 1988). Several hundred letters from Millie to Susan and to Elizabeth are preserved in the SCS Papers. Elizabeth continued to talk regularly with Susan Lawson Brown until the 1990s. Such relation-ships may be exceptions, but lifelong intimacies developed which modern scholarship has largely chosen to ignore. Such relationships between women may not alter general interpretations of race relations, but they certainly influenced the lives of individual women.

28. Jones, *Tomorrow Is Another Day*, 356.

29. Wolfe, *Daughters of Canaan*, 134.

30. There is a photograph in the family collection of Susan in the Babby outfit Mrs. Clay had made for her. Susan later noted her inclination to act out the characters from the books she read in her article "Apology of a Small Town Poetess," *New York Times Review and Magazine*, Dec. 18, 1921.

31. Carol Dyhouse, *Girls Growing Up in Late Victorian and Edwardian England* (London: Routledge & Kegan Paul, 1981), 121–35; Carroll Smith-Rosenberg and Charles Rosenberg, "The Female Animal: Medical and Biological Views of Woman and Her Role in Nineteenth-Century America," *Journal of American History* 60 (Sept. 1973): 340.

32. "The Forgetmenots," an unpublished story, SCS Papers.

33. Untitled story, SCS Papers. Anne Firor Scott recounted her own reaction to reading *The Little Colonel* in her essay in "Historians Construct the Southern Woman," 95–96. The similarity of experiences is noteworthy. Scott also mentioned being enrolled at birth in the Children of the Confederacy by her great-grandmother just as Susan was enrolled on the Honor Roll of the war relief effort by her Aunt Teetee.

34. Sawitzky, "Apology of a Small Town Poetess."

35. Blanford, "La Petite." Susan wrote in the margin that of her "luny experiments" this one was "the saddest of all."

36. Blanford, "Memories of Our Kentucky Childhood," SCS Papers. Mrs. Clay was aware of Susan's inclination to wander. On one occasion, sensing that her daughter had been quiet too long, she went to find Susan just in time to open the gate to an adjacent field allowing her daughter to escape an irate cow. Susan had forgotten her mother's instructions when she saw elderberry flowers in the field. The cow, normally gentle, had a young calf at the time.

37. Elizabeth Stone, *Black Sheep and Kissing Cousins: How Our Family Stories Shape Us* (New York: Penguin, 1988), 5.

38. Blanford interview with the author.

39. Photograph collection, SCS Papers.

40. Jillson, *Romance and Reality*, n.p.

41. Susan kept booklets in which she pasted newspaper articles and pictures of famous people and places. Even as a young girl she was fond of the Russian and English royal families, the people and places of literature, and actors of the New York and London stages. See SCS Papers.

42. Rothenstein, *Summer's Lease*, 156; Richard Redd, *Reminiscences of Richard Menifee Redd Better Known as Colonel "Dick" Redd from Childhood to Old Age* (Lexington: Clay Printing Co., 1929). Woodridge Spears, in an interview with the author, recalled being surprised by Colonel Redd's behavior.

43. *Lexington Herald*, Apr. 15, 1917; Thomas J. Clay, "A Synopsis of the Life of Thomas J. Clay, U.S. Army, Retired." Slightly different versions can be found in the SCS Papers and in the Thomas J. Clay Papers.

44. Susan to Thomas J. Clay, July 10, 1935, SCS Papers. Thomas J. Clay rode with Henry Ware Lawson and Lieutenant Leonard Wood when Geronimo was captured (Thomas J. Clay, "Notes of Seven Months Field Service in Texas and Mexico," Box 60, Thomas J. Clay Papers). In later years Clay wrote to a number of people about his adventures. See Leonard Wood Papers and Hermann Hagedorn Papers, both in LC.

45. Susan to Thomas J. Clay, July 10, 1935, SCS Papers.

46. The high spirit may have been a euphemism for the depression that many members of the family experienced. That is not uncommon among leading families. See Bertram Wyatt-Brown, *The House of Percy: Honor, Melancholy, and Imagination in a*

Southern Family (New York: Oxford University Press, 1994), 13. Wyatt-Brown notes the battle with melancholia experienced by others such as Sylvia Plath, Winston Churchill, and Franz Kafka. Each of Henry Clay's sons experienced depression at various times in their lives. Three sons sought treatment for it.

47. Susan to Ria Clay, Oct. 10, 1933, SCS Papers.

48. The Clay Papers appear to have been purged of material pointing to known foibles of Henry Clay. There are no references to the heavy drinking, gambling, or womanizing which other sources indicate. Teetee had learned from her mother that, because of jealousy and envy, some people liked to emphasize anything that could detract from the reputation of a great man. She also felt very keenly the need to uphold the values of the family and, one suspects, she believed that Henry Clay's heart had been in the right place even if he strayed occasionally. Such destructiveness was not intended to alter history but to assure its proper interpretation. Moreover, some articles were suppressed to save others from pain or because genteel people did not mention certain things. For example, Teetee Clay edited a letter from Susan M. to James B. Clay (July 9, 1863) now located in the Hunt Morgan Papers, 1862–63, University of Kentucky Special Collections. Teetee removed the name of a man Susan M. Clay said had been rude to Henrietta Morgan because, in Teetee's words, he was "considered a kindly good citizen" after the war. Elizabeth Blanford also expressed strong reservations about including names and quotations for the same reasons. For example, she wished to suppress a letter from her father to Uncle George chastising George Clay for wanting to sell the family papers. Her father was correct, she said, in his assertion that the papers belonged to the family, but the letter might leave an unfair impression of Uncle George. Once a doubt is placed in people's minds, she argued, it takes precedence over more favorable qualities. Such concerns extended beyond the family. A poem entitled "To Elizabeth" was written about a friend of Susan's. Even at risk of the reader believing it was about her, Elizabeth Blanford feared there might be relatives of the woman who would be hurt or offended unnecessarily. Both Susan M. Clay and Teetee were also ridiculously defensive about the reputations of family members. Their biography creates a man of absolute perfection. See "Henry Clay and His Slanderers," Box 55, and "Newspaper Clippings," Box 61, Thomas J. Clay Papers. The Clay Papers in the Library of Congress also contain letters to editors of newspapers across the country responding angrily to criticisms of Henry or James B. Clay. At one point, Mrs. Clay even adopted a pseudonym. See Box 61, Thomas J. Clay Papers.

49. Lucretia Clay, "The Hilliards," an unpublished novel, SCS Papers. Two versions by different titles can be found in Box 59, Thomas J. Clay Papers. One is entitled "Money-Mad" and the second is "A House Party at Inverloch."

50. Blanford, "La Petite."

51. The influence of family values may be most apparent in a later action by Susan's youngest brother, Robert Pepper Clay. He attended West Point and served with distinction in World War II and Korea. Clay wanted to earn a general's stars but retired from the U.S. Army, like his father, as a colonel. The following conversation occurred, according to Elizabeth Blanford, between Bob Clay and a friend who was promoted to the higher rank. The friend asked, "Pep, do you know how I got these stars? I never made an enemy." Bob Clay responded, "I would be ashamed to admit it." Remarkably

similar to Henry Clay's "I would rather be right than President," it speaks to the internalization of family values the children, male and female, experienced.

52. As is so often the case, Elizabeth Blanford's account is collaborated by other sources. Leonard Wood notes the incident in his journal of the time. See also Hermann Hagedorn to Thomas J. Clay, July 25, 1929, Box 3, Hagedorn Papers. Hagedorn was a biographer of Leonard Wood.

53. Harry Clay, Memoir, Mar. 8, 1881, SCS Papers; A. W. Greely to H. Clay, Aug. 16, 1881, Box 46, Thomas J. Clay Papers; A. L. Todd, *Abandoned: The Story of the Greely Expedition, 1881–1884* (New York: McGraw-Hill, 1961), 21–22; Bessie Rowland James, ed., *Six Came Back: The Arctic Adventure of David L. Brainard* (Indianapolis: Bobbs-Merrill, 1940), 23; Lieut. A. W. Greely to Lucretia Clay, Sept. 1884, SCS Papers. See Lindsey Apple, "In Search of a Star: A Kentucky Clay Goes to the Arctic," *Filson Club Historical Quarterly* 71 (Jan. 1997): 3–26. Teetee also told the children about Jim Clay, another uncle, riding south after Appomattox to let the Confederates know the war was over. Tired and hungry, she said, he rode on so that lives would not be lost unnecessarily. She did not tell them about the letter he wrote to his mother celebrating the murder of Lexington blacks serving in the Union army by General Breckinridge's troops after the Battle of Saltville. Family histories are inclined to omit facts that do not support their purpose.

54. Abraham Lincoln had called Thomas Hart Clay the "one true son of Henry Clay." Though such a remark was a reference to James B. Clay's Confederate leanings, Teetee chose to see it as a compliment because it was made by a president of the United States. Neither she nor the children sensed the contradiction.

55. Blanford interview with the author. Blanford tells a story of being handed a George Washington letter to hold when she was about ten years old. The letter split at the crease just as it settled into her hands. She spoke emotionally some seventy-five years later of the anguish she felt even though she had done nothing to cause the damage.

3. Youth

1. Blanford interview with the author.

2. J. Winston Coleman Jr., *The Private School of Ella M. Williams of Lexington, Kentucky* (Lexington: Winburn Press, 1980); Gladys V. Parrish, "The History of Female Education in Lexington and Fayette County" (M.A. thesis, University of Kentucky, 1932), 67; Jo Della Alband, "A History of the Education of Women in Kentucky" (M.A. thesis, University of Kentucky, 1934).

3. Parrish, "History of Female Education," 67, states that "special classes were given for young ladies." Alband notes ("History of the Education of Women in Kentucky," 154–55) that female education was based on the tradition of the "Select Schools for Young Ladies" and that academic studies were "superficial." Coleman, who left the school in 1912 to enter Morton School, said only one male graduated from Miss Ella Williams' School in 1912. There were no males in the graduating classes of 1913 or 1914 (*Private School of Ella M. Williams*, 19).

4. Alband, "History of the Education of Women in Kentucky," 154–55; Parrish, "History of Female Education," 67.

5. See scrapbooks, photographs, and school assignments in SCS Papers.

6. Parrish, "History of Female Education," 67.

7. Susan to Mr. and Mrs. Charles D. Clay, Feb. 7, 1912, SCS Papers.

8. Ibid., Feb. 10, Apr. 1, May [n.d.], 1912, SCS Papers.

9. Ibid., Feb. 7, 10, 1912, SCS Papers.

10. Susan to Mrs. Clay, Feb. 10, 1912, SCS Papers. A separate sealed letter to her mother was enclosed in the correspondence to both parents.

11. Susan to Mr. and Mrs. Charles D. Clay, Feb. 1912, SCS Papers.

12. Susan to Mrs. Clay, Feb. 7, 1912, SCS Papers.

13. Susan to Charles D. Clay, May 1912, SCS Papers.

14. Untitled notebook, SCS Papers.

15. Suzanne Juhasz, *Naked and Fiery Forms: Modern American Poetry by Women, a New Tradition* (New York: Octagon Books, 1976), 1–2. The dependency of nineteenth-century women on male models is implied in many literary studies, for example, by Elaine Showalter in the title of her work, *A Literature of Their Own* (Princeton: Princeton University Press, 1977). Gilbert and Gubar, *Madwoman in the Attic*, 83, note that "almost all nineteenth century women were in some sense imprisoned in men's houses." See also Carol S. Manning, *The Female Tradition in Southern Literature* (Urbana: University of Illinois Press, 1993), 49.

16. SCS Papers; only fragments of the report exist.

17. Blanford interview with the author. Blanford quoted her mother as saying the task "would be impossible!" Susan read far too much for her mother to read it all first. In discussing Ellen Glasgow's novel *Virginia*, Anne Goodwyn Jones notes that southern women, though praised for physical beauty, piety, and sacrifice, were "forbidden" to search for truth. Susan Clay was certainly discouraged from asking questions that might have led beyond the myths. See Jones, *Tomorrow Is Another Day*, 241. See also Wolfe, *Daughters of Canaan*, 97; Welter, *Dimity Convictions*, 28–29.

18. Welter, *Dimity Convictions*, 23; Jones, *Tomorrow Is Another Day*, 8–9.

19. Barbara Welter, "The Cult of True Womanhood, 1820–1860," *American Quarterly* 18 (Summer 1966): 151–74.

20. Untitled book of poems, SCS Papers. Corrections in spelling were also evident for the first time.

21. Ibid.

22. Ibid.

23. Ibid. See also SCS Papers for examinations and lecture notes taken in 1926 in University of Kentucky history classes.

24. "Lines to a Butterfly," untitled book of poems, SCS Papers.

25. Concern about overtaxing young women with mental exertion, particularly in fields like mathematics and the sciences, was common. See Smith-Rosenberg and Rosenberg, "The Female Animal," 340–41; Dyhouse, *Girls Growing Up in Late Victorian and Edwardian England*, 121–35.

26. It seems doubtful that Charles Clay would have allowed either of his sons to terminate their study of mathematics. In letters from Charles Clay to his sons, Charley and Bob, academics was stressed only as a means to pass the exam for admission to West Point.

27. Susan Clay, "A Christmas Disappointment," *Lexington Leader*, Dec. 21, 1913.

28. *Lexington Herald*, Mar. 10, Apr. 11, July 11, Sept. 5, 1915.

29. Irwin, *Women in Kentucky*, 91. William Chafe argues that the suffrage issue brought few of the changes envisioned by its proponents. The underlying structure of society remained unchanged (*Women and Equality*, 29). That was particularly true of the Bluegrass gentry. See also Forderhase, "The Clear Call of Thoroughbred Women," 19; Scott, *Southern Lady*, 180–81; Klotter, *The Breckinridges*, 193, 212–13; Tapp and Klotter, *Decades of Discord*, 95–96. The society columns of local newspapers continued to present accounts of gentry social functions as frequently and in the time-honored fashion long after the successful conclusion of the suffrage issue.

30. Baker, *Mary Todd Lincoln*, 53–73; Rothenstein, *Summer's Lease*, 156.

31. Irwin, *Women in Kentucky*, 91; Wolfe, *Daughters of Canaan*, 131. Anne Goodwyn Jones notes that writers like Frances Newman, Ellen Glasgow, and Zelda Fitzgerald left the South, but it did not always leave them (*Tomorrow Is Another Day*, 274). She also noted (p. 320) that Margaret Mitchell often retreated within the image of the southern lady.

32. Simpson, *Enchanted Bluegrass*, preface.

33. Wyatt-Brown, *Southern Honor*, 239–40.

34. Clay, "Apology of a Small Town Poetess." Students of women in almost any era note that women who show their intelligence in a relationship often jeopardize that relationship.

35. Maxine P. Atkinson and Jacqueline Bales, "The Shaky Pedestal: Southern Ladies Yesterday and Today," *Southern Studies: An Interdisciplinary Journal of the South* 24 (Winter 1985): 399.

36. Graduation program, 1914, Howard Curry Papers, Special Collections, University of Kentucky; Blanford interview with the author.

4. *Matilda, the Same Thing Has Happened to Me!*

1. Judith M. Bordwick and Elizabeth Douvan, "Ambivalence: The Socialization of Women," in *Woman in Sexist Society: Studies in Power and Powerlessness*, ed. Vivian Garnick and Barbara K. Moran (New York: New American Library, 1971), 232.

2. Much of the literature suggests that young women experienced in adolescence a sense of loss, restriction, or confinement. See Paula J. Kaplan, *Barriers Between Women* (New York: Spectrum Publications, 1981), 37–38; Gerda Lerner, *The Female Experience: An American Documentary* (Indianapolis: Bobbs-Merrill, 1977), xxvi; Carolyn G. Heilbrun, *Reinventing Womanhood* (New York: Norton, 1979), 17.

3. Charles Clay returned to the military during World War I, retiring the final time with the rank of colonel. He was quick to note that his rank was "earned on the nation's battlefields," not received as an honorary title (Blanford interview with the author).

4. One suspects that Clay, like many Victorian men, was far more comfortable with his daughters when they were small children than when they became young women. Like Tom Clay, he was open and engaging with Susan when she was a baby. On those occasions when he could be with his family, he had taught Susan nursery rhymes and songs and had overcome his formality to play on the floor with her. He did the same

thing with Metzie when he returned in 1908. Elizabeth recalls him allowing her to go to the fields with him and carrying her back when she tired. With Susan, however, he was more reserved after 1908, and the difference between image and reality drove a wedge between them. She later claimed that a "cold wind" blew between them. See untitled notebook, SCS Papers.

5. Charles to Ria, Nov. 16, 1901, SCS Papers. The educational process started early and was pursued consistently. In 1901, when Susan was three years old and Charley two, he sent a foldout botanical garden for Susan's Christmas gift, toy soldiers and cannons for Charley. Christmas gifts consistently followed the stereotypical pattern. His letters to the children were also instruments of instruction, urging them to follow particular modes of conduct. In 1899 Clay declared his son the "Charley of the future." Nobility of character, duty, and manly virtues were frequent topics in letters. Clay later remarked that he had always dreamed of walking down Lexington's Main Street flanked by his two sons in the uniforms of the U.S. Army. In 1928, Mrs. Clay stated in sworn testimony that the family understood that the education of Charley and Robert was the first priority. If anything happened to their father, the care of Mrs. Clay, Susan, and Elizabeth would be the sons' responsibility. See deposition sworn in Fayette County Court, Mrs. Charles D. Clay, 1928, SCS Papers. The testimony was required to receive federal payments owed Charley Clay.

6. Blanford interview with the author.

7. Ibid.

8. Cleo Dawson Smith, interview with the author, Lexington, Kentucky, Sept. 23, 1986. Smith, a professor of Spanish at the University of Kentucky, befriended a young Elizabeth Clay. A Texan with a take-charge attitude, she sent young men to call on Elizabeth but recalled many of them sensing that they were not truly welcome.

9. Blanford interview with the author. Mrs. Blanford recalled with some delight her youngest brother's means of avoiding the family scrutiny. Bob Clay met his future wife on a military base and gave her an engagement right before bringing her to meet the family. The Clays therefore could not ask the usual probing questions. They did let Bob know, however, that they would have preferred to meet her before he proposed. Susan and Metzie were certain he planned his strategy to avoid the endless questions and fault-finding of the family and were delighted that he had succeeded.

10. Heilbrun, *Reinventing Womanhood*, 17.

11. Wolfe, *Daughters of Canaan*, 135, 141; Wheeler, *New Women of the New South*, 40–46; Hay, *Madeline McDowell Breckinridge*, 219–20.

12. Even those who were freer in many instances had their fling before returning to traditional roles. The appearance of liberation was greater than its reality. Jones, *Tomorrow Is Another Day*, 271–72; Chafe, *Women and Equality*, 29–30.

13. Juhasz, *Naked and Fiery Forms*, 3.

14. The butterfly, of course, later became the symbol of the women's movement.

15. "The Butterfly," unpublished poem. SCS Papers.

16. Untitled poem, SCS papers.

17. *Lexington Leader*, Dec. 21, 1913. Susan did not realize that she was confronting the contradictions in the values attributed to the southern lady. Jones, *Tomorrow Is Another Day*, 4, notes the contradiction between image and reality and its consequences.

18. Bordwick and Douvan, "Ambivalence," 232; Wolfe, *Daughters of Canaan*, 132–33.

19. Bordwick and Douvan, "Ambivalence," 232–33. Bordwick and Douvan are writing about a later generation of women and make no references to class.

20. The young Lexington women who achieved success professionally as well as those who became activists for reform seemed to have had strong family support or families whose male members were so harsh that it was relatively easy to make a clean break. For example, James Klotter notes in *The Breckinridges, 194–96,* that Sophonisba Breckinridge, who was older than Susan, received "strong support" from her parents when she entered graduate school at the University of Chicago. Madeline Breckinridge received the support of both her father and her husband (Hay, *Madeline McDowell Breckinridge,* 16, 219). Laura Clay reacted strongly to the unfair treatment of her mother by her father (Fuller, *Laura Clay,* 15–17; see also Wheeler, *New Women of the New South,* 61). Susan's father was not an ogre, but he certainly offered no support beyond that of a traditional parent.

21. "The Pine Tree," unpublished poem, SCS Papers.

22. Clay, "Apology of a Small Town Poetess." Such attitudes toward Lexington's gentry can be seen in letters that will be cited later. Susan carried suspicions all her life. She spoke frequently of the pettiness, cruelty, and gossip of Lexington's gentry. The same feelings are apparent in Blanford's conversations. When she was in her eighties, removed from Lexington for over fifty years, the memories of slights and hurtful comments still brought an emotional response. None of the Clay children established a home in Lexington. See Susan to Elizabeth Blanford, July 23, 1951, SCS Papers.

23. Mrs. Clay to Charley, Oct. 6, 13, 1913; Colonel Clay to Charley, June 30, 1918; Mrs. Clay to Bob, n.d. [internally dated 1923]. Mrs. Clay writes, "Bobby, please take no risks in swimming, canoeing or too violent exercise or balancing over some height." She added boating to the list in a letter of June 18,1924. Robert Clay to Mrs. Clay, Sept. [n.d.], 1923, Sept. 24, 1923; Mrs. Clay to Bob, May 15, 1924; Robert Clay to Mrs. Clay, June 18, 1924, all in SCS Papers.

24. Chafe, *Women and Equality,* 29–30.

25. *Lexington Leader,* Jan. 1, 1917.

26. Both Robert Seager and Melba Porter Hay, editors of the *Clay Papers,* have expressed doubt about the family account in conversations with the author. Robert Remini accepts the story at face value in *Henry Clay: Statesman for the Union* (New York: Norton, 1991), 31.

27. Susan did not discover Mary Chesnut's critique of southern definitions of beauty for many years, but she described beauty the same way. See Susan Clay, *Poems by Susan Clay* (Chicago: Ralph Fletcher Seymour, 1923), 20–23.

28. Susan M. Clay to Charles Clay, Oct. 31, 1882, SCS Papers. In a harsh letter, Susan M. Clay told her son to stop thinking of marriage because he had no money and the girl had none. She cited several examples within the extended family where poverty had led to unpleasant marriages and argued that she had required Tom Clay to break off a relationship for the same reason. Finally, she cited the quip that when poverty comes in the door, love flies out the window. Just as bluntly, she warned her sons against drinking, gambling, unacceptable friends, and a host of other shortcomings (Susan M. Clay to Harry Clay, Oct. 3, 1876, Box 46, Thomas J. Clay Papers). Susan M.

Clay had exercised significant authority over Charles's decisions, and he sought to do the same with his children.

29. The family did not dismiss her threats of suicide, but they were inclined to believe them merely expressions of her "high spirit" or her overly dramatic nature rather than a legitimate threat. Mrs. Clay called her daughter "Susan Over-do" (Blanford interview with the author).

30. Many of her drawings have been preserved. They indicate some talent, but the subject matter speaks most clearly to her discontent.

31. *Poems by Susan Clay*, 12.

32. Ibid., 16.

33. Ibid., 15.

34. *Town and Country Magazine* 89 (Oct. 15, 1922): 34.

35. Unpublished poem, SCS Papers.

36. *Poems by Susan Clay*, 25–26.

37. Gilbert and Gubar, *Madwoman in the Attic*, 83. Susan Clay also seemed to be experiencing the struggle of the woman poet described by Susan Juhasz. Given the contradictory definitions of woman and poet, Juhasz denotes a tension in the work of female poets. They experience what she calls the "double bind." She also notes the tendency to suicide (*Naked and Fiery Forms*, 3).

38. *Poems by Susan Clay*, 11.

39. SCS Papers. Susan Clay wrote the same short expression on several scraps of paper.

5. Escape

1. Ria Clay said as much in letters written to Susan years later. She also used essentially the same argument when Elizabeth suffered a similar sense of despair for the same reasons.

2. *Poems by Susan Clay*, 31.

3. Blanford interview with the author.

4. Clay, "Apology of a Small Town Poetess."

5. *Poems by Susan Clay*, 20–22.

6. Ibid.

7. Ibid., 30.

8. Ibid., 10.

9. Susan to Metzie, Nov. 12, 1931, SCS Papers.

10. Mrs. Clay to Susan, Jan. 11, 1920, SCS Papers.

11. See Bordwick and Douvan, "Ambivalence," 232–33. Susan shared the difficulties of breaking free with many more modern women. The authors note that "women have not been fundamentally equipped and determined to succeed." Susan was not equipped to work effectively or to live independently. She did not sew, cook, or clean, nor did she have the skills to acquire employment that would allow her to purchase such services. Moreover, she was so emotionally dependent on her family as a result of her upbringing that the normal uncertainty that accompanies new freedom surely compounded her discomfort. Then there was the burden of guilt. Many women of Susan's era who

succeeded in attaining a measure of independence or a career seem to have had the support of a parent, brother, or husband or to have had such a negative relationship that a total break with family was possible. Susan was caught between the two, lacking the support of her parents, but not yet ready to defy them.

12. Wolfe, *Daughters of Canaan,* 86–87.

13. The novel reflects the impact of Victorian myth-making as well as Clay myths. Copies of the novel may be found in the SCS Papers and the Thomas J. Clay Papers.

14. Lucretia Clay to Susan, Jan. 1, 1920, SCS Papers.

15. Sara M. Evans says female solidarity was "eroded" by new currents (*Born For Liberty: A History of Women in America* [New York: Free Press, 1989], 145).

16. Karen J. Blair, *The Torchbearers: Women and Their Amateur Arts Associations in America, 1890–1930* (Bloomington: Indiana University Press, 1994), 4, 7, 9.

17. *Springfield* (Ohio) *Sunday News,* Jan. 30, 1921. The article was saved among Susan Clay Sawitzky's papers.

18. Clippings from newspapers, SCS Papers.

19. William Sawitzky to Charles Clay, May 14, 1927, SCS Papers.

20. Tom Smith, interview with the author, July 7, 1988. A Pepper cousin, Tom Smith lived in Charles Clay's home while attending the University of Kentucky and later spoke frequently with Sawitzky in New York and Connecticut.

21. William Sawitzky to Charles Clay, May 14, 1927, SCS Papers. He had even been honored by having a bird discovered on the expedition named after him.

22. William Sawitzky to Susan Clay, [n.d.], SCS Papers.

23. The remark was attributed to a family friend and Christian Science practitioner, Lyda Sandifer Hord.

24. "Passion," unpublished poem, SCS Papers.

25. Untitled fragment, SCS Papers.

26. Ibid.

27. Helen Lowry to Susan, [n.d.—1921], SCS Papers.

28. Mrs. Clay to Susan, July 12, 1921, SCS Papers.

29. Susan to Mrs. Clay, [n.d.—internally dated July 1921], SCS Papers.

30. Cesare, later a cartoonist for the *New York Times,* and his wife, Ann, became close friends of Susan and William Sawitzky.

31. Susan to Mrs. Clay, July 2, 1921, SCS Papers.

32. Ibid.

33. Mrs. Charles Clay to Susan, July 12, 1921, SCS Papers.

34. See family photograph albums, SCS Papers.

35. *Louisville Herald,* Oct. 30, 1921. Susan complained that the editor altered her articles because he did not understand her literary references.

36. Ibid., Sept. 25, 1921. See also article of Oct. 2, 1921.

37. Ibid., Oct. 23, 1921.

38. Ibid., Nov. 6, 1921.

39. See Evans, *Born for Liberty,* 178–79.

40. Mrs. Clay to Susan, Dec. 1921, SCS Papers.

6. Romance

1. Ria Clay to Susan, Dec. 1921, SCS Papers.

2. Susan Clay's actions illustrate the dilemma of young women seeking independence. She had been taught to see the positive rather than to evaluate critically so when she confronted the difficulties of living alone and the critical reactions of her editor she chose to hear Edna Ferber, the editor of her poetry, and her own hopes for success and marriage. Two additional aspects are worthy of note. If she had become a successful poet during her lifetime, a biographer would be inclined to interpret her resignation as dedication to her goal and the willingness to take risks to achieve success. Since "success" was limited, her decision can be described as a sign of weakness and poor judgment. Second, the myth required women to be subservient to men, but there were subtle nuances to it. Susan was of a higher social class and, to her way of thinking, better educated than the editor. He deserved respect in public, but she was not inclined to accept his revisions. Women of the leadership class were superior to men of lower station though respectfully so.

3. Unpublished poem, SCS Papers.

4. Unpublished poem, SCS Papers.

5. *Poems by Susan Clay*, 9.

6. Ibid., 18.

7. Susan wrote often of the destiny that brought them together. They had in her mind always been one despite the distance or the difference in age. "Even in your childhood / When I was not born yet / I was with you." See manuscript collections, SCS Papers.

8. William Sawitzky to Susan Clay, Oct. 9, 1922, SCS Papers.

9. Hortense Flexner King sometimes wrote under her name and at other times used her husband's name.

10. Hortense King to Susan Clay, Dec. 1921; Draft letter, Susan Clay to William Sawitzky, [n.d.—later remarks indicated letter was written in August 1926], SCS Papers.

11. Blanford interview with the author.

12. The family was inclined to make a saint of Charley Clay after his death, but there is evidence that both he and his brother Bob carried the same burden of duty to family and noblesse oblige that earlier generations of the family had carried. Charley constantly championed the underdog. The headmaster at Episcopal High School in Alexandria, Virginia, wrote to his parents that Charley was hurting his reputation with the other boys by taking up for any student who was hazed (L. M. Blackford Jr. to Mr. and Mrs. Clay, Nov. 9, 1913; Mrs. Clay to Charley Clay, Oct. 10, 1913). Charles Clay wrote back urging Charley to use more discretion in choosing his causes. Charles Clay to Charley, Oct. 10, 1913. Apparently he had the same problem at West Point. Bob wrote to his parents during his plebe year that he had experienced trouble "about Charley" (Robert Clay to Colonel and Mrs. Clay, Sept. 20, 1921, SCS Papers). Bob also experienced the problem to a lesser degree. In an interview with the author, July 23, 1985, Dunster Foster Petit, who knew the family well, noted that Charley had a strong sense of honor and fair play.

13. There is evidence to suggest a less favorable account, but the Clays tended to put the best face on adversity. Just as Susan's sense of family loyalty and her worldview consistently clouded her judgment, Charley's apparent need to act out his sense of "nobility" created difficulties for him too frequently for its importance to be denied. The Clays chose, however, to make Charley's desire to fight in the war a part of the family saga.

14. This may be another incidence of rewriting the evidence. Both Bob and Susan referred to the possibility of suicide in letters. Bob said he had believed Charley's death a suicide at first but changed his mind (Bob to Mrs. Clay, Jan. 23, 1923). Susan stated in a letter to Sawitzky that the family never knew for sure (Susan Clay to William Sawitzky, Aug. 1926, SCS Papers). Admonishing Bob against drinking liquor, Mrs. Clay later claimed that Charley's character had been "perfect but for the mistake of ever touching whiskey" (Mrs. Clay to Bob, May 15, 1924, SCS Papers). The board of inquiry had noted that Charley was drinking heavily before his death.

15. Petit interview with the author, July 23, 1985. The Fosters introduced Charley Clay to their friends, and Dunster was allowed to go just about anywhere with Charley and his friends. Her mother answered criticism from within her social circle by stating that Charley Clay was as trustworthy as if he were a member of the family. The freedom allowed a young lady had limits in St. Paul, Minnesota, similar to those found in Lexington, Kentucky.

16. D. T. Spencer to Colonel H. B. Clay, Feb. 11, 1923, SCS Papers. Spencer was writing to Charles D. Clay.

17. Telegram, General R. C. Davis to Colonel Charles Clay, Mar. 8, 1923, SCS Papers.

18. Copy of the Minutes, U.S. Army Board of Inquiry, Fort Snelling, Minnesota, Apr. 24, 1923, SCS Papers.

19. Robert P. Clay to Mrs. Clay, Mar. 1, 1923, SCS Papers.

20. Blanford interview with the author. Much of Blanford's account is corroborated in William Sawitzky to Susan Clay, Oct. 9, 1926, SCS Papers.

21. Grade reports, University of Kentucky, SCS Papers.

22. G. Terrell to Susan Clay, Apr. 21, 1924. Susan had just published a poem in the *Kentucky Kernel,* the student newspaper, and won a prize of two dollars for it.

23. Mrs. Clay to Robert P. Clay, n.d.

24. Mrs. Clay to Bob, Dec. 12, 1924, Feb. 1, 1925, SCS Papers.

25. Susan Clay to William Sawitzky, [n.d.—Aug. 1926], SCS Papers.

26. William Sawitzky to Susan Clay, Oct. 9, 1926 (earlier letter), SCS Papers.

27. Ibid., Oct. 9, 1926 (later letter). It is difficult to determine whether he was really naive enough to think the Clays would accept his explanation or if he was trying to convince Susan.

28. Ibid.

29. Ibid.

30. Ibid.

31. Jones, *Tomorrow Is Another Day,* 274, 320; Smith, *Killers of the Dream,* 9; Manning, *Female Tradition,* 47–48; Wolfe, *Daughters of Canaan,* 134.

32. William Sawitzky to Susan Clay, Dec. 23, 1926, SCS Papers.

33. Ibid., Apr. 14, 1927.

34. Ibid., Apr. 17, 1927.

35. Ibid., Apr. 20, 1927.

36. Ibid., Apr. 27, 1927. From the time of their secret meeting, Susan called Sawitzky Vassili, his family name.

37. Ibid.

38. Ibid.

39. Susan to William Sawitzky, Apr. 29, 1927, SCS Papers.

40. Ibid., Apr. 28, 1927 (registered letter).

41. Ibid., Apr. 28, 1927 (regular letter).

42. Vassili to Susan, Apr. 29, 1927, SCS Papers.

43. Susan to Vassili, Apr. 30, 1927, SCS Papers.

44. Ibid., May 2, 1927.

45. Vassili to Susan, May 3, 1927.

7. After the Wedding

1. Susan to Colonel and Mrs. Charles D. Clay, May 7, 1927, SCS Papers.

2. Ibid.

3. Ibid.

4. William Sawitzky to Colonel and Mrs. Charles D. Clay, May 7, 1927, SCS Papers.

5. William Sawitzky to Mrs. Clay, May 11, 1927, SCS Papers.

6. Carroll Smith-Rosenberg notes the closeness between mothers and daughters in nineteenth-century America. That was certainly true of Mrs. Clay and Susan, and it assured a reconciliation after Susan's elopement (Smith-Rosenberg, "The Female World of Love and Ritual: Relations Between Women in Nineteenth-Century America," *Signs* 1 [1975]: 1–29).

7. William Sawitzky to Colonel Charles D. Clay, May 14, 1927, SCS Papers.

8. Ibid.

9. Ibid.

10. Ibid.

11. Newspaper clippings, SCS Papers.

12. Blanford interview with the author. Blanford remained convinced that there were no bad feelings between the two men.

13. William Sawitzky to Mrs. Charles D. Clay, July 7, 1927, SCS Papers.

14. Susan to Mrs. Clay, [n.d.]. Internal details indicate the letter was written just after they arrived in New York.

15. Susan to Elizabeth Clay, June 5, 1927, SCS Papers.

16. Susan to Mrs. Clay, June [n.d.], 1927, Aug. 15, 1927, SCS Papers.

17. Susan to Mrs. Clay, Aug. 15, 1927, SCS Papers.

18. Ibid., Sept. 15, Oct. 13, 1927.

19. Ibid., Oct. 13, 1927.

20. Ibid.

21. See photograph collection, SCS Papers.

22. Susan to Mrs. Clay, Dec. 21, 1927, SCS Papers.

23. Ibid., Jan. 13, 1928.

24. Telegram, Susan to William Sawitzky, Apr. 7, 1928, SCS Papers.

25. Susan to Vassili, Apr. 8, 1928, SCS Papers.

26. Ibid.

27. Ibid.; Vassili to Susan, Apr. 14, 1928, SCS Papers.

28. Dunster Foster Petit, interview with the author, July 23, 1985; Susan to Vassili, Apr. 8, 1928, SCS Papers.

29. Susan to Vassili, Apr. 8, 1928.

30. Ibid., Apr. 12, 1928.

31. Ibid., Apr. 18, 1928.

32. Ibid., Apr. 17, 1928.

33. Ibid., Apr. 12, 1928.

34. Ibid.

35. Smith-Rosenberg, "The Female World of Love and Ritual," 1–29.

36. Tom Smith, interview with the author, Sept. 15, 1986.

37. Vassili to Mrs. Clay, Jan. 12, 1928, SCS Papers.

38. Vassili to Susan, Apr. 11, 1928, SCS Papers.

8. The Making of a Poet

1. Jones, *Tomorrow Is Another Day*, 23–24.

2. Ibid., 91, 136, 232, 353–54. Jones notes a split between an inner vision and a desire to conform in the life and writing of the southern women she studies. That struggle confronted Susan Clay Sawitzky throughout her life.

3. William Sawitzky to Charles D. Clay, May 7, 1928, SCS Papers.

4. Susan to Mrs. Clay, May 9, 1928, SCS Papers.

5. Unpublished poem, SCS Papers.

6. Journal, SCS Papers.

7. Notebook, SCS Papers. Susan Sawitzky kept notebooks and journals in a very disorganized fashion. They can sometimes be dated from practice letters contained in them, but she appears to have kept several notebooks simultaneously.

8. Journal, SCS Papers.

9. Unpublished poem. The poem can be found in several versions in her papers.

10. Spears, ed., "The Circling Thread," 28.

11. Ibid., 32.

12. Ibid., 25.

13. Ibid., 31.

14. *Poems by Susan Clay*, 16.

15. Journals, SCS Papers.

16. Marjorie H. Buffum to Susan Sawitzky, Mar. 29, 1933, SCS Papers. Buffum suggested readings from *Science and Health* dealing with human thought and Divine spirit: 371:14–19, 21:9–12, 451:14–18, 129:22–24, 2:23–30, 3:4–11, 248: 12–29, 445:1–26, 469:7–11, 282:26–27, 3:17–26. (Readings from *Science and Health* are noted by page number followed by line numbers.) She also suggested readings from the Bible and

other inspirational books. See also fragments of letters and journal entries in SCS Papers; Mary F. Bednarowski, "Outside the Mainstream: Women's Religion and Women Religious Leaders in Ninteenth-Century America," *Journal of the American Academy of Religion* 48 (June 1980): 217.

17. Unpublished poem, SCS Papers.

18. Journal, SCS Papers.

19. Spears, ed., "The Circling Thread," 29.

20. Ibid., 17. Susan's interest in Darwinism may have resulted from her trip to Kentucky shortly before the miscarriage. She had been invited to lunch by Frances Jewell McVey, the wife of the president of the University of Kentucky, who was embroiled in a struggle with fundamentalists over the teaching of Darwinism at the institution.

21. Ibid., 19.

22. Unpublished poem, SCS Papers. She titled the poem "Leonids" for a band of meteors that appear in November. From Sawitzky's letter to Mr. and Mrs. Clay, it may be assumed that the child was conceived in late November or early December.

23. *Poems by Susan Clay,* 27–28.

24. Unpublished poem, SCS Papers.

25. Spears, ed., "The Circling Thread," 47.

26. Stephen Gottschalk, *The Emergence of Christian Science in American Religious Life* (Berkeley: University of California Press, 1973), 94–95; Robert Peel, *Mary Baker Eddy: The Years of Discovery* (New York: Holt, Rinehart and Winston, 1966), 197; Mary Baker Eddy, *Science and Health with Key to the Scriptures* (Boston: First Church of Christ, Scientist, 1971), 291, 426–30.

27. Unpublished poem, SCS Papers.

28. Spears, ed., "The Circling Thread," 27.

29. Ibid., 31.

30. Ibid., 46.

31. Unpublished poem, SCS Papers. See also Spears, ed., "The Circling Thread," 40–41. In the latter version she changes the first person pronoun to third person. "Let *us* lie too."

32. Unpublished poem, SCS Papers.

33. Unpublished poem, SCS Papers. Later, the poem was entitled "Renewed." See Spears, ed., "The Circling Thread," 37.

34. Unpublished poem, SCS Papers.

35. Unpublished poem, SCS Papers.

36. Journal entry, Sept. 15, 1940, SCS Papers.

37. Unpublished poem, SCS Papers.

38. Jones, *Tomorrow Is Another Day,* 37.

9. The Comfort of Familiar Things

1. William Sawitzky to Colonel Charles D. Clay, May 14, 1927, SCS Papers.

2. One might legitimately question whether "life" hurt Susan Clay Sawitzky because she was a poet and an artist or because she was protected to such a degree that reality frightened her.

3. Unpublished poem, SCS Papers.

4. Notebook, SCS Papers. In one of her notebooks Susan Sawitzky listed poems under several topics, possibly with the intent of publishing them.

5. Susan to Colonel and Mrs. Clay, Dec. 6, 1932, SCS Papers.

6. See series of letters June 7–21, 1929, May 29–June 12, 1930, Nov. 1–15, 1931, July 5–18, 1933, SCS Papers.

7. See Thomas J. Clay Papers. After the death of Teetee Clay in 1924, Tom and George moved to the Lafayette Hotel in Lexington. They attempted for a time to live at Balgowan but found it impossible without Teetee's guiding hand.

8. Colonel Charles Clay to William Sawitzky, June 9, 1930, SCS Papers.

9. Thomas J. Clay Papers. See also letters, Apr. 1930, SCS Papers.

10. See letters, Apr. 1930, Sept. 1932, SCS Papers.

11. See letters and postcards, July and Aug. 1930, SCS Papers.

12. Susan to Colonel Clay, Oct. 10, 1933, SCS Papers.

13. Susan to Mrs. Clay, Oct. 5, 1933, SCS Papers.

14. Susan to Metzie, Dec. 13, 1932; Susan to Colonel and Mrs. Clay, Dec. 23, 1932; Jan. 31, 1933, SCS Papers. Actually, Mrs. Clay had been worried for many years by Susan's "disordered ideas" (Mrs. Clay to Bob Clay, Feb. 1, 1925, SCS Papers).

15. Susan to Vassili, June 21, 1935, SCS Papers.

16. Ibid., [n.d.—internally dated June 1929], SCS Papers.

17. Ibid., July 11, 1933, SCS Papers.

18. Ibid., July 14, 1933, SCS Papers.

19. Susan to Colonel and Mrs. Clay, July 29, 1933, SCS Papers.

20. Susan to Papa, June 13, 1935, SCS Papers.

21. Susan to Uncle Tom, Jan. 31, 1935, SCS Papers.

22. Ibid., July 10, 1935, SCS Papers.

23. Susan to Uncle George, Oct. 18, 1933. Susan also wrote about the old servants and recalled parts of the farm or special memories. The letters indicate a quiet rural upbringing free of want or worry and far removed from the depression she was experiencing. See also Susan to Uncle Tom, Feb. 11, 1934, July 10, 1935, SCS Papers.

24. Such sentiments were common among southern women writers. The home carried the image of internal order, of ideal community. It signified the security many women craved. See Jones, *Tomorrow Is Another Day*, 361.

25. Unpublished fragment, SCS Papers.

26. Spears, ed., "The Circling Thread," 20–22.

27. Susan to Metzie, Nov. 12, 1931, SCS Papers. Susan was beginning to read Hindu philosophy, and she declared that she, Elizabeth, and Charley were Brahmins, their brother Bob and father of a caste that included more army people.

28. Spears, ed., "The Circling Thread," 38.

29. Ibid., 25.

30. Susan to Colonel and Mrs. Clay, Dec. 23, 1932, SCS Papers.

31. Unpublished fragment, SCS Papers.

32. Spears, ed., "The Circling Thread," 30.

33. *Poems by Susan Clay*, 10.

10. Depression

1. Susan to Colonel and Mrs. Clay, Apr. 3, Aug. 26, Oct. 5, 1933, SCS Papers. It was easy to convince Susan because she shared the southern view that men's careers were far more important. See Middleton-Keirn, "Magnolias and Microchips," 100–101.

2. Susan Clay Sawitzky, "Another Miniature by Gilbert Stuart," *Antiques* 21 (1932): 214–16.

3. Susan to Elizabeth, Feb. 11, 1932, SCS Papers.

4. G. Terrell to Susan Clay, Apr. 21, 1924, SCS Papers.

5. Susan to Elizabeth, Dec. 13, 1932; Susan to Colonel and Mrs. Clay, Dec. 23, 1932; Susan to Vassili, July 14, 1933, SCS Papers.

6. Susan to Colonel and Mrs. Clay, Jan. 31, 1933, SCS Papers.

7. Susan to Elizabeth, Aug. 3, 1935, SCS Papers.

8. Susan to Colonel and Mrs. Clay, Dec. 23, 1932, SCS Papers.

9. Notebook, SCS Papers. Susan frequently wrote drafts of letters she intended to send.

10. See Gilbert and Gubar, *Madwoman in the Attic*, 45–51; Juhasz, *Naked and Fiery Forms*, 1–5. Elizabeth Fox-Genovese notes the same tendencies in elite southern women a century before Susan Clay Sawitzky. Southern women rarely published, and even in their private reflections, Fox-Genovese claims, they saw little connection to the views of other women. The "loneness" in Susan Sawitzky's poem "Mariner" is very much the isolation that Fox-Genovese notes (*Within the Plantation Household: Black and White Women of the Old South* [Chapel Hill: University of North Carolina Press, 1988], 245–46).

11. Susan to Elizabeth, [n.d], SCS Papers. The letter can be dated by its contents.

12. Susan to Colonel and Mrs. Clay, Oct. 26, 1932, SCS Papers.

13. Susan to Vassili, July 7, 1933, SCS Papers.

14. Susan to Mrs. Clay, Sept. 30, 1932; Susan to Colonel and Mrs. Clay, Dec. 21, 1932. See also Vassili to Susan, July 5, 1933; Susan to Vassili, July 7, 1933; Susan to Mrs. Clay, May 5, 1934, SCS Papers.

15. Susan to Mrs. Clay, Nov. 24, 1934, SCS Papers.

16. Susan to Colonel and Mrs. Clay, June 16, 1933, SCS Papers.

17. When Mrs. Clay visited Susan, Bob jokingly asked her how she liked eating two meals a day in restaurants (Bob Clay to Mrs. Clay, Sept. 11, 1938). Susan noted the practice in letters to her mother and kept a list of expenses in her journals. See SCS Papers.

18. Susan to Mrs. Clay, Feb. 6, 1935; Susan to Colonel and Mrs. Clay, Dec. 30, 1934, SCS Papers. Sara M. Evans suggests that the stress of unemployment and economic deprivation was likely to cause difficulties between husbands and wives. The Depression actually brought William and Susan Sawitzky closer together. See Evans, *Born for Liberty*, 199.

19. Susan to Colonel and Mrs. Clay, Dec. 30, 1934, SCS Papers.

20. Susan to Thomas J. Clay, Jan. 31, 1935, SCS Papers.

21. Susan to Mrs. Clay, Jan. 13, 1933, SCS Papers.

22. Bob Clay to Mrs. Clay, Sept. 1, 1938. See also journals and notebooks, SCS Papers.

23. Susan to Colonel Clay, Oct. 10, 1933; Susan to Colonel and Mrs. Clay, Nov. 22, 1933, SCS Papers.

24. Susan to Colonel and Mrs. Clay, Mar. 10, 20, 1935, SCS Papers.

25. Susan to Mrs. Clay, Aug. 5, Oct. 25, 30, Dec. 9, 1934; Mar. 11, May 4, 1935, SCS Papers.

26. Susan to Mrs. Clay, Nov. 30, 1933, SCS Papers.

27. Ibid., May 5, 1936.

28. Ibid., Feb. 6, 1935.

29. Susan Brown, interview with the author, Sept. 5, 1988. Brown is the daughter of Millie Lawson.

30. Colonel Charles D. Clay to William Sawitzky, May 22, 1932, SCS Papers.

31. *New York Times,* Mar. 14, 1931; *International Studio,* Apr. 1931, 35, 71–72.

32. Susan to Mrs. Clay, Sept. 30, 1932, SCS Papers.

33. Susan to Colonel and Mrs. Clay, Dec. 21, 1932, SCS Papers.

34. Susan to Colonel Clay, Jan. 9, 1933, SCS Papers.

35. Ibid.

36. Susan to Mrs. Clay, Jan. 13, 1933, SCS Papers.

37. Susan to Colonel and Mrs. Clay, Apr. 4, 1935, SCS Papers.

38. Colonel Charles D. Clay to Susan, Sept. 19, 1935, SCS Papers.

39. Mrs. Clay to Susan, Nov. 18, 1935, SCS Papers. Susan's sister, Elizabeth, noted in an interview with the author that she had sent her laundry home in 1931 when she had visited her brother Bob and his wife at Fort Sill, Oklahoma.

40. Susan to Vassili, Dec. 5, 1935, SCS Papers.

11. Recovery

1. Practice letter to Mrs. Clay, Mar. 8, 1939, Notebook, SCS Papers.

2. A copy of the will is among the papers of Elizabeth Clay Blanford. Tom Clay completed the will several years before his death and added a codicil at Susan's suggestion allowing Vassili to enjoy the benefits of the trust should Susan die first. Upon Susan's death the benefits went entirely to her sister. The circumstances of Tom Clay's will raise an interesting dilemma regarding Susan in particular and Tom Clay's attitude toward women. There seems little doubt that he was following traditional Clay values by giving Bob his inheritance outright and creating a trust for his two nieces, but it was a wise decision. Susan, particularly, was incapable by training and temperament of investing the money. She would later sell the family heirlooms left to her. It seems fair to say she would have spent her share very quickly had she been given complete control. Protection does seem to enhance the legitimate need for it.

3. Vassili to Susan, July 6, 1937; Susan to Mrs. Clay, Oct. 30, 1938, SCS Papers.

4. Susan to Mrs. Clay, Jan. 21, 1934, SCS Papers.

5. Susan to Colonel and Mrs. Clay, Oct. 30, 1933, SCS Papers.

6. Susan to Mrs. Clay, Oct. 5, 1933, SCS Papers.

7. Ibid., Aug. 25, 1933, SCS Papers.

8. Susan to Colonel and Mrs. Clay, Dec. 30, 1933, SCS Papers.

9. Mrs. Bruce Kennedy to Elizabeth Blanford, July 11, 1984; Susan to Rita (Vassili's

niece), Mar. 9, 1941; Susan to Elizabeth, May 4, 1933, SCS Papers; Blanford interview with the author.

10. Susan to Mrs. Clay, May 24, 1936; Susan to Colonel and Mrs. Clay, Feb. 21, 1935, SCS Papers.

11. Susan to Colonel and Mrs. Clay, May 22, 1935, SCS Papers.

12. Ibid., Aug. 1, 1935.

13. Ibid., Aug. 5, 1934. See also Susan to Mrs. Clay, Aug. 1, 1935, SCS Papers.

14. Susan to Colonel and Mrs. Clay, July 7, 1934, SCS Papers.

15. Practice letter to her parents, June 6, 1934, SCS Papers.

16. Susan to Mrs. Clay, Nov. 4, 1938, SCS Papers.

17. Ibid., Feb. 18, 1938.

18. Ibid., June 14, 1938.

19. Manning, *Female Tradition in Southern Literature*, 49. Manning notes that writing in isolation was common among southern women writers.

20. Susan Clay Sawitzky, "Mariner," 306. The poem was also included in Spears, ed., "The Circling Thread," 34–35. There are also manuscript copies in her papers.

12. Poetry

1. The effort was not uncommon in southern women writers. See Jones, *Tomorrow Is Another Day*, 356–62.

2. Dorothy M. Brown, *Setting a Course: American Women in the 1920s* (Boston: Twayne, 1987), 222–25.

3. Unpublished poem, Notebook, SCS Papers.

4. Notebooks, SCS Papers.

5. Many writers have pointed to the seclusion in which southern women wrote. See Margaret Homans, *Women Writers and Poetic Identity: Dorothy Wordsworth, Emily Brontë, and Emily Dickinson* (Princeton: Princeton University Press, 1980), 5; Manning, *Female Tradition in Southern Literature*, 49; Jones, *Tomorrow Is Another Day*, xi–xii.

6. Susan to Elizabeth, Jan. 22, 1951, SCS Papers.

7. Spears, ed., "The Circling Thread," 33.

8. Susan made the statement in a conversation with Frank Martin, a Christian Science practitioner and friend (Frank Martin, interview with the author, Apr. 17, 1984). Elizabeth Blanford noted that Susan had said the same thing to her.

9. Hortense King to Susan Sawitzky, Mar. 18, 1962, SCS Papers.

10. Spears, ed., "The Circling Thread," 23–24.

11. Ibid., 18.

12. Ibid., 28.

13. "The Shifting Void," unpublished poem, SCS Papers.

14. Notebook, SCS Papers.

15. Fragment, SCS Papers.

16. Unpublished poem, SCS Papers.

17. Fragment, SCS Papers.

18. Fragment, SCS Papers.

19. Unpublished poem, SCS Papers.
20. Unpublished poem, SCS Papers.
21. Unpublished poem, SCS Papers.
22. Fragment, SCS Papers.
23. Unpublished poem, SCS Papers.
24. Fragment, SCS Papers.
25. Spears, ed., "The Circling Thread," 43.
26. Ibid., 44.

13. Fear of Forever

1. Though Carroll Smith-Rosenberg writes about nineteenth-century women, her discussion of the closeness between mothers and daughters applies to Susan and Ria Clay ("The Female World of Love and Ritual," 1–29).

2. Susan to Mrs. Clay, May 5, 1938, SCS Papers.

3. Bob Clay to Mrs. Clay, June 10, 1927, SCS Papers. Mrs. Clay had written to Bob indicating that Papa was concerned that a young man Metzie was seeing was poor. Bob questioned his father's protectiveness and argued in favor of love, to no avail.

4. Even before the death of her parents, Susan had demonstrated such protectiveness. While she was visiting at home in 1933, an issue had arisen concerning the proper conduct of a lady. Elizabeth had been writing a play with a professor at the University of Kentucky. She wanted to telephone him about some aspect of the play, but the family doubted that that was proper. Susan was inclined to support her parents' view until Vassili suggested that because the subject was business, the call would probably not damage Elizabeth's reputation. See letters exchanged between Susan and Vassili during her visit home in July 1933, SCS Papers.

5. James T. Flexner, "Obituaries, William Sawitzky, 1879–1947," *College Art Journal* 6 (1947): 301–2.

6. Notebook, SCS Papers.

7. Unpublished poem, SCS Papers.

8. Susan to Elizabeth, May 26, July 19, 1950, SCS Papers. The theme, stated directly and indirectly, runs through the letters written from Vassili's death well into the 1960s.

9. Ibid., Feb. 11, 1955, SCS Papers.

10. Ibid., May 18, 1950.

11. Charles Baker to Susan Sawitzky, Sept. 13, 1950, June 26, July 26, 1951, SCS Papers.

12. Ibid., Feb. 28, 1951, SCS Papers.

13. Susan Sawitzky to the New-York Historical Society, Feb. 11, 1955, copy in SCS Papers.

14. See Susan Clay Sawitzky, "Reuben Moulthrop: A Checklist of William Sawitzky," *The New-York Historical Society Quarterly* 39 (Oct. 1955): 385–404.

15. Susan Clay Sawitzky, "New Light on the Early Work of Reuben Moultrop," *Art in America* 44 (Fall 1956): 8–11.

16. Susan Clay Sawitzky, "Abraham Delanoy in New Haven," *New-York Historical Society Quarterly* 41 (Apr. 1957): 193–206.

17. Charles Baker to Susan Sawitzky, Nov. 21, 1956, May 6, 1959, SCS Papers.

18. Susan to Elizabeth, July 19, 1948. In other letters Susan complained of having little to show for her work and that her work progressed at "the speed of a tortoise." See Susan to Elizabeth, Mar. 15, May 18, 1950, SCS Papers.

19. Ibid., May 18, 1950.

20. Susan to the New-York Historical Society, Feb. 11, 1955, copy in SCS Papers.

21. Charles Baker to Lawrence B. Goodrich, Jan. 30, 1957. A copy has been preserved in the SCS Papers.

22. Susan Sawitzky to L. B. Goodrich, Feb. 1, 1957, copy in SCS Papers.

23. Susan to Elizabeth, July 23, 1951, SCS Papers.

24. Frank Martin, interview with the author, Apr. 14, 1984.

25. Susan to Elizabeth, June 1, 1953, SCS Papers.

26. William and Elizabeth Blanford interview with the author. Mr. Blanford reiterated his account in a telephone conversation on May 30, 1995.

27. Susan to Elizabeth, Sept. 24, 1954, SCS Papers.

28. Ibid., June 8, 1950, Mar. 7, 1963.

29. Blanford interview with the author; Martin interview with the author, Apr. 14, 1984.

30. Martin interview with the author, Apr. 14, 1984.

31. Unpublished poems, SCS Papers.

32. See notes in SCS Papers.

33. Eddy, *Science and Health with Key to the Scriptures* 468:27–29. See notes, SCS Papers.

34. See notes, SCS Papers.

35. Susan, in her grief, developed a dependency upon alcohol. As a child she had been warned repeatedly that the "high spiritedness" which characterized the Clays would not tolerate drinking. Her "ouija board" records attributed Vassili with the suggestion that she drink in moderation or not at all, but she raised the issue.

14. Circle Complete

1. Susan Sawitzky to Hortense King, Mar. 11, 1962, Hortense Flexner King Papers, Rare Books and Special Collections, University of Louisville Libraries (hereafter cited as HFK Papers).

2. Hortense King to Susan Sawitzky, Mar. 18, 1962, SCS Papers. The phrase "A new one by H. F." refers to a poem by King. She wrote under her own name, Hortense Flexner.

3. Susan Sawitzky to Hortense King, Mar. 11, 1962, May 12, 1966, HFK Papers.

4. Ibid., Feb. 24, 1963, Mar. 27, 1964.

5. Ibid., May 12, 17, 1862.

6. Ibid., Apr. 7, 1962.

7. Ibid., June 25, 1966.

8. Ibid., Jan. 10, 1967.

9. Ibid., Jan. 7, 1964.

10. Ibid., Mar. 11, 1962.

11. Jones, *Tomorrow Is Another Day,* 320; McMillen, *Southern Women,* 1; Wolfe, *Daughters of Canaan,* 134. Anne Goodwyn Jones says in "Southern Literary Women," 79–80, that Mary Chesnut sought to erase "self" from her diary. In a sense Susan Clay Sawitzky sought the same end and, like Chesnut, created a persona by doing so.

12. Susan Clay Sawitzky to Hortense King, Aug. 29, 1963, HFK Papers. She also noted her appreciation of the biblical poets in a line of an unpublished poem, SCS Papers.

13. Unpublished poem, SCS Papers. See appendix.

14. Unpublished poem, SCS Papers.

15. Unpublished poem, SCS Papers.

16. Unpublished poem, SCS Papers.

17. Unpublished poem, SCS Papers.

18. Unpublished poem, SCS Papers.

19. Unpublished poem, SCS Papers.

20. Unpublished poem, SCS Papers.

21. Unpublished poem, SCS Papers.

22. Susan to Elizabeth, Dec. 21, 1968, SCS Papers.

23. Unpublished poem, SCS Papers. See appendix.

15. Give Me Death

1. Blanford interview with the author. Susan implied as much in her letters to Hortense King as well.

2. Susan Sawitzky to Hortense King, May 17, 4, 1962, HFK Papers.

3. Ibid., Mar. 27, Aug. 13, 1964.

4. Ibid., Jan. 7, 1964.

5. Ibid., Nov. 8, 1969.

6. Hortense King to Susan Sawitzky, May 18, 1962, SCS Papers; Frank Martin, interview with the author, Apr. 14, 1984; Blanford interview with the author.

7. Martin interview with the author, Apr. 14, 1984. Frank Martin, who owned apartments himself, was astounded that she would demand such security measures in Louisville. Elated initially that she wanted to move to Louisville, he was secretly relieved that she decided against it. Blanford noted that property owners in Gloucester also refused to consider such changes.

8. Blanford interview with the author.

9. Susan Sawitzky to Hortense King, Aug. 26, 1963, HFK Papers.

10. Blanford interview with the author. Others have substantiated such information.

11. Blanford mentioned the arrangement. I subsequently spoke by telephone with Mrs. Timmerman who described the role she and her husband played.

12. Jones, *Tomorrow Is Another Day,* 356–62.

13. Susan Juhasz notes in *Naked and Fiery Forms,* 58, that women in transition from old traditions to new ones found it necessary to "abstract and generalize" their experi-

ences to give them validity. It was not until Sylvia Plath and Anne Sexton that women could consistently emphasize their experience in their art. Denise Levertov, according to Juhasz, was a transitional figure. Susan Clay Sawitzky's mature poetry treats the struggle shared by all.

14. Wolfe, *Daughters of Canaan*, 134; Jones, *Tomorrow Is Another Day*, 23–24.

15. Stone, *Black Sheep and Kissing Cousins*, 31.

16. Degler, *At Odds*, 28–29.

17. Wolfe, *Daughters of Canaan*, 204.

18. Juhasz, *Naked and Fiery Forms*, 85–116.

19. Juhasz also argues (ibid., 3) that for a woman and a poet to be able to live at all, to survive, may be the nearest thing to victory.

Bibliography

Abbott, Shirley. *Womenfolk: Growing Up Down South.* New York: Ticknor and Fields, 1983.

Alband, Jo Della. "A History of the Education of Women in Kentucky." M.A. thesis, University of Kentucky, 1934.

Alpern, Sara, Joyce Antler, Elizabeth Israels Perry, and Ingrid Winther Scobie, eds. *The Challenge of Feminist Biography: Writing the Lives of Modern American Women.* Urbana: University of Illinois Press, 1992.

Anderson, William Kyle. *Donald Robertson and His Wife Rachel Rogers of King and Queen County, Virginia, Their Ancestry and Posterity.* Detroit: Privately printed, n.d.

Apple, Lindsey. "In Search of a Star: A Kentucky Clay Goes to the Arctic." *The Filson Club History Quarterly* 71 (January 1997): 3–26.

Atkinson, Maxine, and Jacqueline Bales. "The Shaky Pedestal: Southern Ladies Yesterday and Today." *Southern Studies: An Interdisciplinary Journal of the South* 24 (Winter 1985): 398–406.

Baker, Jean H. *Mary Todd Lincoln: A Biography.* New York: W. W. Norton, 1987.

Bednarowski, Mary F. "Outside the Mainstream: Women's Religion and Women Religious Leaders in Nineteenth-Century America." *Journal of the American Academy of Religion* 48 (June 1980): 207–31.

Bernhard, Virginia, Betty Brandon, Elizabeth Fox-Genovese, Theda Perdue, and Elizabeth Hayes Turner, eds. *Hidden Histories of Women in the New South.* Columbia: University of Missouri Press, 1994.

Bingham, Sallie. *Passion and Prejudice: A Family Memoir.* New York: Applause Books, 1989.

Blair, Karen J. *The Torchbearers: Women and Their Amateur Arts Associations in America, 1890–1930.* Bloomington: Indiana University Press, 1994.

Blake, William. *The Complete Works of William Blake.* Edited by Geoffrey Keynes. London: Oxford University Press, 1966.

Blanford, Elizabeth Clay. Interviews by Lindsey Apple and Bettie Kerr, May 18, 19, 21, 22, 23, 1987, cassette tape, Special Collections, Margaret I. King Library, University of Kentucky, Lexington, Kentucky; interviews by Lindsey Apple, July

17–20, 1984, cassette tape in the possession of the author, Georgetown, Kentucky; telephone, interviews by Lindsey Apple, 1984–93.

Bordwick, Judith M., and Elizabeth Douvan. "Ambivalence: The Socialization of Women." In *Woman in Sexist Society: Studies in Power and Powerlessness,* edited by Vivian Garnick and Barbara K. Moran, 225–41. New York: New American Library, 1971.

Brown, Dorothy M. *Setting a Course: American Women in the 1920s.* Boston: Twayne, 1987.

Brown, Susan. Telephone interview with the author. September 5, 1988.

Chafe, William H. *Women and Equality: Changing Patterns in American Culture.* New York: Oxford University Press, 1979.

Clay Family Papers, 1807–1909, Mary Clay Kenner Collection [microfilm], Special Collections, Margaret I. King Library, University of Kentucky, Lexington, Kentucky; original in possession of Kenner family.

Clay, Susan. "Apology of a Small Town Poetess." *New York Times Review and Magazine,* December 18, 1921.

———. *Poems by Susan Clay.* Chicago: Ralph Fletcher Seymour, 1923.

———. "Poppies." *Town and Country Magazine* 89 (October 15, 1922): 34.

Clay, Thomas J. Papers. Manuscript Division, Library of Congress, Washington, D.C.

Clinton, Catherine. *Plantation Mistress: Women's World in the Old South.* New York: Pantheon Books, 1982.

Coleman, J. Winston Jr. *The Private School of Ella M. Williams of Lexington, Kentucky.* Lexington: Winburn Press, 1980.

Crook, George. *General George Crook: His Autobiography.* Edited and Annotated by Martin F. Schmitt. 1946. Reprint. Norman: University of Oklahoma Press, 1986.

Curry, Howard. Papers. Special Collections, Margaret I. King Library, University of Kentucky, Lexington, Kentucky.

Degler, Carl N. *At Odds: Women and the Family in America from the Revolution to the Present.* Oxford: Oxford University Press, 1980.

Dierks, Jack Cameron. *A Leap to Arms: The Cuban Campaign of 1898.* Philadelphia: J. B. Lippincott, 1970.

Dillman, Caroline Matheny. "Southern Women: In Continuity or Change?" In *Women in the South: An Anthropological Perspective,* edited by Holly F. Mathews, 8–17. Athens: University of Georgia Press, 1989.

Dyhouse, Carol. *Girls Growing Up in Late Victorian and Edwardian England.* London: Routledge & Kegan Paul, 1981.

Eaton, Clement. *Henry Clay and the Art of American Politics.* Boston: Little, Brown, 1951.

Eddy, Mary Baker. *Science and Health with Key to the Scriptures.* Boston: First Church of Christ, Scientist, 1971.

Evans, Sara M. *Born for Liberty: A History of Women in America.* New York: Free Press, 1989.

Faulk, Odie B. *The Geronimo Campaign.* New York: Oxford University Press, 1969.

Flexner, James T. "Obituaries, William Sawitzsky, 1879–1947." *College Art Journal* 6 (1947): 301–2.

Forderhase, Nancy K. "The Clear Call of Thoroughbred Women: The Kentucky Federation of Women's Clubs and the Crusade for Educational Reform, 1903–1909." *Register of the Kentucky Historical Society* 83 (1985): 19–35.

Fox, Margery. "Protest in Piety: Christian Science Revisited." *International Journal of Women's Studies* 1 (July–August 1978): 401–16.

Fox-Genovese, Elizabeth. *Within the Plantation Household: Black and White Women of the Old South.* Chapel Hill: University of North Carolina Press, 1988.

Freidel, Frank. *The Splendid Little War.* New York: Bramhall House, 1958.

Fuller, Paul E. *Laura Clay and the Woman's Rights Movement.* Lexington: University Press of Kentucky, 1975.

Gilbert, Sandra M., and Susan Gubar. *The Madwoman in the Attic: The Woman and the Nineteenth-Century Literary Imagination.* New Haven: Yale University Press, 1979.

Gottschalk, Stephen. *The Emergence of Christian Science in American Religious Life.* Berkeley: University of California Press, 1973.

Hagedorn, Hermann. *Leonard Wood: A Biography.* 2 vols. 1931. Reprint. New York: Kraus Reprint Co., 1969.

———. Papers. Manuscript Division, Library of Congress, Washington, D.C.

Hawks, Joanne V., and Sheila L. Skemp, eds. *Sex, Race, and the Role of Women in the South.* Jackson: University Press of Mississippi, 1983.

Hay, Melba Porter. *Madeline McDowell Breckinridge: Kentucky Suffragist and Progressive Reformer.* Ann Arbor: University Microfilms International, 1980.

Heilbrun, Carolyn G. *Reinventing Womanhood.* New York: Norton, 1979.

———. *Writing a Woman's Life.* New York: Ballantine Books, 1988.

Hewitt, Nancy A., and Suzanne Lebsock, eds. *Visible Women: New Essays on American Activism.* Urbana: University of Illinois Press, 1993.

Homans, Margaret. *Women Writers and Poetic Identity: Dorothy Wordsworth, Emily Brontë, and Emily Dickinson.* Princeton: Princeton University Press, 1980.

Hunt-Morgan Papers, 1862–63. Special Collections, Margaret I. King Library, University of Kentucky, Lexington, Kentucky.

Irwin, Helen Deiss. *Women in Kentucky.* Lexington: University Press of Kentucky, 1979.

Jacob-Johnson Papers. Filson Club, Louisville, Kentucky.

James, Bessie Rowland, ed. *Six Came Back: The Arctic Adventure of David L. Brainard.* Indianapolis: Bobbs-Merrill, 1940.

January Papers. Special Collections, Margaret I. King Library, University of Kentucky, Lexington, Kentucky.

Jillson, Willard Rouse. *Romance and Reality.* Frankfort, Ky.: Roberts Printing Co., 1953.

Jones, Anne Goodwyn. "Southern Literary Women as Chroniclers of Southern Life." In *Sex, Race, and the Role of Women in the South,* edited by Joanne V. Hawks and Sheila L. Skemp, 75–93. Jackson: University Press of Mississippi, 1983.

————. *Tomorrow Is Another Day: The Woman Writer of the South, 1859–1936.* Baton Rouge: Louisiana State University Press, 1981.

Juhasz, Suzanne. *Naked and Fiery Forms: Modern American Poetry by Women, a New Tradition.* New York: Octagon Books, 1976.

International Studio. 1931.

Kaplan, Paula J. *Barriers Between Women.* New York: Spectrum Publications, 1981.

Kentucky Gazette. February 23, 1793–December 31, 1799.

Kerber, Linda K. "Separate Spheres, Female Worlds, Woman's Place: The Rhetoric of Women's History." *Journal of American History* 75 (June 1988): 9–39.

King, Hortense Flexner. Papers. Rare Books and Special Collections, University of Louisville Libraries, Louisville, Kentucky.

Klotter, James C. *The Breckinridges of Kentucky.* Lexington: University Press of Kentucky, 1986.

Lee, Rebecca Smith. *Mary Austin Holley: A Biography.* Austin: University of Texas Press, 1962.

Lerner, Gerda. *The Female Experience: An American Documentary.* Indianapolis: Bobbs-Merrill, 1977.

————. *The Majority Finds Its Past: Placing Women in History.* New York: Oxford University Press, 1979.

Lewis, Sinclair. *Main Street.* New York: Harcourt, Brace, 1920.

Lexington Leader. 1905–45.

Louisville Herald. September–December 1921.

Manning, Carol S. *The Female Tradition in Southern Literature.* Urbana: University of Illinois Press, 1993.

Martin, Frank. Interview with Lindsey Apple, April 17, 1984.

McGuire, Sue Lynn. "The Little Colonel: A Phenomenon in Popular Literary Culture." *Register of the Kentucky Historical Society* 89 (Spring 1991): 121–46.

McMillen, Sally G. *Southern Women: Black and White in the Old South.* Arlington Heights, Ill.: Harlan Davidson, 1992.

Middleton-Keirn, Susan. "Magnolias and Microchips: Regional Subcultural Constructions of Femininity." *Sociological Spectrum* 6 (1986): 83–107.

Morzek, Donald J. "The Habit of Victory: The American Military and the Cult of Manliness." In *Manliness and Morality: Middle-Class Masculinity in Britain and America, 1800–1940,* edited by J. A. Mangin and James Walvin, 35–51. New York: St. Martin's Press, 1987.

Nagel, Paul C. *Descent from Glory: Four Generations of the John Adams Family.* Oxford: Oxford University Press, 1983.

New York Times. 1921–47.

O'Toole, G. J. A. *The Spanish War: An American Epic, 1898.* New York: Norton, 1984.

Parrish, Gladys V. "The History of Female Education in Lexington and Fayette County." M.A. thesis, University of Kentucky, 1932.

Peel, Robert. *Mary Baker Eddy: The Years of Discovery.* New York: Holt, Rinehart and Winston, 1966.

Pettit, Dunster Foster. Interview with Lindsey Apple, July 23, 1985.

Redd, Richard. *Reminiscences of Richard Menifee Redd Better Known as Colonel "Dick" Redd from Childhood to Old Age.* Lexington: Clay Printing Co., 1929.

Remini, Robert V. *Henry Clay: Statesman for the Union.* New York: Norton, 1991.

Rothenstein, John. *Summer's Lease: Autobiography, 1901–1938.* London: Hamish Hamilton, 1965.

Sawitzky, Susan Clay. "Abraham Delanoy in New Haven." *New-York Historical Society Quarterly* 41 (April 1957): 193–206.

———. "Mariner." *Poetry: A Magazine of Verse* 57 (1941): 306.

———. "New Light on the Early Work of Reuben Moultrop." *Art in America* 44 (Fall 1956): 8–11.

———. Papers. In the possession of Elizabeth Clay Blanford.

———. "Portraits of William Johnston: A Preliminary Checklist." *New-York Historical Society Quarterly* 39 (January 1955): 79–89.

———. "Thomas McIlworth (active 1758 to c. 1769)." *New-York Historical Society Quarterly* 35 (April 1951): 117–39.

Sawitzky, William. *The American Work of Benjamin West.* An offprint from the *Pennsylvania Magazine of History and Biography.* October 1938.

———. *Matthew Pratt, 1734–1805.* New York: New-York Historical Society/Carnegie Corporation of New York, 1942.

———. *Ralph Earl, 1751–1801.* An exhibit catalog, Whitney Museum of American Art, New York, October 16–November 21, 1945; Worcester Art Museum, Worcester, Massachusetts, December 13, 1945–January 13, 1946.

Sawitzky, William, and Susan Sawitzky. "Portraits by Reuben Moulthrop." *New-York Historical Society Quarterly* 39 (October 1955): 385–404.

Scott, Anne Firor. "Historians Construct the Southern Woman." In *Sex, Race, and the Role of Women in the South,* edited by Joanne V. Hawks and Sheila L. Skemp, 95–110. Jackson: University Press of Mississippi, 1983.

———. *Making the Invisible Woman Visible.* Urbana: University of Illinois Press, 1984.

———. "On Seeing and Not Seeing: A Case of Historical Invisibility." *Journal of American History* 71 (June 1984): 7–21.

———. *The Southern Lady: From Pedestal to Politics, 1830–1930.* Chicago: University of Chicago Press, 1970.

Showalter, Elaine. *A Literature of Their Own.* Princeton: Princeton University Press, 1977.

Simpson, Elizabeth Murphey. *The Enchanted Bluegrass.* Lexington: Transylvania Press, 1938.

Smith, Cleo Dawson. Interviews with the author, September 23, 1986, May 4, 1987, May 6, 1988.

Smith, Lillian, *Killers of the Dream.* New York: Norton, 1949.

Smith, Tom. Letter to Elizabeth Clay Blanford. July 7, 1988, in the possession of the author.

Smith, Zachary F., and Mary Rogers Clay. *The Clay Family.* Louisville: Filson Club, 1899.

Smith-Rosenberg, Carroll. "The Female World of Love and Ritual: Relations Between Women in Nineteenth-Century America." *Signs* 1 (1975): 1–29.

Smith-Rosenberg, Carroll, and Charles Rosenberg. "The Female Animal: Medical and Biological Views of Woman and Her Role in Nineteenth-Century America." *Journal of American History* 60 (September 1973): 332–56.

Spears, Woodridge, ed. "The Circling Thread: Poems by Susan Clay Sawitzky." *Kentucky Poetry Review*, January 1984.

———. Interview with the author, September 3, 1985.

Stone, Elizabeth. *Black Sheep and Kissing Cousins: How Our Family Stories Shape Us.* New York: Penguin, 1988.

Tapp, Hambleton, and James C. Klotter. *Kentucky: Decades of Discord, 1865–1900.* Frankfort, Ky.: Kentucky Historical Society, 1977.

Time. May 31, 1976.

Todd, A. L. *Abandoned: The Story of the Greely Expedition, 1881–1884.* New York: McGraw-Hill, 1961.

U.S. Army. Copy of Minutes, Board of Inquiry, Fort Snelling, Minnesota, April 24, 1923. Copy in Susan Clay Sawitzky Papers.

Utley, Robert M. *Frontier Regulars: The United States Army and the Indian, 1866–1891.* Lincoln: University of Nebraska Press, 1973.

Welter, Barbara. "The Cult of True Womanhood: 1820–1860." *American Quarterly* 18 (Summer 1966): 151–74.

———. *Dimity Convictions: The American Woman in the Nineteenth Century.* Athens: Ohio University Press, 1976.

Wheeler, Marjorie Spruill. *New Women of the New South: The Leaders of the Woman Suffrage Movement in the Southern States.* New York: Oxford University Press, 1993.

Wilson, Robert Burns. *Until the Day Break.* New York: Charles Scribner's Sons, 1900.

Wolfe, Margaret Ripley. *Daughters of Canaan: A Saga of Southern Women.* Lexington: University Press of Kentucky, 1995.

———. "Fallen Leaves and Missing Pages: Women in Kentucky History." *Register of the Kentucky Historical Society* 90 (1992): 64–89.

Wood, Leonard. Papers. Manuscript Division, Library of Congress, Washington, D.C.

Wooster, Robert. *Nelson A. Miles and the Twilight of the Frontier Army.* Lincoln: University of Nebraska Press, 1993.

Wright, John D. Jr. *Lexington: Heart of the Bluegrass.* Lexington: Lexington–Fayette County Historical Commission, 1982.

Wyatt-Brown, Bertram. *The House of Percy: Honor, Melancholy, and Imagination in a Southern Family.* New York: Oxford University Press, 1994.

———. *Southern Honor: Ethics and Behavior in the Old South.* New York: Oxford University Press, 1982.

Index

Cautious Rebel

was composed in 10.5 /13.5 Fairfeild
on Power Macintosh 7100/80 using PageMaker 6.0
at The Kent State University Press;
printed by sheet-fed offset
on 50# Glatfelter Supple Opaque Natural
notch case bound over binder's boards
in ICG cloth
and wrapped with dust jackets printed in two colors
on 100# enamel stock finished with film lamination
by Braum-Brumfield, Inc.
designed by Diana Gordy
and published by

THE KENT STATE UNIVERSITY PRESS
Kent, Ohio, 44242